Genesis as Torah

Genesis as Torah

Reading Narrative as Legal Instruction

Brian Neil Peterson

CASCADE *Books* • Eugene, Oregon

GENESIS AS TORAH
Reading Narrative as Legal Instruction

Copyright © 2018 Brian Neil Peterson. All rights reserved. Except for brief quotations in critical publications or reviews, no part of this book may be reproduced in any manner without prior written permission from the publisher. Write: Permissions, Wipf and Stock Publishers, 199 W. 8th Ave., Suite 3, Eugene, OR 97401.

Cascade Books
An Imprint of Wipf and Stock Publishers
199 W. 8th Ave., Suite 3
Eugene, OR 97401

www.wipfandstock.com

PAPERBACK ISBN: 978-1-5326-3583-0
HARDCOVER ISBN: 978-1-5326-3585-4
EBOOK ISBN: 978-1-5326-3584-7

Cataloging-in-Publication data:

Names: Peterson, Brian Neil, author.
Title: Genesis as torah : reading narrative as legal instruction / Brian Neil Peterson.
Description: Eugene, OR: Cascade Books | Includes bibliographical references and indexes.
Identifiers: ISBN: 978-1-5326-3583-0 (paperback) | ISBN: 978-1-5326-3585-4 (hardcover) | ISBN: 978-1-5326-3584-7 (ebook).
Subjects: LCSH: Bible. Genesis—Criticism, interpretation, etc. | Law (Theology)—Biblical teaching.
Classification: BS1235 P65 2018 (print) | BS1235 (ebook).

Manufactured in the U.S.A.

Scripture quotations marked (NASB) taken from the New American Standard Bible® (NASB), Copyright © 1960, 1962, 1963, 1968, 1971, 1972, 1973, 1975, 1977, 1995 by The Lockman Foundation. Used by permission. www.Lockman.org/.

This book is dedicated to my daughter Maddie (Madeline), my firstborn child. Genesis is replete with both explicit and implicit instruction on God's blessing to be fruitful and multiply. It also depicts the joy that children can bring to a couple (Gen 21:6). My wife and I were truly blessed by God when our baby girl came into the world. You have taught me how to love as a father. My prayer is that you will love God and his Word as much as we do and even more.

Contents

Acknowledgments | ix
Abbreviations | x
Preface | xiii

1. **An Introduction to Reading Genesis as Torah** | 1
2. **Genesis 1–2**
   Creation as Foundational to God's Torah | 18
3. **Genesis 3–4**
   The Analogical Role of the Fall of Humanity | 41
4. **Genesis 5–11**
   The Flood and Babel: How to Avoid the Judgment of God | 61
5. **Genesis 12–25**
   Abraham as an Example of Righteous Behavior | 76
6. **Genesis 26–36**
   "Israel" as an Example for Israel | 100
7. **Genesis 37–50**
   The Life of Joseph: How to Live in Exile | 121
8. **Conclusions** | 140

Bibliography | 145
Subject Index | 155
Scripture Index | 161

Acknowledgments

I would like to express my gratitude and thanks to the administration of Lee University, Cleveland, Tennessee, for extending to me various means of funding to bring this project to completion. First, I want to thank my department Chair, Dr. Skip Jenkins, for believing in me and this project and helping to fund my summer research in Toronto, Canada, through a Department of Theology grant. Second, I want to extend my appreciation to the Faculty Council of Lee University for voting to award me a summer 2017 Research Grant through the office of Dr. Debbie Murray, Vice President of Academic Affairs. Finally, I want to thank Dr. Paul Conn, President of Lee University, for consistently supporting my research efforts both financially and through his words of encouragement.

Abbreviations

AB	Anchor Bible
ABD	*Anchor Bible Dictionary*, edited by David Noel Freedman. 6 vols. New York: Doubleday, 1992
AfO	*Archiv für Orientforschung*
ANE	ancient Near East
ANEP	*The Ancient Near East in Pictures Relating to the Old Testament*, edited by James Pritchard. 2nd ed. Princeton: Princeton University Press, 1969
ANET	*Ancient Near Eastern Texts Relating to the Old Testament*, edited by James Pritchard. 3rd ed. Princeton, NJ: Princeton University Press, 1969
b.	Babylonian Talmud
BA	*Biblical Archaeologist*
BASOR	*Bulletin of American Schools of Oriental Research*
BBR	*Bulletin of Biblical Research*
Bib	*Biblica*
BibIntSer	Biblical Interpretation Series
BSac	*Bibliotheca Sacra*
BTB	*Biblical Theology Bulletin*
BTS	Biblical Tools and Studies
BZAW	Beihefte zur Zeitschrift für die alttestamentliche Wissenschaft
CBC	The Cambridge Bible Commentary
CBQ	*Catholic Biblical Quarterly*
CBQMS	Catholic Biblical Quarterly Monograph Series

Abbreviations

CBR	*Currents in Biblical Research*
CC	Continental Commentaries
COS	*The Context of Scripture*, edited by William W. Hallo and K. Lawson Younger Jr. 3 vols. Leiden: Brill, 1997–2017
EBC	Expositor's Bible Commentary
EvQ	*Evangelical Quarterly*
EvT	*Evangelische Theologie*
HLR	*Harvard Law Review*
HTR	*Harvard Theological Review*
HUCA	*Hebrew Union College Annual*
IEJ	*Israel Exploration Journal*
Int	*Interpretation*
IBT	Interpreting Biblical Texts
JANESCU	*The Journal of the Ancient Near Eastern Society of Columbia University*
JBL	*Journal of Biblical Literature*
JETS	*Journal of the Evangelical Theological Society*
JLR	*Journal of Law and Religion*
JNSL	*Journal of Northwest Semitic Languages*
JPSTC	Jewish Publication Society Torah Commentary
JSOT	*Journal for the Study of the Old Testament*
JSOTSup	Journal for the Study of the Old Testament: Supplement Series
m.	Mishnah
NAC	New American Commentary
NIB	*The New Interpreter's Bible*, edited by Leander E. Keck et al., 12 vols. Nashville: Abingdon, 1994–2004
NIBC	New International Bible Commentary
NICOT	New International Commentary on the Old Testament
NIVAC	The NIV Application Commentary
NT	New Testament
OBT	Overtures to Biblical Theology
OIUC	Oriental Institute of the University of Chicago
OT	Old Testament

Abbreviations

OTL	Old Testament Library
OTT	Old Testament Theology
PRSt	*Perspectives in Religious Studies*
PTMS	Princeton Theological Monograph Series
RGG	*Die Religion in Geschichte und Gegenwart: Handwörterbuch für Theologie und Religionswissenschaft*, edited by Kurt Galling et. al. 6 vols. 3rd ed. Tübingen: Mohr/Siebeck, 1959
RPP	*Religion Past and Present: Encyclopedia of Theology and Religion*, edited by Hans Dieter Betz et. al. 14 vols. Leiden: Brill, 2007–2013
SBL	Society of Biblical Literature
SBLit	Studies in Biblical Literature
SBLSCA	Society of Biblical Literature Septuagint and Cognate Studies
SBLSP	Society of Biblical Literature Seminar Papers
SBLSS	Society of Biblical Literature Semeia Series
SBTS	Sources for Biblical and Theological Study
SJOT	*Scandinavian Journal of the Old Testament*
UCOIS	University of Chicago Oriental Institute Seminars
VT	*Vetus Testamentum*
VTSup	Supplements to Vetus Testamentum
WBC	Word Biblical Commentary
YES	Yale Egyptological Studies
YJLH	*Yale Journal of Law and the Humanities*
ZAW	*Zeitschrift für die alttestamentliche Wissenschaft*

Preface

For anyone who has grown up in church and attended Sunday school on a regular basis the narratives of Genesis are no doubt some of the first stories they encountered as children. If asked, I am sure, they would quickly recall the accounts of creation, Adam and Eve, Cain and Abel, Noah and the flood, Babel, Abraham, Isaac, Jacob, and of course Joseph and his famous "coat of many colors." For readers and hearers throughout Israel's history and later, these stories would have indeed been entertaining and memorable. Today, even though the average person may not be able to recall the order of the various laws of Exodus, Leviticus, Numbers, and Deuteronomy—or even the Ten Commandments for that matter—they almost certainly will be able to recollect the stories of Genesis and their basic order. The genre of story has a natural built-in pedagogical facet that enables the reader or hearer to recount the basic structure and plot line of a given account. To be sure, Genesis falls into this genre category.

Yet, it is also true that Genesis is not isolated to one genre alone. On the contrary, scholars have identified a number of genre forms within this book: genealogy, saga, etiology, legend, and novella, to name but a few.[1] Such variation elicits a variety of queries such as: Why did the author use so many genres to tell *these* specific accounts while excluding other events? Surely he had numerous stories from which to choose?[2] What was the reason for the presentation of Genesis in this fashion? Or what was the instructive purpose of Genesis? I will attempt to address these and similar questions in later chapters.

---

1. For a discussion on the role of etiology in the OT and particularly in Genesis 2–3, see Lohfink, *Theology*, 18–34. On the Joseph narrative as novella, see Humphreys, *Joseph and His Family*, 15–31.

2. See also the comments by Longman, *How to Read Genesis*, 62.

Preface

At the same time, the Genesis accounts have been the focus of fierce debate. On the one hand, some argue that the stories of Genesis present a historical recollection of the early period of the earth and Israel's founders. On the other hand, many scholars now see in these accounts nothing more than quasi-historical material at best, or straight up fiction at worst, which have ample parallels with other ancient Near Eastern accounts. As such, many now categorize the opening eleven chapters of Genesis as myth. Now to be sure, there are various shades of what the term "myth" means to various scholars;[3] but at the heart of these discussions lies the belief that the material found in these chapters is not to be read as history as much as it is to be read for its aesthetic value and as in some way *instructive* either, theologically, ethically, etiologically, or some combination of all three. While for some (e.g., the ancient Jewish sages[4]) reading Genesis as "history" is vital to the interpretive discussion—something I feel strongly about myself—it is the *instructive* aspect of the Genesis material that I will focus on throughout this book.[5] After all, Genesis is the opening book of what has become known for centuries as "Torah" (i.e., instruction/law). Those who placed Genesis in this position must have had a good reason for doing so. Due to this fact, perhaps we moderns should take note of this importance as well.[6]

In what follows, I will attempt to show that the author had a distinct purpose for his presentation beyond a mere recitation of ancient accounts that purport to predate Israel as a nation. I will argue that the author sought to present not only the early history of the world and how Israel became a nation, but more importantly he sought to present specific instruction on key legislative aspects of the Torah. In other words, the author appears to have wanted to show what certain laws actually looked like in a "real life" setting. In this light, I will demonstrate that good portions of Genesis served much in the same fashion as case law is used in court settings today.[7] This is also known as the setting of precedents, that is, an invoking of a real-life scenario where a particular judgment was rendered or a specific outcome happened.

3. See Rogerson, *Myth*, 1, 6–7, 9, 12–13.

4. So Neusner, *Genesis and Judaism*, 127.

5. Rosenberg ("Bible: Biblical Narrative," 63) notes that the narratives of the OT "in some sense purports to be history" even though he goes on to note that it should not be evaluated as history in a modern sense.

6. Fretheim, "Reclamation," 355.

7. Some rabbis propose that the laws of Genesis served as "memory devices" or "reminders" for their traditions and Sinai laws. See Polin, "Jewish Law," 38.

Preface

Jacob Milgrom (1923–2010), a renowned OT scholar who has written extensively on the Jewish law, notes the role of narrative as setting the precedent for law. He states, "The law is incomprehensible without its framing narrative, which illustrates both the application and the limit of the law. Thus not only casuistic (case) law of which Scripture abounds describes the parameters of a law's application, but even apodictic law, despite its imperative nature, can be traceable to particular circumstances from which it arose."[8] Similarly, biblical scholar Joel Rosenberg rightly notes that "narrative and nonnarrative materials of the Bible must not be read in isolation from one another."[9] He goes on to point out the institution of the law of circumcision, which is rooted in the narrative of Genesis 17, as a primary example of this very fact.

Therefore, in many ways, Genesis and broader Pentateuchal narratives serve as a commentary on the Law.[10] Due to this fact, James W. Watts is mistaken when he asserts that some of the narrative accounts (e.g., Jacob and Joseph) contain no reference to the law.[11] This is simply to miss the importance of these Genesis narrative accounts (see more below in chapters 6 and 7). After all, as Watts himself correctly notes a little later, narratives such as the account detailing Zelophad's daughters' complaint to Moses on inheritance rights in Numbers 27 clearly have legal precedents attached to them.[12] This is no less the case concerning the close connection between the narrative of Leviticus 10 related to the untimely death of Nadab and Abihu and the ensuing laws against intoxicated priests (Lev 10:8–11). And the narrative of Exodus 32–34 certainly teaches about the dangers related to idolatry and breach of covenant!

Nevertheless, Watts is correct that the stories of the Torah cannot be reduced simply to "legal case studies."[13] Rhetorically they teach both history *and* law in a memorable and persuasive way. However, the reader needs to be alert to the fact that in some cases, the laws of Sinai not only reiterate laws already present in the narratives of Genesis (or vice versa depending on one's perspective dating schema), in some cases it also alters previously

---

8. Milgrom, *Leviticus 23–27*, 2103–4.
9. Rosenberg, "Bible: Biblical Narrative," 65.
10. So, too, Damrosch, *Narrative Covenant*, 35–36.
11. Watts, *Reading Law*, 85.
12. Ibid., 87; and Jackson, *Wisdom Laws*, 425–27.
13. Watts, *Reading Law*, 88.

Preface

practiced customs such as patriarchal sacrifice—a cultic practice that became the prerogative of the tribe of Levi.[14]

Finally, when Israel read or heard the stories of Genesis they were not only entertained[15] and educated about some facet of the ancient eras of the world and their own early history,[16] they were also instructed on what to do, or not to do, vis-à-vis specific statutes and commandments of YHWH found in Exodus through Deuteronomy. From this perspective, the narratives of Genesis become Torah and therefore should be read from that vantage point in order to determine what the author was attempting to teach Israel as a nation. Indeed, Calum Carmichael, a prolific author in comparative literature and Jewish law, rightly notes that "A thesis that argues for a close link between the laws and narratives in the Bible need not occasion much surprise, even if the results are unexpected."[17] And if scholars have been rightly faulted for skipping over the extensive legal portions of the Pentateuch in order to focus on the more "interesting" and evocative narrative/"story" portions,[18] they are also to be faulted for focusing too heavily on the narratives as a source of "story"/"myth" and "history" to the exclusion of their legal teaching. By doing this, scholars have minimized the value of the Genesis narratives as Torah. It is this imbalance which I seek to correct in this book.

---

14. See also comments by Polin, "Jewish Law," 41.

15. So the conclusion of Coats ("Joseph Story," 296) when speaking of the Joseph account; and Rendsburg, "David and His Circle," 446.

16. See Sailhamer, *Genesis Unbound*, 28. See also the comments of Rogerson, et al., *Genesis and Exodus*, 72–74.

17. Carmichael, *Law and Narrative*, 18.

18. See the critique by Damrosch, *Narrative Covenant*, 33–34, 261–62.

I

An Introduction to Reading Genesis as *Torah*

In this opening chapter I will discuss a number of issues directly related to my thesis and the content of the chapters that follow. While I will integrate discussions of my methodological approach throughout, here I will focus mainly on a number of premises that will be adopted throughout this book. I have not attempted to offer an exhaustive handling of the scholarly source material related to Genesis; rather I have been selective in nature due to the vastness of Genesis scholarship. Moreover, in the chapters that follow, I will refrain from entering into detailed discussions on the historical-critical approaches to the text (e.g., tradition, form, redaction history), which has been handled at length by others.[1] Instead I will focus most of my attention on the final form of the text and how the implied audience(s) may have understood it. Whether that audience was from the period of Moses or long after cannot be known for certain. With this caveat, I will begin by looking at the meaning of the term *torah* vis-à-vis Genesis.

Torah Defined

What is *torah*? Broadly defined *torah* means law or instruction (Gen 26:5; Exod 12:49; 13:9; 18:16 etc.). When assessing the Pentateuch, *torah* can

---

1. On the topic of the origins of Israelite law, see the classic presentation of Alt, *Essays on Old Testament History and Religion*, 81–132.

Genesis as Torah

be more narrowly defined as instruction in the ways and commands of YHWH (Exod 16:4; cf. 24:12).[2] Frank Crüsemann adds that "it comprises legal, moral, cultic, religious, theological and historical statements."[3] When most scholars speak of *torah*, it is quite clear that Genesis does not immediately come to mind.[4] Instead they generally turn their focus to the obvious portions of the Pentateuch[5] that engender the concept of law, namely, the Book of the Covenant (Exod 20:22—23:33); the Holiness Code of Leviticus 17–26; the Deuteronomic Law (Deut 12–26); or the Decalogue of Exodus 20 and Deuteronomy 5.[6] A fine example of this is the approach used by Albrecht Alt (1883-1956), who when discussing the origins of the law in Israel only mentions Genesis in one passing footnote.[7]

It is obvious that scholars struggle with using the term *torah* in its strictest sense when classifying the book of Genesis. Characteristic of this line of thought is Terence Fretheim's definition of *torah*. He states, "The Hebrew word *torah* can be more properly used if it is broadly defined as instruction, and hence could include both law and narrative. But, given the usual meanings of the word 'law,' it should not be used as a shorthand reference to the Pentateuch in its entirety" (italics original).[8] While I can appreciate what Fretheim is trying to say, I disagree with his conclusion that the word "law" should not encapsulate the whole of the Pentateuch. Not only are such definitions too narrow, they also fail to give proper weight to the *torah* instruction found in narratives throughout Genesis in particular. Moreover, these narrow definitions go against Jewish tradition, which identifies Genesis not only as part of the Torah, but as its very introduction!

At the same time, care must be taken not to diminish the juridical force of the law in favor of its value as "religious instruction."[9] While using

---

2. See also the comments by Sanders, *Torah and Canon*, 1–3.

3. Crüsemann, *Torah*, 9.

4. See for example Longman, *How to Read Genesis*, 44.

5. On the possible source development of the Pentateuch, see Whybray, *Pentateuch*, 235–42.

6. See for example Greenstein, "Biblical Law," 84; Beyerlin, *Origins and History* (1965); or Crüsemann, *Torah*, 7. Crüsemann is an excellent example of the scholarly focus on the strict legal portions of the Torah while failing to note the *torah* nature of the narratives in the Pentateuch, Genesis in particular.

7. Alt, *Essays on Old Testament*, 81 n2.

8. Fretheim, *Pentateuch*, 20. See a similar conclusion by Wenham, *Exploring the Old Testament*, 4; and Speiser, "The Biblical Idea of History," 214.

9. This is the position taken by Greenstein, "Biblical Law," 84. However, see Milgrom's

the term "instruction" in a general sense may help alleviate the tension, Genesis can also rightly be termed "law" or "case law" in a variety of situations where God in fact brought forth judgment (see next section below).[10] Therefore, focusing mainly on the overt legal portions of the Torah as the primary legal instruction[11] within the Pentateuch is in fact to miss the importance of the implicit legal instruction present within the narratives of Genesis.[12] And, as just noted, such designations fail to take seriously the longstanding Jewish practice of labeling the entirety of the first five books of the Hebrew canon as Torah.

Some of today's scholarly neglect in reading Genesis as Torah may be due to the fact that the NT authors tended to use Genesis in a theological manner (see Rom 5:14; 1 Cor 15:22, 45; 1 Tim 2:13–14; Heb 11:7–22).[13] Now that is not to say that some scholars have not noted the legal teaching of Genesis, but rather that today scholars tend to be more focused on the theological dimension of Genesis as it relates to Israel and the Church[14] as opposed to how the book served as legal instruction/*torah*. Due to this lacuna, I will preface my detailed discussion of Genesis as Torah in the following chapters by doing a brief overview of the types of legal instruction found within the narratives of Genesis. While it is true that the genre of narrative may not immediately come to mind when speaking of legal material, this reality does not in any way diminish the legal instruction housed within narrative.

Genesis Narratives as *Torah*

Narrative dominates the first third of the Pentateuch (Genesis—Exodus 19).[15] With Genesis making up the greatest portion of this block, it is easy to see why many have chosen to label this first book as something other than law. Apart from the designation of Genesis as the prehistory/background for the nation of Israel, scholars tend to use titles such as "theological history,"

---

refutation of it in *Leviticus 17–22*, 1348.

10. Contra Wenham, *Exploring the Old Testament*, 4.
11. See comments by Watts, *Reading Law*, 156.
12. This was a similar conclusion reached by Maimonides (*Mishneh Torah, Hil. Melakhim* 9.3). As noted by Polin, "Jewish Law," 38.
13. Briggs and Lohr, *Theological Introduction*, 26.
14. Ibid., 28.
15. Fretheim, *Pentateuch*, 27.

an "extended introduction,"[16] to the Pentateuch or, as Rolf Knierim asserts, an "introduction to the *Vita Mosis*," that is, the life of Moses (see more on this below).[17] Despite these labels, the dominant narrative genre of Genesis has the appeal of demonstrating both the practical and the technical aspects of the Law through memorable events in Israel's history.[18] Indeed, narrative in any context begs to be interpreted in order to understand its moral and its purpose.[19]

It is no secret that narrative plays a powerful role in juridical procedure, even in today's legal system.[20] A good story told in narrative format has a way of shaping one's perspective while "staying with" the hearer or reader in a memorable way. One could argue that Genesis did this very thing for its Israelite audience while instructing on legal case law.[21] Thus, both narrative and law should be taken seriously when defining what constitutes *torah* instruction. Steven D. Fraade, however, warns that "the history of scholarship has often superimposed upon this distinction between law and narrative the presumption that while narratives might be fanciful, laws must be realistic, aiding and abetting their hermetic, categorical isolation from one another (as between the scholars who study them)."[22] Whether or not one adopts the language of "fanciful" or "realistic," the fact remains that the narratives do in fact teach legal realities and therefore should not be isolated from the strict legal portions of the Torah.

Fortunately, the identification of *torah* instruction within the narratives of Genesis has not gone completely unnoticed. Some scholars have noted that important regulations, especially for later Jewish communities (e.g., of the exilic and Diaspora periods) come from the Genesis narratives thus proving that legal instruction is not isolated to the law codes. As I will

---

16. Longman, *Genesis*, 7–8; Longman, *How to Read Genesis*, 61–62; Watts, *Reading Law*, 155; and Wenham, *Exploring the Old Testament*, 2. See also the perspectives of the Jewish sages in Neusner, *Genesis and Judaism*, 1.

17. Knierim, "Composition," 414, and also 395.

18. While many propose that Genesis 1–11 is based in mythology, the text is written in such a way that it wants to be read as history.

19. Cover, "Nomos and Narrative," 5.

20. See ibid., 4–68, esp. 4–5 and 19–25; Brooks, "Narrative Transactions," 1–28; and Brooks, "Literature as Law's Other," 349–67 esp. 360.

21. Throughout, I do not use the phrase "case law" as a synonym for casuistic law. While there are similarities, there is a distinction due to the absence of the "if . . . then" clauses.

22. Fraade, *Legal Fictions*, 13.

demonstrate in more detail in the following chapters, instructions on keeping Sabbath (2:2; cf. *Rashbam*[23]), prohibitions against eating blood (9:4), capital punishment (9:5–6), circumcision (17:11–27), and endogamous practices (27:46—28:9) are just a few examples of legal instruction that find expression in the opening book of the Torah and are later expanded in the legal portions of the Pentateuch.[24] Indeed, some scholars have gone so far as to insist that many of the laws of Sinai have allusions in the narratives of Genesis.[25] From this perspective, it is clear that the narratives of Genesis demonstrate for an Israelite audience what many of the Sinai laws look like in practice,[26] that is, Genesis is a practical application of law and/or instruction.

The thesis that law and narrative have correspondences should not be surprising in light of the connections made within the Torah itself. For example, the creation account in Gen 1:1—2:4 is clearly stated as the reason for the giving of the Sabbath commandment in Exod 20:9–11. At the same time, there are also diverse perspectives on which portion/genre of the Pentateuch influenced what. For example, Gershon Hepner suggests that the narratives of Genesis were birthed out of the legal portions of the Torah at a much later date.[27] Conversely, Carmichael in his many works related to the Law and the narratives of Genesis insists that it is just the opposite.[28] Although speaking more specifically of narratives outside of Genesis, namely, those in Exodus through Deuteronomy, Milgrom offers a mediating perspective by suggesting that law and narrative may have been written simultaneously.[29] Regardless of which perspective one adopts, most scholars tend to date the material of both the Law and Genesis to a

---

23. Rashbam interpreted Genesis 1 as the basis for Sabbath observance based upon Exod 20:11. See Kamin, "Rashbam's Conception," 100.

24. Crüsemann, "Der Pentateuch," 263–64. See also Watts, *Reading Law*, 124; and Polin, "Jewish Law," 37.

25. See specifically the numerous works of Calum Carmichael cited throughout this work and the perspective of Hepner, *Legal Friction*, 18, 25.

26. So, too, ibid., 27.

27. Ibid., 351. Hepner dates Genesis to the exilic and postexilic eras. While this is indeed possible, the fact remains that the date for the writing of Genesis is up for debate. Here I argue that it was written after Sinai but before the entrance into the land.

28. See for example his statements in the *Origins of Biblical Law*, 20.

29. Milgrom, *Leviticus 17–22*, 1347–48; and Milgrom, *Leviticus 23–27*, 2103. Jackson ("Ideas of Law," 198) also notes the close interchange between law and narrative in the Covenant Code.

much later period of Israel's history. Of course no matter how fanciful one's theory is for such a perspective, there simply is no way to know for certain how the material came to its final form. We can be assured, however, that the material was instructional.

It also should not be surprising that the actual legal tradition of Exodus through Deuteronomy does not make frequent note of the laws of Genesis. This should not be expected if Genesis serves to *explain* in narrative format *pre-existing* law. Read as a whole, Genesis compliments the rest of the Pentateuch and allows the reader to gain an understanding of what specific laws looked like in a practical or a "historical" setting. In this regard, James Bruckner notes that "The unconditional implied imperatives of Genesis 1—Exodus 18 provide a fruitful narrative context for the unconditional commandments given at Sinai."[30] Thus, the reinforcement of *torah* instruction through narratives served to aid the reader/listener in the particulars of the law, especially those relating to life and death issues.

Could Readers Identify Legal Instruction in Narrative?

It makes sense that an author would use narrative for instruction pertaining to legal matters especially in a predominantly aural society. To a degree, one could argue that in the same way today's biblically informed movie goer has no problem identifying biblical allusions and analogies found within the Chronicles of Narnia series and the Tolkein trilogy so, too, the ancient Israelite reader would have easily drawn legal instruction from their inspired narratives. This is particularly true when one considers that Torah reading was to be a regular part of the Israelites' lives (Deut 6:6–9; 11:18–20). On an individual level, the king and Joshua were instructed to read the law regularly (Deut 17:19; Josh 1:8). For the nation as a whole, general instruction was to play a key role in their daily lives (Lev 10:11; cf. Deut 33:10; 2 Chr 17:7–9). John Sailhamer rightly notes that "The Torah was written to be read more than once. In fact, much of its message comes into focus only after one has read through the whole Pentateuch several times."[31] Apart from individual study (Deut 6:6–9; 11:18–20), the Hebrew Law was to be read aloud every seven years during the Feast of Booths (Deut 31:10–13). With the repetition of the stories of Genesis came clear instruction on how to keep the Law and what actions to avoid. In this regard, Dale Patrick

---

30. Bruckner, *Implied Law*, 221.
31. Sailhamer, *Pentateuch*, 144.

and Allen Scult note that "narratives either recommend and promote or condemn and repress the action they portray."[32]

There is also a debate on what actually constituted *torah* instruction for the nation. On the one hand, scholars have argued that this instruction did not appear to include an extensive law code—perhaps only some form of Deuteronomy (2 Kgs 23:2–3; 2 Chr 34:30–31). On the other hand, even though scholars have long struggled with the concept of Israel having the "entire" law (i.e., good portions of the Pentateuch) read to them, some actually propose that this was possible and even likely.[33] Ezra's reading of the Law seems to intimate that the book of the Law was extensive due to the fact that he read the Law over several days (Neh 8:1–5, 13, 18; 9:3). Some scholars now believe that Ezra in fact was reading the entire Pentateuch at the time of the postexilic period. If this was the case, Genesis would have been read at that time as Law.[34]

Gaining an understanding of the Torah through familiarity with the narratives of Genesis would make even more sense in an aural society where repetition and stories were central to learning. As I will demonstrate in the following chapters, it appears that at least in some cases the author did in fact choose specific stories and content when telling the prehistory of Israel in order to teach specific laws. Therefore these stories carried weight beyond historical and theological importance; they also offered *torah* instruction. It is perhaps best to take to heart the words of Gabriel Josipovici, who notes that, "the Israelites placed their laws within a narrative context, in a book along with stories, genealogies, poems and prophecies, and even, as in Exodus, within the same portion of the book. Are we being good readers when we split up what has been put together in this way? Is it not up to us to try and understand what that putting together might imply?"[35] On his last question, I believe one has to answer in the affirmative, especially when dealing with the narrative content of Genesis.

Taken from this perspective the comments of Bruckner become poignant. He notes that in Genesis one does not find many direct commands against particular things that are sinful, what he calls "oughts and ought nots"; rather in Genesis they are implied in the narratives.[36] He continues,

32. Patrick and Scult, *Rhetoric*, 114.
33. Watts, *Reading Law*, 23–24.
34. So, too, ibid., 20.
35. Josipovici, *Book of God*, 92.
36. Bruckner, *Implied Law*, 18.

"In contrast to the biblical text's depiction of God's revealing of the law to Moses on the mountain, the oughts of Genesis are not explicitly delivered or revealed. Rather, they are woven into creational motifs in the plot and dialogue of the narrative."[37] Bruckner also notes that "Historical interests in law have served to reconstruct the history of legal sources, forms and settings that lie behind the biblical text, but little attention has been given to interpreting law in its canonical and narrative context."[38] (Again, it is this lacuna that I wish to address in this book.)

As an example of this type of instruction, Bruckner concludes that the sin of coveting is a central teaching in the pre-Sinai narratives.[39] Now while coveting is indeed a central concept—as I will demonstrate in the following chapters—Bruckner's focus is by far too limiting of what the Genesis narratives are actually teaching the "implied audience." In this vein, it is important to ask who exactly were the Genesis narratives written for? And who could have written them? Does it even matter to our discussion? It is to these topics that I now turn my attention.

The "Implied" Audience of Genesis

In recent decades it has become common fare for scholars to look to the final form of the Pentateuch as evidence that the "implied readers" were at least from the exilic period and far removed from the land.[40] However, in cases like this, it is important to distinguish between material that *implies* an earlier period or context versus notations that show clear signs of *updating* at a later period (Gen 11:28, 31; 14:14;15:7; 28:19; 35:6; Deut 1:1, 5; 2:10–12; 3:9; 4:41, 46–49 etc.). That Genesis went through a series of edits is to be understood (e.g., references to Canaanites [13:7]; Ur of the Chaldees [11:28, 31; 15:7]; Dan [14:14]; and Israel's kings [36:31]).[41] However, the

---

37. Ibid., 200.

38. Ibid., 23.

39. Ibid., 222–23. For example, Bruckner notes that pharaoh and Abimelech coveted Sarah (chs. 12; 20); Sarah coveted Hagar's sexuality (ch. 16); Jacob coveted Esau's birthright and blessing (ch. 27); Shechem coveted Dinah and the possessions of Jacob and his family (ch. 34); Joseph's brothers coveted Jacob's favor (ch. 37); etc.

40. Fretheim, *Pentateuch*, 40–43. This is most evident in the book of Deuteronomy as demonstrated by Fretheim. Blenkinsopp (*Abraham*, 20) posits a late date and editing of the Abraham account.

41. Wenham, *Genesis 1–15*, xliv. These issues were noted as early as Baruch Spinoza (seventeenth century). See his *Theologico-Political Treatise*, 103–9 (118–124 in C.

prehistory of the text is still very much open to debate. A clear counter argument to the late date for Genesis is the conclusion of Gordon Wenham who allows for the antiquity of many parts of Genesis and argues persuasively against a late date (i.e., exilic and postexilic) by suggesting that the editing/revision of Genesis took place in the period of the United Monarchy.[42] Similarly, some scholars of the recent past have also tried to connect Genesis and the patriarchal narratives in particular to the political milieu of David's day, thus interpreting them through the lens of political critique.[43]

Wenham appears to be on the right track.[44] Some form of the earliest text—whether in oral form or not one cannot be sure—appears to reflect content from the period of Moses at least in an implied sense.[45] From this vantage point, the "implied readers" in the text are the Israelites encamped on the Plains of Moab prior to entering the land of Canaan.[46] Whether these implied readers are a literary fiction as some posit is a matter of debate.[47] The reason that this is important to our discussion will become evident in the following chapters where I will demonstrate that some of the *torah* instruction in Genesis makes the most sense in a Mosaic context.

Of course coming to the conclusion that the author or editors wanted to present Moses as the author does not negate the fact that when the Pentateuch reached its final form that it would have been instructional for all Israel at later periods as well. The use of the divine name, YHWH, is a case in point. For example, even though the patriarchal period is distinct in its instruction/portrayal of the earlier period, at times it betrays Mosaic monotheism and Yahwism.[48] It is clear that the narratives of Genesis are being told from a later Yahwistic perspective and are intended to be read as such by an audience from a much later time than that portrayed by the

---

Gebhardt's vol. 3 1925 edition).

42. Wenham, *Story as Torah*, 41–43.

43. See von Rad, *The Problem of the Hexateuch*, 166–204, esp. 169, 172. See also, Brueggemann, "David and His Theologian," 156–81; Rendsburg, "David and His Circle," 438–46; and Ho, "Stories of the Family," 514–31. For a critique of Rendsurg's and Ho's methodological approach, see Noble, "Esau, Tamar, and Joseph," 222–28.

44. Wenham (*Genesis 1–15*, xliv) suggests a date between 1250 BCE (following a late date for the exodus) and prior to 950 BCE.

45. Briggs and Lohr, *Theological Introduction*, 24.

46. See also Keiser, *Genesis 1–11*, 150; and Watts, *Reading Law*, 127–29.

47. Carmichael (*Law, Legend, and Incest*, 103) suggests that the implied audience is in fact "fictional."

48. Moberly, *Old Testament of the Old Testament*, 104.

accounts.[49] The blending of the divine name with the more generic term for God, Elohim, proves that the narratives of Genesis were meant to be instructive for a later audience. Of course this later audience could just as easily have been from the pre-conquest period in light of the revelation of the divine name prior to the exodus (cf. Exod 3:13–15; 6:3). Yet, if the implied audience is pre-conquest Israel, it not only presupposes, but expects, that Moses is the dominant speaker/writer. Even though this is no longer the accepted stance within scholarship today,[50] it nonetheless appears to be the way later editors wanted the Pentateuch to be read. This naturally leads to the topic of authorship and the unity of Genesis.

Singularity of Authorship: Does it Point to Moses?

Over the past 150 years, diachronic and synchronic approaches to the study of the Pentateuch have dominated scholarly discussions. Both of these approaches directly affect the issues of authorship and the unity of Genesis. Scholars approaching Genesis from the former perspective insist that it is naïve to view the book as anything but an amalgamation of sources collected over time and supplemented by a variety of editors/redactors. However, source-critical approaches have led to the fragmentation of the final form and in turn the fragmentation of its message.[51] The effects of source theory taken as a whole have diminished the message of Genesis as *torah*. Indeed, the atomistic tendencies of the historical-critical approaches of the past,[52] especially that of source and form criticism, made it almost impossible to draw any real meaning out of the final form of the text, which, it is argued, was "the product of varied schools of thought operating over a period of several hundred years."[53] Gerhard von Rad (1901–1971) sums up the problem well when he states, "On almost all sides the final form of the Hexateuch has come to be regarded as a starting-point barely worthy of

---

49. See the detailed discussion on the divine name in Genesis and Exodus in ibid., 36–78.

50. See the discussion by Nigosian, "Moses," 339–44; and Nicholson, "The Pentateuch," 10–21.

51. For an excellent overview of the state of historical-critical studies, see Lim, *Grace*, 1–9.

52. See the astute and concise assessment of Clines, *Theme*, 7–10.

53. Damrosch, *Narrative Covenant*, 9.

An Introduction to Reading Genesis as Torah

discussion, from which the debate should move away as rapidly as possible in order to reach the real problems underlying it."[54] In this light, approaches that attempt to show a unified message based upon the final form are often dismissed as naïve and lacking scholarly importance.[55] This is unfortunate because of the obvious desire of the later editors who clearly wanted to have Genesis and the Torah as a whole read as though it was written by Moses prior to his death on the Plains of Moab on Mt. Nebo.

Nevertheless, there are a few positive aspects of the historical-critical method that shed light on Genesis as *torah*. Some form-critical work on Genesis does allow insights into the text that can be helpful in isolating *torah* instruction. Apart from etiological accounts (e.g., tithing—14:20; 28:22, and food laws—32:32),[56] a good example of the benefits of form criticism is highlighted by Bruckner, who lists the following legal instruction from genre forms in Genesis: "1. Commercial law (e.g. contracts of sale and family law) in the purchase of Ephron's field (Gen. 23) and in Jacob's marriage contract (Gen. 24). 2. Treaties between men (Gen. 21, 26, 31) and covenants with God, accompanied by cultic sacrifice (Gen. 8, 12, 13, 15, 26, 33, 35). 3. Juridical procedure (secular and sacral), as in the arraignments of Abimelech (Gen. 20), of Sodom (Gen. 18–19), of Jacob (Gen. 31) and of Tamar (Gen. 38)."[57] Of particular interest in this list is the fact that the juridical proceedings noted here reflect a period prior to the institution of civil authority/kingship.[58] As such, many of the legal nuances would have fit a period in Israel's history when a similar situation was the norm. This once again may point to the author's desire to connect these accounts to the early period of Israel's history when this type of instruction was needed.

Those holding to a synchronic approach to the Scriptures assert that the Pentateuch—and Genesis in particular—should be read as it now stands in its canonical form and context.[59] Being fully aware of the complexities that often accompany literary-historical approaches to the text, I still feel

---

54. Von Rad *The Problem of the Hexateuch*, 1.

55. Fortunately, some are beginning to see the value of the narrative coherence of Genesis and perhaps the work of an author, not merely a redactor, pulling this material together. See for example the comments by Noble "Esau, Tamar, and Joseph," 244–49 esp. 249.

56. See more in Long, *Etiological Narrative*; Schmid, *Moses Story*, 81; and von Rad, *The Problem of the Hexateuch*, 169.

57. Bruckner, *Implied Law*, 14. See also Westermann, *Genesis 12–36*, 79–83.

58. So Westermann, *Genesis 12–36*, 83.

59. See comments by Clines, *Theme*, 7–15.

Genesis as Torah

there is benefit in examining how the final form would have been heard or read by its audience, whether pre-exilic, exilic, or postexilic is impossible to know with certainty, although some messages clearly fit most appropriately in a given time period.[60] Whether the earliest readers of Genesis understood the events of the book as actually happening as they are recorded is not of importance in this particular discussion because in reality we can never answer this question with certainty. The final form of the text that we have, however, does present a message that can be analyzed with the purpose of determining, in at least some ways, how the first readers would have interpreted their history and legal texts.

As I will demonstrate in the chapters that follow, rhetorical, narratival, and structural features of Genesis betray the author's desire to offer clear instruction on a variety of matters. Over the past three decades, more and more scholars are recognizing the existence of at least a central controlling editor/compiler of the Pentateuch.[61] Moreover, many have come to recognize that the book of Genesis reflects one controlling "mind" (e.g., the Yahwist) in its composition.[62] Now whether that is one person or a group of people working together cannot be determined. It is also impossible to know what portions of the narratives are based upon earlier source material, oral tradition, and/or divine revelation.

Despite the rhetorical and narrative unity of Genesis, most Pentateuchal scholars have rejected Mosaic authorship *a priori*. Of course, to posit the very idea that Moses may have had a hand in writing the books that contain so much information about his life and work is at best to invite cackles and scoffs and at worse to be accused of "special pleading" or labeled naïve and unscholarly. Yet few scholars who posit such a stance (i.e., for Mosaic authorship and/or influence) would reject the notion that editing (accounting for changes in vocabulary) and updating (perhaps accounting for anachronisms) has occurred (see above). And while the date of this final editing is up for debate, one cannot deny that the setting, which the author(s) wished to present, is indeed Mosaic for the most part.[63] That

---

60. On the possibility of reading Genesis 12-36 in the Persian period, see Heard, *Dynamics of Diselection*.

61. See Whybray, *Pentateuch*, 221-35.

62. See for example the argument for unity by Brodie, *Genesis*, 5-25; and Lim, *Grace*, 90.

63. Fretheim, *Pentateuch*, 31; and Carmichael, *Origins of Biblical Law*, 13-14. Whybray (*Pentateuch*, 241) propounds that the author of the laws is not the same as the author of the historical narratives. However, he offers no proof for his claim other than

is, the Pentateuch wants to be read as though it was "transmitted to Israel by God through Moses."[64] The truth is no one can be one hundred percent certain as to what portions are non-Mosaic. As I noted above, in some cases, only Mosaic authorship makes sense of some of the details.[65] Even if the author is not Moses, someone certainly wanted to portray him as such.

At the same time, one must contend with the reality that authority for Genesis as *torah* comes from the fact that in both historical (e.g., Josephus, Philo, Nahmanides [1194-1270][66]) and textual traditions (Nehemiah 9; Luke 24:27, 44; John 1:17, 45; 5:46; 7:19, 22; Acts 28:23) Moses has been identified as the author.[67] This connection to Moses brought force to the teaching components of the narratives that a simple record of Israel's history—assigned to an unknown author—did not have. Even if one refuses to acknowledge the connection between the author and Moses, the fact that the Torah is presented as a direct revelation from God certainly is meant to bring legitimacy to the narratives of Genesis.

Before leaving this discussion concerning the authorship of Genesis one more aspect needs to be addressed which seems to point to the reality that the author wanted to present Moses' dominant role in formulating the narratives not only in Exodus through Deuteronomy, but also Genesis. This is made evident by the fact that the Pentateuch reflects biographical material related to Moses.

Genesis as Biography

Despite possible debates to the contrary, one is hard pressed not to recognize and admit the fact that the Pentateuch reflects biographical material directly related to Moses' life. Furthermore, the content is heavily weighted in that direction. Comprising 25 percent of the Pentateuch, Genesis reflects *all* of history before the time of Moses. On the other hand, Exodus to Deuteronomy—the remaining 75 percent—covers only the 120 years of

---

his basic assertion that it seems logical to draw such a conclusion.

64. Crüsemann, *Torah*, 6. See also the discussion by Watts, "Legal Characterization," 415–26.

65. Contra Emmerich ("Temptation Narrative," 19–20), who argues for a late date from a circular perspective. Just because *scholars* label something "Deuteronomic" does not mean that it did not reflect Mosaic traditions or that it necessarily has to be of a later date.

66. See discussion by Sperling, *Original Torah*, 14–16.

67. See comments by Watts, *Reading Law*, 89–90.

Genesis as Torah

Moses' life.[68] Of course it is not new to see the Pentateuch as a biography of Moses.[69] Now whether it is to be understood as something along the lines of a "sacred biography" versus "historical biography"[70] is a matter of debate. Nevertheless, as we will see throughout the following chapters, certain features of the book of Genesis have striking parallels with the life of Moses[71] even though his name never appears in the book.[72] While I will address more of these parallels as I move forward, at this point a few examples should suffice to prove my point.[73]

1. God starts anew with Adam, Noah, and Abraham, and threatens to do so with Moses (Exod 32:10).[74]

2. Abraham and Moses are intercessors (Gen 18:23–33; 20:7; Exod 33:12–16; Num 14:13–19).[75]

3. Moses and Jacob are forced to flee their homelands in a self-imposed exile.

4. Both find a wife/wives and have a family while in a foreign land (Genesis 29; Exodus 2).

5. Both return to their people with God's blessing (Gen 31:3; Exod 3:10)

6. Both give a blessing to the tribes of Israel before they die (Genesis 49; Deuteronomy 33).[76]

---

68. Knierim, "Composition," 395.

69. See discussion by Watts, *Reading Law*, 154–57. See also the works of Sailhamer, *Pentateuch*, 62–66; Henn, *The Bible as Literature*, 191–94; Nigosian, "Moses," 345–48 (Nigosian calls it "sacred biography" not "historical biography"); Knierim, *The Task of Old Testament Theology*, 372–79 esp. 377; Knierim, "Composition," 395–96, 409–15; Kirsch, *Moses* (1998); Blenkinsopp, *Pentateuch*, 52; and Wenham, *Exploring the Old Testament*, 2–3, 36.

70. Nigosian, "Moses," 344.

71. Contra Watts, *Reading Law*, 156.

72. For a chart on the frequency of Moses' name in the OT, see Nigosian, "Moses," 346.

73. Based upon Homeric studies, Alter (*Biblical Narrative*, 47–62 esp. 56–58) identified these types of scenarios as "type-scenes." In particular, this one he calls "the betrothal type-scene" (52).

74. Postell, *Adam as Israel*, 147.

75. Many of these are as noted by Wenham, *Exploring the Old Testament*, 3.

76. So, too, Josipovici, *Book of God*, 88; and Schmid, *Moses Story*, 84–85.

7. And as is often noted, Jacob and Moses represent, in a collective sense, the people of Israel.

By noting these parallels I do not wish to imply that one should read every part of Genesis as in some way reflecting biographical material of Moses.[77] On the contrary, but it does appear that the final editor made sure that Moses' "fingerprints" were all over the text in order to alert his readers to the reality that Moses was to be identified as the implied author or at least a central figure even in the book of Genesis. In this vein, Knierim notes that "just as Moses is seen as the one decisive person for all of humanity's history and existence so is he the decisive person for all of humanity's history and existence."[78] As such, reading Genesis through a Mosaic lens, especially in an instructive manner, should be a natural means of aiding in its interpretation.

The Legal Instruction of Genesis versus the Laws of Sinai

Before moving on to our analysis of Genesis it is vital that we examine one final issue. This deals with how to handle some of the actions of the characters within the narratives of Genesis that are at odds with the laws delivered at Sinai. How can these narratives be instructional for a post-Sinai audience? A good example of this type of conflicting instruction can be found in the marital choices of Abraham and Jacob. Abraham married his half-sister and Jacob married two women who were sisters. In both cases, the later law forbade such nuptial pairings (cf. Lev 18:11; 20:17 and Lev 18:18 respectively). Another issue is the apparent disregard for the law of primogeniture (Deut 21:15–17).[79] This issue is played out in the lives of Cain and Seth, Isaac and Ishmael, Jacob and Esau, Joseph and his brothers (note also Perez and Zerah), and Ephraim and Manasseh (cf. Gen 25:23; 48:14–20; 1 Sam 16:12–13; 1 Chr 22:9).[80] Of course from an instructional standpoint it is possible that the continued appearance of the motif of the younger sibling ruling over the elder, or in some way being favored by God,

---

77. See the warnings of Sailhamer, *Pentateuch*, 65–66.

78. Knierim, "Composition," 414.

79. Stahl, *Law and Liminality*, 17. For a more detailed study on primogeniture, see Greenspahn, *Brothers*, 9–29.

80. See also comments by Cover, "Nomos and Narrative," 20–21.

may in fact reflect God's choice of Israel—a newly formed nation—over the "older" and more "mature" nations like Egypt and those in Mesopotamia (Exod 19:3–5; Deut 7:7; 32:8–9).[81]

Apart from these specific examples, it is important to note that a number of the questionable actions of the patriarchs and matriarchs of Israel may not have necessarily been included simply to show an editor's slavish loyalty to his sources but rather that these accounts were included for the purpose of showing Israel *why* the Mosaic Law was needed in the first place. Indeed, when law is absent anarchy can reign, especially when someone is ignorant of specific God-ordained laws (see Gen 29:26).

Finally, one must remember that while in *some* cases actions in the Genesis narratives appear in conflict with the Sinai tradition, in reality the giving of the law at Sinai was, according to Fretheim, "not a new reality . . . Sinai is a drawing together of previously known law, and some natural extensions thereof; it intensifies their import for this newly shaped community. In most respects, Sinai is simply a regiving of the law implicitly or explicitly commanded in creation. Sinai reiterates for those redeemed the demands of creation."[82] Similarly, Walter Kaiser notes that the commands of the Decalogue already appear in the Genesis narratives, a fact I will note throughout this work.[83]

Conclusion

Having dealt with a variety of concerns related to reading Genesis as *torah*, I will now pull together some of my preliminary conclusions and premises, which will govern my discussions that follow. First, *torah* instruction can come in a variety of genres, narrative is indeed a dominant one. Second, Genesis should not be read in isolation from the rest of the Torah as a mere retelling of Israel's prehistory, it is a fundamental part of Israel's instruction. Third, while frequent reading of the law would have allowed for a level of familiarity with the law, the narratives of Genesis would have afforded the Israelites a means of remembering key parts of the Torah through the genre of story. This in turn would have facilitated a passing on of the law to the next generation. Fourth, no matter what methodological approach one takes to Genesis, it is clear that the final form assumes Mosaic authorship

---

81. Kaminsky, "Election," 151.
82. Fretheim, "Reclamation," 363. See also Fretheim, "The Book of Genesis," 483–84.
83. Kaiser, *Old Testament Ethics*, 81–82.

and that the implied audience is Israel encamped on the Plains of Moab prior to the conquest. As such, we will see that the legal instruction found in Genesis often reflects this milieu. Finally, even though a number of events and actions in Genesis appear to be in conflict with the Sinai tradition, more often than not, the narratives of Genesis serve as instruction, which reinforces creation mandates *and* by extension, the laws of Sinai.

As I now move to an analysis of the text of Genesis a final word of warning seems in order for those who have been steeped in the historical-critical method, which, at first glance, may appear to be at odds with my approach in the following chapters. Watts notes well the fact that "Though the training of modern biblical scholars usually introduces them to historical theories about the text before they have read most of it, methodologically the text must be read sympathetically (i.e. described as it stands) before historical questions and evidence can be adduced from it . . . The evidence of Israel's reading practices [leads] . . . to a fundamentally rhetorical orientation that understands persuasion, rather than literary art, to be the overriding purpose of the text's composition."[84] If *persuasion* is the "overriding purpose of the text's composition" then one must ask of what exactly was the author of Genesis trying to persuade his audience? In what follows I hope to answer this very question.

---

84. Watts, *Reading Law*, 132.

2

Genesis 1–2

Creation as Foundational to God's Torah

Anyone who has ever read Genesis 1 and 2 with the purpose of appreciating their artistic features will quickly recognize that these chapters record what appear to be two very different perspectives of the creation event. On the one hand, Genesis 1 pictures a watery chaos brought into submission at the mere command of God/Elohim. God creates the universe, sky and oceans, dry land, and the respective "inhabitants" of these spaces (i.e., the sun, moon, stars, the birds and fishes, the creeping things, and humans etc.) and in turn God declares that all these things are good (1:4, 10, 12, 18, 21, 25, 31). On the other hand, Genesis 2 depicts a dry and barren wasteland in need of the close attention of the creator God, YHWH Elohim. In this latter account, the author brings into sharp focus the creation of Adam and Eve and a garden made specifically as their home. The creation of Adam is personal: God fashions him (2:7), and later, the animals (2:19), as a potter would fashion a clay vessel.[1] The creation of Eve is no less personal. After removing a rib from Adam's side, YHWH "builds" (*banah*) the perfect helper and companion for the man (2:18, 21–22).

Scholars have long noted the distinctions between these two accounts from a source-critical perspective.[2] Genesis 1 has been assigned to the hand of the putative Priestly source and chapter 2 to the hand of the theo-

---

1. So, too, von Rad, *Old Testament Theology*, 1:149.
2. For example, see ibid., 1:139–53.

Genesis 1–2

retical "J"/Yahwistic author.[3] While the arguments related to the dating of these texts can be pedantic, the fact remains that in their final form they are meant to be read as synoptic accounts of the same event.[4] As an introduction to the Torah, they must have originally been read—or understood in their oral form—as being in some way instructional for the Israelites.[5] Whether the audience was pre-monarchic, pre-exilic, or postexilic or some combination of the three cannot be determined with any degree of certainty. Nevertheless, if one takes at face value the claims of the Torah, namely, that these are the words of Moses to the children of Israel prior to their entering the land of Canaan, then one may find a fuller appreciation of what these texts were trying to teach the first and second generations of Israel and beyond.

In this chapter, I will examine a number of ways these two opening chapters may have been viewed as *torah* instruction for Israel. Now to be sure, any number of minor intertextual and motif connections could be made between Genesis 1 and 2 and later *torah* instruction.[6] For example, scholars have noted the connections between the splitting of the waters in Genesis 1 and the dividing of the Red Sea.[7] Or one could note the obvious interconnectedness of the creation of the sun, moon, and stars for appointed seasons (1:14) as a precursor to the appointed times of Israel's feasts

---

3. The dates of these theoretical sources are debated. The Priestly source is often dated to the late sixth or even to the fifth century BCE, with some scholars insisting that it predates the J-source. See for example, Wenham, *Genesis 1–15*, xxxi–xxxii. The Yahwistic source has been almost universally dated to the tenth century BCE.

4. So Longman, *Genesis*, 46–47; Sailhamer, *Genesis Unbound*, 88–90; Mathews, *Genesis 1—11:26*, 188–89; and Arnold, *Genesis*, 55. Wenham ("Sanctuary Symbolism," 404) suggests that the opening three chapters have more in common thematically/symbolically than most acknowledge. As such, could one conclude that perhaps they may come from the same author/editor?

5. Carmichael (*Origins of Biblical Law*, 45–50) argues that the Priestly author fashioned the "ten sayings" of creation in Genesis 1 after the ten words of the Decalogue (cf. m. *Pirqe Aboth* 5:1).

6. Noble ("Esau, Tamar, and Joseph," 219–52) rightly notes the inherent pitfalls of making intertextual connections without a defined methodology. While many of Noble's points are valid, he may be too stringent in his methodological criteria. Based upon his criteria, virtually none of the midrashic connections would have ever been made; yet, Jewish interpreters did make what appear at times to be very tangential connections. The truth is ancient readers/hearers no doubt understood/read their texts very differently than we understand/read ours.

7. Postell, *Adam as Israel*, 33 n37.

Genesis as Torah

(Exod 12:16; Lev 23:2–37).[8] Even the ordering of creation into "kinds" (*min*; 1:11, 12, 21, 24, 25) prepares the reader for the various food laws and the restrictions placed upon the nation of Israel (Leviticus 11; Deuteronomy 14).[9] While at particular points in this chapter I will draw upon what could be classified as micro-connections such as these, generally speaking I will examine larger motifs and parallels along with some of the theological nuances of these opening two chapters.[10] I will not examine in any detail the role that Eden and Adam play vis-à-vis Israel; that discussion will be reserved for the next chapter.

Instruction on the Ten Commandments

Initiating our discussion with the parallels between creation and the Ten Commandments seems a fitting place to begin in light of the Decalogue's role as an overview of general *torah* instruction.[11] While a number of laws will be addressed throughout this chapter, none play quite as an important a role as do the Ten Commandments. In the dual creation accounts of Genesis, the author highlights a number of these commandments by what he says and, in some cases, by what he does not say or include in the narrative. When the entirety of chapters 1 and 2 are considered, it becomes clear that they in some way address the first five of the Ten Commandments either directly or indirectly. On the other hand, commandments 6–10 become more pronounced in later chapters.

Commandments 1 and 2

To begin, the monotheistic thrust of the creation narratives clearly reflect the instruction found within the first two commandments, namely, do not have any other gods before YHWH and do not make idols.[12] The monothe-

---

8. Ibid., 108 n126; Vogels, "Calendars," 133–48; and Gorman, "Priestly Rituals," 354–57.

9. See for example Douglas, "Forbidden Animals," 16–18; Douglas, *Purity and Danger*, 51–71 esp. 69; Greenstein, "Biblical Law," 91, 96; and Gorman, *Ideology*, 39–45, 52.

10. For a detailed theological treatment of Genesis 1–11, see Lim, *Grace* (2002).

11. This is particularly the case for Deuteronomy where the Decalogue of chapter 5 serves as an outline of sorts for the remainder of the stipulations section of chapters 6–26.

12. Patrick ("Structure," 107–18 esp. 107–13) and Bruckner (*Implied Law*, 221–22) argue that the first commandment does not appear in Genesis 1—Exodus 18. While both are correct that no explicit statement is made about other gods, perhaps with the

istic perspective of these opening narratives draws a stark contrast with the polytheistic nature of other ANE creation accounts.[13] Although I will be handling this topic in more detail below, suffice it to say that the opening lines of Genesis 1 make it clear that there are no other gods on par with Israel's creator God: Israel's God stands alone *and* creates alone.[14] Unlike so many of the ANE creation myths, Israel's God does not create other deities to join him in governing the cosmos, nor does he have a consort. For those of the first generation after the exodus (the implied audience of the text) coming from Egypt where there was a panoply of gods, the opening lines of Genesis 1 would have been jarring. This would have been no less the case for a later audience, which had grown up in exile in Babylon surrounded by numerous creation myths about a multiplicity of gods and goddesses. In this regard, the author's refusal to mention the actual names for the sun and the moon when speaking of their creation (1:16) is one of the stronger arguments reflecting the author's intentions to place Israel's God above all others.

The sun and moon are simply called the lesser and the greater lights (1:16). In Hebrew the terms for sun (*shemesh*) and for the moon (*yareach*) are also parallel terms/names for the sun and moon gods in other cultures. For example, in Babylon the sun god Shamash (Shapash at Ugarit) was worshipped regularly while the moon god Yarikh (a cognate of *yareach*) was an important god at ancient Ugarit.[15] Interestingly, in Mesopotamia the moon god was believed to have begotten the sun and thus was seen as greater than the sun god. In the case of Genesis, the author even undermines this concept by placing the greater light (i.e., the sun) ahead of the lesser light (i.e., the moon).

Also of interest is the fact that the moon god was believed to be a judge over human fate while the sun was often depicted as the giver of life (e.g., the Egyptian sun god Aten; cf. *ANET*, 369–71). Within the creation account, it is YHWH who gives life (2:7), and throughout the Torah it is YHWH who judges (Gen 6:1–7; 15:14; 18:25; 19:13, 24; Exod 5:21; 14:17–28; Lev 10:2; Num 11; 12; 14; 16; 25 etc.). Furthermore, in the ANE where gods created other gods and birthed lesser deities, the author of Genesis

---

exception of Jacob's request in 35:2–4, the implicit teaching is deafening.

13. See also Collins, "Historical Adam," 153.
14. See also Patrick and Scult, *Rhetoric*, 112, 115.
15. In Mesopotamia, the moon god was known by three different names: Suen/Sin, Nana, and Ashimbabbar.

removes all doubt about the uniqueness of God (cf. Deut 6:4–6). That is why Israel was not to worship any of the hosts of the heavens—they are merely created things (Gen 1:14–16; Deut 4:19; 17:3; cf. 2 Kgs 21:3; 23:5, 11; Jer 8:2; Ezek 8:16).

By diminishing the pride of place given to the sun, moon, and stars as deities, as was common in the ANE, the author of Genesis speaks volumes from an instructional perspective. If the hosts of heaven are mere creations, then Israel should never make images of them for the purpose of worship. Also, beyond the anthropomorphic details ascribed to God in both of these chapters, God is never likened to any *thing* per se (e.g., the hosts of heaven, natural phenomena, or animals), which should discourage Israel from fashioning an image in his likeness. If anything, the author's presentation of God in the creation accounts stresses that it is only humanity that is made in God's image, nothing else. God stands on his own, transcendent and apart from his creation, yet, relational and immanent enough to get his "hands dirty" by creating humankind from the dust of the earth.

By stressing the first commandment within the opening chapter of the Torah, the author is showing the central and most vital aspect of the Torah—there is but one God with whom Israel is to be in relationship. For as Fretheim rightly notes, "Only as the community remains in a right relationship with God (see Deut. 6:5) is obedience of the law truly possible."[16]

Commandment 3

Closely connected to the source theory for dating and interpreting Genesis 1 and 2 is the author's use of different divine names in each of these chapters.[17] Genesis 1 exclusively uses the generic term for God, namely, Elohim; whereas Genesis 2 uses YHWH Elohim. Source theorists argue that the Priestly author chose to use Elohim in an effort to avoid defaming the sacred covenant name of YHWH. To a degree, this thinking is rooted in *torah* instruction found within the third commandment, which forbids the taking of God's name in vain (Exod 20:7). While this is indeed possible, as we will see in our discussion below there may be another reason for this anomaly.

---

16. Fretheim, "Reclamation," 365.

17. I use the term "author" for ease of discussion even though more than one may have been involved in the writing of the text.

Genesis 1–2

Commandment 4

Instruction related to the Ten Commandments continues with the institution of the Sabbath day rest, a direct link to the fourth commandment (Gen 2:2–3; Exod 20:8–10).[18] In fact, in Exod 20:11 Moses uses God's resting at the end of the creation week as a means of justifying the Sabbath day rest for Israel.[19] Even though God could have created the universe in a moment of time, some have seen in the six-day creation week further instruction for Israel: following God's design, Israel's work week was to be six days followed by a day of rest.[20] Now to be sure, it could be argued that the Sabbath rest of God is ongoing and therefore the parallel is not one-to-one. While this is perhaps a correct way of viewing God's ongoing "Sabbath," the fact remains that for Israel, this was an important part of who they were as a nation (cf. Jer 17:19–27).

The importance of the Sabbath is strengthened by the fact that this particular regulation appears across a variety of legal material in the Torah (e.g., Exod 31:12–17; 35:1–3; Lev 23:1–3; Deut 5:12–15; cf. Exod 16:29). Sabbath in essence became the sign of the Sinai covenant (Exod 31:13, 17; cf. Ezek 20:12, 20).[21] So important was this day of rest that the Law required the death penalty for those who did not adhere to it (Exod 35:2; Num 15:30–36). In many ways, Sabbath made Israel distinct among the surrounding nations. Nothing quite like it has been found within other ANE cultures.[22]

One of the unique features of the Israelite Sabbath was how it was applied universally within society. According to Exod 23:12 (cf. Deut 5:14), even foreign sojourners, servants/slaves, and animals were to rest from their work whether the Sabbath fell during planting season or harvest (Exod 34:21). The example set by God brought into sharp focus the importance for the Israelites to take the time to cease from their labors and to reflect upon who their God was and what he had done for them in bringing them out of Egypt and promising them a land of their own. As we will see in the next chapter, some scholars are now drawing a direct connection

---

18. Contra von Rad, *Old Testament Theology*, 1:148. For a discussion on the Sabbath, see Tsevat, *Meaning*, 39–52.

19. So, too, Wenham, *Story as Torah*, 26–27.

20. Sailhamer, *Genesis Unbound*, 95.

21. Hasel, "Sabbath," 852.

22. Some posit that the Akkadian concept of *shapattu* is the forerunner of Sabbath in Israel (see *ANET*, 68 and n84).

between the blessing of Eden given to Adam and the promise of Canaan given to Israel.

Commandment 5

The fifth commandment—to honor one's father and mother—finds a number of narrative parallels in Genesis (e.g., 9:20–27; 26:34–35; 27:7–46; 28:1–4 etc.). In the creation narrative, this is no less the case. The narrative comment of 2:24, which encourages a man to leave his father and mother and to cling to his wife, in many ways undermines ancient patriarchal customs. While some have seen in this verse the remnants of a matriarchal society, in reality this is a warning to young men and women that the marriage bond is supposed to be greater than the kinship ties to one's parents. Even though a son still was to honor his parents, the husband-wife union was to be greater.[23] The bedrock of the covenant community was the family unit and was therefore not be threatened by parental interference in a God-sanctioned marriage relationship. Finally, God's creation of humans in his image and then the portrayal of YHWH Elohim intimately fashioning Adam and Eve present God as a "father" figure of sorts. Humanity, and by extension Israel, were to honor their Creator/Father for who he truly was—the giver of life and all of creation's goodness!

Commandments 6–10

The portion of the Ten Commandments related more to the interrelationships of the covenant community does not find fitting parallels in Genesis 1 and 2 due to the fact that these commandments deal with sins that become prevalent *after* the fall. Nevertheless, within the remaining chapters of Genesis, on numerous occasions we will see the breach of the rest of the commandments: Cain murders his brother and lies about it (4:8–9), and Lamech murders a young man for a minor offense (4:23; cf. 6:1–8); Pharaoh and Abimelech covet what was not rightly theirs and almost commit unintentional adultery in the process (12:10–20; 20:1–18; 26:7–10); Eve also covets and takes that which is not rightly hers as does Jacob (3:6; 27:35); Adam and Eve bear false witness against others, and Joseph's brothers lie to their father (3:12–13; 37:31–32), a similar sin committed by Jacob himself against his own father Isaac (27:9–25).

---

23. Hartley, *Genesis*, 63.

Genesis 1–2

Throughout the book of Genesis it becomes clear that narrative accounts have a greater purpose than telling a pre-history of the nation, they also paint a vivid picture of what the breaking of the Ten Commandments looked like and the repercussions for doing so. Whether one was a native-born Israelite or whether a person was a servant/slave or a sojourner, the Ten Commandments and the broader laws of Israel still applied. In this vein, it is important to remember that Genesis was not only written as instruction for Israel, but also for those who had assimilated with the nation throughout their journeys. This assimilation began as early as their departure from Egypt when a "mixed multitude" joined the fledgling nation on their trek to the Promised Land (Exod 12:38).

Instruction for the "Mixed Multitude"

Closely connected to the monotheistic concepts that lay behind the first three of the Ten Commandments is the possible reason why God is identified only as Elohim in Genesis 1. While scholars have appealed to source theory as the reason for the proposed anomaly, there may be a practical reason for the author's use of the term, namely, the implied context of the writing of the Torah. Jewish tradition assigns the writing of the Torah sometime after Israel's departure from Egypt and prior to their entering of the land of Canaan. As an introduction to the Torah—specifically Genesis 1–11, which focuses broadly on all the nations—Genesis 1 in many ways served to instruct a variety of people,[24] Israel included, on what god was actually responsible for creation. As just pointed out, Israel was not alone when they left Egypt, a mixed multitude came with them (Exod 12:38). Whether one associates the earliest forms of the Torah with the period of Moses or later, the fact remains that foreign people groups joined with the nation of Israel throughout their history.[25] Apart from the mixed multitude just noted, scholars have posited that some Bedouin tribes may also have associated themselves with Israel during Israel's time in the wilderness.[26] Indeed, Moses' invitation to his Midianite father-in-law to join Israel in their trek to Canaan intimates as much (Num 10:29). Of course Rahab and her family as well as the Gibeonites joined the nation shortly after the

---

24. Fretheim, "Reclamation," 356–57.
25. See also Fretheim, *Pentateuch*, 45.
26. The Kenizzites from which Caleb—who is associated with Judah—came is often posited as joining Israel while they were in the wilderness.

Genesis as Torah

conquest began (Josh 6:17–25; 9–10), and after his capture of Jerusalem, David seems to have incorporated the Canaanites in the city into the nation (2 Sam 5:5–9; 24:18–24; 1 Chr 21:21–25).[27]

In light of the diversity within the fledgling nation, the author could very easily have chosen to adopt the more generic term for God—Elohim—in order to instruct the nation, and those who had aligned themselves to Israel, on exactly what god was responsible for the beginning of all things.[28] This is bolstered by the fact that derivatives of Elohim were used across cultures to reflect the generic concept of deity.[29] The God who created everything was in fact the same God, YHWH, who entered into covenant with Israel at Sinai![30]

Israel's assimilation of other people groups also helps explain why the second, more focused, creation account of chapter 2 uses the rare doubled name for God, YHWH Elohim, which appears most frequently in chapters 2 and 3 (2:4, 5, 7, 8, 9, 15, 16, 18, 19, 21; 3:1, 8 [2x], 9, 13, 14, 21, 22, 23) and only one other time in the Torah (Exod 9:30).[31] Therefore, the use of YHWH Elohim in Gen 2:4 is not necessarily the result of later editing or due to Mesopotamian influence as proposed by some,[32] but may simply have the rhetorical purpose of showing that YHWH is in fact the same God who created all things as seen in chapter 1.[33] With such a variety of people associated with the new nation, instruction related to the creation of the universe would have been needed in light of the numerous myths circulating within many of the ANE cultures. It is to this topic that we now turn our attention.

---

27. Some assert that Bathsheba was of Canaanite descent. See for example, Legrand, *Culture*, 21.

28. This is similar to Daniel's use of Aramaic for the portion of his book when he is speaking of the events related to the Babylonian and Persian courts where Aramaic was the lingua franca. For a discussion on the use of YHWH in Genesis, see Wenham, "Religion," 177–83.

29. Kikawada and Quinn, *Before Abraham*, 18; and Brett, *Genesis*, 25–26.

30. So, too, Sailhamer, *Genesis Unbound*, 83.

31. Cf. 2 Sam 7:25; 2 Kgs 19:19; 1 Chr 17:16, 17; 28:20; 2 Chr 1:9; 6:41 (2x), 42; Pss 59:6; 72:18; 80:4, 20; 84:9, 12.

32. Westermann, *Genesis 1–11*, 198.

33. So, too, Wenham, *Genesis 1–15*, 57. See also comments by Whybray, *Pentateuch*, 75–76.

Genesis 1–2

The Creation Narratives as Polemic

The idea that the creation narratives were meant to serve as a polemic against the ANE creation myths is certainly nothing new within the world of scholarship. It is clear that the author sought to instruct the nation of Israel concerning how the universe came into being and who was responsible for doing so. Apart from the mixed multitude mentioned above and the many traditions that they would have brought with them, when one considers the fact that the children of Israel spent over 400 years in captivity (cf. Exod 12:40–41; Judg 11:26; 1 Kgs 6:1) surrounded by temples and imagery devoted to Egyptian deities then the importance of this type of instruction becomes clear. What is more, Israel was about to enter the land of Canaan, which in turn, had its own belief system of creation no doubt heavily influenced by Mesopotamian thought processes. And for those in the Babylonian exile, similar teaching would certainly have been appropriate.

The cross-pollination of cultures is not something unique to our modern era where the internet is ubiquitous. Ancient sources and archaeological discoveries make it clear that cross-cultural borrowing and/or influence was prevalent in the ANE.[34] The creation traditions behind Genesis 1–2 certainly predate the writing of the book; yet, this does not preclude the possibility of the truthfulness of the basic tenets of these chapters. Indeed, is it not possible that someone like a Moses figure, trained in the house of pharaoh, would have had access to copies of Mesopotamian myths, which were rooted in some form of reality? Or is it so farfetched to believe that the Bedouin culture of the Midianites, in which Moses lived for 40 years, would not have heard of the different accounts of creation circulating within the ANE? After all, the Midianites were known as caravan traders and as such would have had interactions with a variety of people groups (37:28–36). And as we will see in the next chapter, the account of the fall of humanity in ways reflects the Mesopotamian Adapa myth (*ANET*, 100–103), which was actually found at Tell el-Amarna, thus confirming that at least some Mesopotamian literature found its way to Egypt as early as the fourteenth century BCE.[35] Of course we also have evidence of international relations detailed within the Amarna Letters, and the Instruction of Amenemope certainly had some influence on the author of Prov 22:17—23:14. Therefore, it is easy

---

34. E.g., Machinist, "Literature as Politics," 455–82 esp. 468–74; and Lambert, "Fragments," 40–50.

35. Wenham, *Genesis 1–15*, 52.

Genesis as Torah

to see how similar traditions and motifs made their way into the biblical text. Due to the influence of divergent cultural perspectives one can appreciate why instruction on the origins of humanity and the universe from a monotheistic perspective was so important to the author of Genesis.[36]

Within ANE creation myths, the begetting of lesser deities through the procreative acts of first-tier/supreme male and female gods was a common occurrence.[37] Also, the creation of the universe often involved conflicts between the gods. The Babylonian creation myth, *Enuma elish*, comes to mind in this regard. Here the young upstart deity named Marduk challenges the goddess Tiamat and ultimately kills her in battle. After splitting her body into two pieces, Marduk creates the heavens and the earth. Later, he kills Tiamat's military general, Kingu, and creates humans from his blood (*ANET*, 60–72).

At the same time, some ANE creation myths show striking parallels to the Genesis account. In the Egyptian Memphis creation account, the god Ptah creates merely by his spoken word,[38] a striking parallel to Genesis 1 (*ANET*, 4–6).[39] And the Atrahasis and Gilgamesh epics also attest a number of similar motifs found within the opening eleven chapters of Genesis.[40] While scholars are mixed when drawing conclusions on how a particular myth may have influenced the author(s) of Genesis, it is almost universally agreed that to a large degree, Mesopotamian parallels and influence predominate. Yet, as noted with the Egyptian creation account, Genesis may also have been influenced by Egyptian myths especially when one considers the implied audience, which had recently moved from Egypt to Sinai and then from there on to the forty years of wilderness wandering.

Due to this *implied* setting, one should take seriously how the ancient *implied* audience would have understood their own pre-history and how that pre-history functioned as instruction for them. Now to be sure, the connections to Mesopotamian myths cannot, and should not, be overlooked; yet it must be remembered that Egyptian connections may make the most sense in the context. As I have already noted, Ptah's creative acts

---

36. Allis, *God Spake*, 13.

37. See Frankfort, *Kingship*, 284.

38. This is also the case in the myth, "Repulsing of the Dragon and the Creation" (*ANET*, 6).

39. So, too, von Rad, *Old Testament Theology*, 1:143.

40. See Kikawada and Quinn, *Before Abraham*, 47–48; Kikawada, "Double Creation," 43–45; Longman, *Genesis*, 47; Garrett, *Rethinking Genesis*, 105–9; and Wenham, *Genesis 1–15*, xxxix, xliv, xlvii, 52.

Genesis 1–2

recorded in the Memphis creation myth have striking parallels with God's similar creative proclamations. As a polemic against one of the Egyptian primary creator deities, Moses could be "setting the record straight" as to what god truly speaks things into existence. Moreover, where Egypt had more than one creator deity (e.g., Re-Atum, Ptah, or Khnum),[41] in the Hebrew text, God acts alone!

YHWH and Khnum Paralleled

Similar to the parallels noted above, the creative acts of YHWH Elohim in Genesis 2 smacks of Egyptian influence when viewed through the historical lens of *torah* instruction for those of the first and second exodus generations in Israel. God's fashioning of Adam from the dust of the ground in Gen 2:7 is perhaps one of the clearest parallels to Egyptian mythological depictions of their creator god Khnum.

The worship of Khnum had a long history in ancient Egypt extending from the Third Dynasty to the period of the Ptolemies.[42] Khnum was most often depicted sitting at his potter's wheel fashioning the pharaoh and his *ka* (i.e., life force/alter ego). In Egypt, pharaoh, the son of Ra, ruled at the behest of the gods and was seen as deity. In Genesis, YHWH fashions Adam as a "son" of sorts to rule the earth/Eden as God's viceroy.[43] Where Khnum fashioned the pharaoh as an incarnation of deity, God fashioned humans, in his image (1:26–27) to rule on his behalf over God's creation. In this historical/mythological milieu, it should not be surprising when Eve attempts to usurp the divine prerogative in Genesis 3 in order to be like God—something forbidden by God's commands in 2:17. Moreover, as the incarnation of deity, the pharaoh was believed to live forever with the gods. In Adam and Eve's case, the tree of life was to supply a similar longevity. Of course sin curtailed this benefit when God had to secure the garden entrance with cherubim and a flaming sword (3:24).

It is no surprise that many scholars have made the connection between Genesis 2 and Khnum, the Egyptian counterpart to YHWH;[44] how-

---

41. Frankfort, *Kingship*, 284.

42. In the Fourth Dynasty, Khufu, the builder of the great pyramid, took on the name Khnum-Khufu (ca. 2650–2600 BCE; cf. *ANET*, 227).

43. See von Rad, *Old Testament Theology*, 1:146–47.

44. See for example Forrester-Brown, *Creation Stories*, 119–20; Hamilton, *Genesis 1–17*, 157; Davidson, *Genesis 1–11*, 30; Westermann, *Genesis 1–11*, 203–5; Sarna, *Genesis*, 17; Wenham, *Genesis 1–15*, 60; Hoffmeier, "Egyptian Cosmology," 47; and Walton,

ever, the problem is that they fail to ask the question of *when* such an image would have been the most instructional for the children of Israel. It is true that the myth of Khnum has ancient roots, as I just noted, but what seems to be most important is the fact that it was during the Eighteenth Dynasty (ca. 1550–1292 BCE) and later that the worship of Khnum and the detailed artistic representations of the god began to flourish and play a central role in Egyptian art and culture,[45] especially among the pharaohs' daily lives.

Although the early vs. the late-date controversy is beyond the scope of this discussion, it nevertheless does come into play when considering the question of when the parallel would make the most sense. As a polemic against one of Egypt's main creator deities, the penning of Gen 2:7–8 and 19 in particular seems to fit best with a period contemporaneous with the Eighteenth Dynasty, and more precisely in the fifteenth century BCE. This conclusion is bolstered by the reality that during the reign of Hatshepsut, Khnum is seen prominently depicted in relief form in Hatshepsut's mortuary temple at Deir el-Bahari. Eugene Merrill has argued that Hatshepsut is a good candidate for the adoptive mother of Moses.[46] If this is the case, then Moses would have grown up seeing this depiction on a regular basis. Even if one opts for a Ramseside date for the exodus, Khnum was still a dominant figure at this time, although perhaps not as prevalent as he was in the earlier period.

To summarize then, as a polemic the creation narratives become instructive from a *torah* perspective in that they undermine the false notions of how the universe, earth, and humanity came into existence. Furthermore, they challenged the belief that humans were simply made to supply food for the gods and to make their workload lighter (*ANET*, 60–72, at 69; 99–100). Instead, it was just the opposite; God provided for his creation and Israel (Gen 1:29; 2:8; cf. Exod 16:15, 35; Num 11:9; Deut 8:3, 16) and sought to make *their* workload lighter (Gen 2:8–25; Exod 2:23–25; Deut 11:9–12). In a covenant community context, especially post-Sinai, Israel quickly learned that YHWH was more than a tribal god; YHWH was the God of all the earth who personally fashioned humans for the purpose of relationship, not to be slaves to the gods. What is made clear here is the importance of intimate fellowship between Israel and her God. No greater intimate relationship could be undertaken by God than for God to come

---

Genesis, 165.

45. Hoffmeier, "Egyptian Cosmology," 47.
46. Merrill, *Kingdom of Priests*, 76–77.

and dwell in the very midst of his people: as God had communed with Adam in the garden, so, too, YHWH came to tabernacle in the midst of Israel. As such, it should not surprise the modern reader that the accounts of Genesis 1 and 2 also reflect temple/tabernacle language, which, once again, was instructive for the children of Israel.

Creation as Tabernacle

It certainly is not new to see in the creation accounts a picture and/or a pattern of the tabernacle of Israel,[47] a reality also present in some ANE creation accounts.[48] Some scholars have even suggested that the seven days of creation parallel the seven speeches of God to Moses concerning the construction of the tabernacle (Exod 25:1; 30:11, 17, 22; 31:1, 12).[49] In both cases, six days/speeches unfold followed by a seventh day where rest/Sabbath is observed (Exod 31:17; Gen 2:3).

Furthermore, the imagery found in Genesis 1 and 2 actually has a number of parallels with how the ancient world viewed the concept of temple in conjunction with the gods.[50] The ordering of chaos into an inhabitable place where God could take up his abode and govern the universe is evident within the creation narratives. For Israel, the instruction would not only have helped them to appreciate the nature of the God they served and the purpose of the created order, but just as importantly, it would have helped them appreciate the specific construction requirements of the tabernacle and its sacredness (Exodus 25–31). In a predominantly oral society where literacy was no doubt limited to a select few, the tabernacle served as a teaching tool to instruct Israel on the holiness and otherness of God. Similar teaching methods were also employed during the Middle Ages in

---

47. E.g., Wenham, "Sanctuary Symbolism," 399–404. See also Sailhamer, *Pentateuch*, 98; Levenson, *Creation*, 86; Moberly, *Theology*, 52; Alexander, *Paradise to the Promised Land*, 119, 123–25; Sailhamer, *Genesis Unbound*, 74–77; Beale, *Temple*, 66–80; Lioy, *Axis of Glory*, 5–15; and Parry, "Garden of Eden," 126–51 (these last four as noted by Hinckley, "Garden Sanctuary," 5 n2).

48. See for example the Instruction of Merikare (*ANET*, 414–18, at 417) or the *Enuma elish* (*ANET*, 67–69) as noted by Kearney, "Creation and Liturgy," 384 n22.

49. Ibid., 375 and esp. 375–78; and Gorman, *Ideology*, 43, 48.

50. See for example the work of Walton, *The Lost World of Genesis One* (2009); Walton, *Genesis 1 as Ancient Cosmology* (2011); and the compendium of essays in Morales ed., *Cult and Cosmos* (2014).

Europe when stain glass windows and the architecture of churches served the double function of aesthetics and instruction for the illiterate masses.

On the macro level, once the chaos of the formless and void world of Genesis 1 was brought to heel at the command of an all-powerful God, and once everything good had been made, God could move forward with his plan to take up his residence within that ordered creation while availing himself to fellowship with his greatest creation, humankind, who had been made in the very image of God (1:26-27). Thus, one could view God's good creation, namely, the cosmos, as a "tabernacle" where deity is at rest (2:3).

Sailhamer offers a variation on this picture when he suggests that Eden is to be identified with the land of Israel whereas the garden itself was only a smaller subsection of it.[51] By viewing the Garden of God—Adam and Eve's home—as being *in* Eden,[52] and not Eden itself, it is then possible to argue that the land of Israel/Eden is the "holy place," and the garden, the holy of holies (perhaps a parallel to Jerusalem?[53]). This would make the rest of the earth, namely, the region outside of Israel, the court of the Gentiles.

Therefore, on the micro level, when the author describes the Garden of Eden in Genesis 2 he is in essence presenting a picture of the inner sanctum of God, that is, the holy of holies (cf. *Jub.* 3:10-12). In Eden, gold and precious jewels were the hallmark of the land (2:11-12). Gold and jewels in particular were used to construct the tabernacle and in the fabrication of the high priest's garments (Exod 25:7; 28:9-14, 20; 35:9, 27; 39:6, 13).[54] Furthermore, as the high priest walked from east to west through the tabernacle, he was alerted that he was approaching and entering the most holy sanctum of YHWH because the furniture, the building, and the Ark of the Covenant were all overlaid or made with pure gold.

Other features found within Eden further support the temple imagery.[55] For example, water is a common element in temples. God's harnessing of water into rivers (2:10-14) and the laver/bronze sea in the tabernacle

---

51. Sailhamer, *Pentateuch*, 98-100.

52. Ibid., 99.

53. See Stager, "Jerusalem," 99-116. Parry ("Garden of Eden," 133-37) parallels the sacred mountain imagery of Eden with the mountain of Jerusalem.

54. Postell, *Adam as Israel*, 113; Chilton, *Paradise Restored*, 33-34; and Beale, *Temple*, 73. Even though onyx is the jewel that is mentioned, bdellium appears as a reference to manna in Num 11:7, which was placed in the tabernacle (Exod 16:33-34).

55. Parry ("Garden of Eden," 126-27) lists eleven different areas of correspondence between Eden and the temple.

Genesis 1–2

and temple[56] are illustrative of God's taming of the primordial chaos (Exod 30:18; 1 Kings 7; 1 Chr 18:8; 2 Chr 4:2–15). Water also served as a picture of fecundity and life (Gen 2:10–14; Ezekiel 47; Ps 46:4; cf. Revelation 22). The tree of life has often been connected to ANE symbols where trees are seen as providing sustenance for life.[57] In later biblical imagery, the tree of life returns with the same purpose of offering life and/or healing for Israel/the nations (Ezek 47:12; Rev 22:2). On the other hand, some Jewish interpreters parallel the tree of life with the Torah itself.[58] By "eating" from the Torah, life is gained. From a figurative standpoint, some scholars have proffered that the multi-branched menorah may have been understood as the counterpart to the tree of life (cf. Exod 25:31–35).[59] Even God's instruction to Adam to "cultivate" (*'abad*) and to "keep" (*shamar*) the garden reflects the language of the priesthood and Levitical order[60] and/or the study and keeping of the Torah and its commands.[61] The priests and Levites were to serve/work (*'abad*; Num 3:7–8; 4:23, 24, 26; 8:26; 18:5–6 etc.) and keep/guard (*shamar*; Lev 8:35; Num 3:7, 8; 10, 28, 32, 38 etc.) the tabernacle as part of their service to God. So, too, Adam and Eve were to serve a royal and priestly function by keeping the sanctuary where God met and walked with them (3:8; cf. Lev 26:12; Deut 23:14; 2 Sam 7:6–7).[62]

The crowning feature of the tabernacle imagery actually appears after the fall of Adam and Eve when God placed the cherubim at the entrance of the Garden of Eden, a fitting parallel with the cherubim that protected the Ark of the Covenant[63] and the entrance to the inner sanctuary in Solomon's

---

56. Due to the mobile nature of the tabernacle, and the limited access to water in the wilderness, the inclusion of a massive bronze sea would not have been practical. That is why it only becomes a part of the temple when it is stationary in Jerusalem. We have no information on whether the tabernacle at Shiloh had anything similar to the bronze sea. See Parry, "Garden of Eden," 129–30.

57. See Emmerich, "Temptation Narrative," 7.

58. Morris, "Exiled," 118.

59. Arnold, *Genesis*, 124; Meyers, *Menorah*, esp. 135–37; Chilton, *Paradise Restored*, 44; Lioy, *Axis of Glory*, 9–10; and Parry, "Garden of Eden," 128–29. See also comments by Hinckley, "Garden Sanctuary," 10.

60. So, too, Beale, *Temple*, 67–69; and Parry, "Garden of Eden," 143–44. For a detailed comparison of Adam as priest, see Hinckley, "Garden Sanctuary," 5–12 esp. 6–7. For an alternate reading of the terms noted here, see Sailhamer, *Genesis Unbound*, 75.

61. Morris, "Exiled," 118.

62. Alexander, *Paradise to the Promised Land*, 124; and Parry, "Garden of Eden," 144.

63. So, too, Hinckley, "Garden Sanctuary," 8.

Genesis as Torah

temple (3:24; Exod 25:18–22; 1 Kgs 6:23–28).[64] Finally, even the orientation of the Garden of Eden reflected the tabernacle and temple. In each case, the entrance faced east (3:24; Exod 25:18–22; 26:31; 1 Kgs 6:23–29).[65]

The value of the temple imagery as *torah* instruction would have been immediately evident to the average Israelite especially with the mobile tabernacle (or later the temple) in their midst. Yet, there are also parallels related to YHWH's relationship with Israel as a whole. In many ways the ordering of chaos into an inhabitable abode for God and his creation (i.e., humanity) finds immediate connections with the way YHWH removed Israel from the wasteland and chaos of Egyptian bondage, parted the Red Sea—a common picture of the primordial waters of chaos (Gen 1:1–10; cf. Job 26:12; Isa 51:9)—provided for their needs (food and water; Exod 16:11–19; 17:5–7; cf. Gen 1:29; Num 11:31–32; 20:5–11) and brought them to rest at the foot of Mount Sinai (Exod 19:1–2; cf. Gen 2:8) with a promise of ultimate rest in Canaan. From the moment of entering into covenant with Israel at Sinai, YHWH himself came to take up his residence with his people in a newly constructed tabernacle (Exod 40:34–38), which was fashioned according to God's own design (Exod 25:9; cf. Genesis 1–2).

Just as humankind were made in the "image of God" and were to function as a reflection of who God is, so, too, Israel and the priesthood were to be a light to the nations and reflect the glory and purity of God (Exod 19:4–6; 34:10; cf. Exod 9:16).[66] Of course it was the family unit that was the central component of the *nation* and which was to be a metaphor reflecting the purity and loving relationship between Israel and her God. It is for this reason that the prophets often presented the Sinai covenant in terms of a marriage covenant (Hosea 1–3; Jeremiah 3; Ezekiel 16; cf. Ephesians 5). For Israel, monogamous marriage reflected the monotheistic concepts present in the exclusive "marriage" of Israel and her God. Not surprisingly, it is monogamous marriage, which is instituted by God himself in the creation account of Genesis 2.

---

64. Wenham, "Sanctuary Symbolism," 401; Beale, *Temple*, 70–71; and Parry, "Garden of Eden," 139.

65. Alexander, *Paradise to the Promised Land*, 124; Lioy, *Axis of Glory*, 12; and Parry, "Garden of Eden," 131–33.

66. Keiser, *Genesis 1–11*, 155; Fretheim, *Pentateuch*, 46–47; and Och, "Creation and Redemption," 336.

Genesis 1–2

Adam and Eve:
God's Design of Monogamous Marriage

It is clear that the sanctity of the union between Adam and Eve in the garden teaches an important life lesson for the nation of Israel. Monogamous heterosexual marriage was always God's intention for his creation in order to build strong families and nations.[67] Marriages founded upon this principle would lead to strong spiritual and emotional ties between couples, and by extension, within a society. On this point, Allen P. Ross aptly concludes that Gen 2:18–25 is "the foundation of the institution of marriage, so it has great bearing on the mainstay of Israel's society. . . God intended that the man and the woman be a spiritual, functional unity, walking in integrity, serving him, and keeping his commandments. If this pattern prevailed, the nation would live and prosper under God's good hand of blessing."[68]

That monogamy is in view in chapter 2 is strengthened by the clear instruction made evident by the fact that all polygamous marriages in Genesis engender strife! This is particularly true of Lamech, Abraham, Jacob, and Esau. It is noteworthy that later *torah* instruction actually attempts to limit the inter-relational animosity generated by bigamous marriages by legislating the inheritance rights of the true firstborn son regardless of how a man loved or did not love one of his wives (Deut 21:15–17).[69] Although it is true that a surface reading of 2:18–25 does not push one immediately to the conclusion that monogamy is the central focus of the text,[70] nonetheless, one is hard pressed not to miss the clear instructive aspects. Indeed, the notion that God creates only one man and one woman, not a multiplicity of humans as is common in other ANE myths (e.g., *ANET*, 99–100) puts a spotlight on the intimacy intended in a monogamous relationship.

In some cases, Jewish interpreters have seen in God's institution of marriage indirect legislation against adultery, bestiality, homosexuality, and incest—sexual pairings that are off limits according to the law of God both before Sinai and after Sinai. In this vein, Rabbi Akiba understood that leaving one's father and mother and cleaving to a wife limited acceptable

---

67. Wenham, *Story as Torah*, 31, 152; Soden, "From the Dust," 60; McKeown, *Genesis*, 34; Allis, *God Spake*, 17; Collins, *Adam and Eve*, 60; and Kaiser, *Old Testament Ethics*, 182–83.

68. Ross, *Creation and Blessing*, 125. See also comments by Brueggemann, *Genesis*, 47.

69. Wenham, *Story as Torah*, 152.

70. Contra von Rad (*Genesis*, 85), who suggests this text is not about monogamy.

marriage relationships. In speaking of the prohibited types of "cleaving" he states, "'His father' means his father's wife [by another marriage, for example]; and 'his mother' refers literally to his mother. "And he shall cleave"—and not to a male. "To his wife"—and not to his fellow's wife. "And they shall become one flesh"—one with whom one can become one flesh [in an offspring], excluding domesticated beasts and wild beasts, who cannot produce an offspring with man" (*b. Sanh.* 58a).[71]

Israel was to practice monogamous marriage for the greater purpose of building a strong community. In fact, divorce was only included in the law due to the hardness of the people's hearts (cf. Deut 24:1–4; Matt 19:8). It is telling of the instructional value of Genesis 2 when one finds within later prophetic texts the metaphor of YHWH being married to *one* metaphorical "woman," that is, Israel/Jerusalem (Jeremiah 3; Ezekiel 16; Hosea 1–3). The intention of God to promote monogamous marriage in the creation account of chapter 2 is clarified even further when Jesus himself quotes Gen 2:24 when asked about the sanctity of marriage (Matt 19:4–6). Interestingly, Jesus actually introduces his reference to 2:24 by noting the dual genders, male and female, which connects chapter 2 with 1:26–27.

Also, Adam's need for a helper looks forward to the harsh realities of life in the Promised Land.[72] After settling in the central highlands of Canaan, women played a key role in working the land with their husbands.[73] The teamwork and coupling of Adam and Eve also allowed for the begetting of children (2:24; cf. 1:28),[74] which played a vital role in an agrarian society. It seems evident that the institution of marriage and the process of becoming "one flesh" in Genesis 2 serve as a more detailed presentation of what Gen 1:26–28 says in a laconic fashion. The nuclear family was to be at the heart of society and the means by which God moved his plan forward for both Israel and the nations. Moreover, God's creation was not complete at the end of the sixth day; God foresaw a populated earth being made possible by the nuclear family, which was also a part of God's "good" creation.[75] Indeed, the begetting of children is how humanity shared in God's creative

---

71. So Polin, "Jewish Law," 39.

72. Meyers, *Discovering Eve*, 93–94.

73. Arnold, *Genesis*, 60; Meyers, Gender Roles," 337–54 esp. 345; and Meyers, *Discovering Eve*, 56–57, 168–173.

74. Von Rad, *Old Testament Theology*, 1:150.

75. Fretheim, "Reclamation," 358.

Genesis 1–2

acts.[76] As Genesis unfolds it becomes apparent that the movement from one man and his barren wife—Abraham and Sarah—to a family—Isaac, Jacob, and his children—develops into a growing clan by the end of the book. By the time the reader reaches the book of Exodus this clan has become a great nation (Exod 1:7).[77]

Finally, while polygamy was often practiced for the purpose of making sure children were born in order to inherit and take care of parents in their old age—a picture played out in Genesis with Abraham, Sarah, and Hagar[78]—the fact remains that Genesis instructs Israel that monogamy is the model established by God. Depending on when one dates the text—pre-conquest or post—instruction on the benefits of marriage would obtain for any agrarian setting, either in the wilderness or in Canaan.

Some Final Parallels between the Creation Event and Life in Israel

Before leaving this topic it is important to note a couple of other parallels between Adam and Eve's life in the garden and Israel's future life in Canaan. First, the highlands of Canaan needed rain in order to produce food. As part of the promises of God to Israel, God assured them that they would not have to water the land by foot (i.e., through irrigation) as was the case in Egypt. Instead, God would send the former and the latter rains as a part of his blessings upon his people (Deut 11:9–15). In 2:6, God was also responsible for watering the earth and garden. In the pre-flood era, this seemed to be done from some form of mist or emanation of water from the earth. For Israel, it came from the sky: they were completely dependent on their God for survival.

Second, it is of particular interest that God causes the grass/herbs (*'eseb*) to grow on the earth in the creation narratives (Gen 1:11, 12, 29, 30; cf. 2:5). This type of provision reminds the reader that it was God who caused the grass to grow through his kind provision of rain (Deut 11:15). Not surprisingly, the curses of the covenant included the removal of vegetation (*'eseb*) so that Israel would perish from the land (Deut 29:22). As we will see in the next chapter, the undoing of God's blessings on Adam and

---

76. Gorman, *Ideology*, 231.
77. See also Fretheim, *Pentateuch*, 45.
78. See Albertz, *Israelite Religion*, 33.

Eve in the garden through the curse against the soil (3:17–18) presents a similar teaching.[79]

The kindness and provision of God are just two of God's many attributes displayed in Genesis 1 and 2. In this vein, these opening chapters of Genesis lay the foundation for theological thinking about who God/YHWH was in relation to Israel. It is with this topic that I will conclude this chapter.

Theological Instruction on the Nature of God

Today, when people want to learn how to think about God or how to discern God's nature and attributes, many turn to a theology textbook and/or to the works of a famous theologian (e.g., Augustine, Aquinas, Calvin, Barth, Moltmann etc.). For the ancient Israelites, their "theological" instruction on the nature and attributes of God came from reading their sacred texts and witnessing the very presence of the God about whom they sought to learn more. For Moses this desire to know God drove him to ask for a face-to-face encounter with God's glory (Exod 33:18–20). Of course God refused to allow such an encounter, at least in the fullest sense of the word. All Moses was allowed to see was the hinder parts/afterglow of YHWH as he passed by. Even then God sheltered Moses in the cleft of a rock in order that he might not perish due to the splendor of YHWH (Exod 33:21–23). This brief encounter brought forth deep theological statements of who YHWH was: "And the Lord passed by before him, and proclaimed, The Lord, The Lord God, merciful and gracious, longsuffering, and abundant in goodness and truth, Keeping mercy for thousands, forgiving iniquity and transgression and sin, and that will by no means clear *the guilty*; visiting the iniquity of the fathers upon the children, and upon the children's children, unto the third and to the fourth *generation*" (Exod 34:6–7 NASB).

Just as theologically poignant is the portrait painted of God in relation to his nature and attributes in Genesis, especially here in chapters 1 and 2.[80] Whether these texts were read aloud to the nation (Deut 31:9–13) or whether they were read by only a select few, the fact remains that Genesis teaches just as much about the theological dimensions of Israel's God as it did the legal precepts enumerated in the remaining legal portions of the

---

79. See comments by Steck, "Die Paradieserzählung," 9–116 esp. 21–35.

80. See also comments of Longman, *How to Read Genesis*, 106–9; and Stratton, *Out of Eden*, 65–66.

Torah such as the Covenant Code (Exod 20:19—23:33), the Holiness Code (Leviticus 17–26), or the Book of Deuteronomy.

In Genesis 1 alone, several theological truths about the nature and attributes of God stand out. Israel's God needs no introduction.[81] He is presented as the omnipotent God who creates by merely speaking things into existence.[82] As the creator of all things,[83] it is easy to envision the teaching that God can, and does, give the land to whomever he chooses (Gen 12:7; 13:15; 15:16–18; Exod 19:5).[84] We also see that God is eternal and outside of time; that he is not only creative, but also a God of order; that he is a God who can appreciate beauty; that he is the giver of law (1:28; 2:16–17; cf. 9:1–7);[85] and that he desires relationship with his creation and in turn blesses it (1:22, 28; 2:3; cf. Gen 5:2; 9:1; 12:3; 24:1 etc.).

In Genesis 2, the reader finds a more anthropomorphic picture of God but one that still depicts the goodness and creative attributes of YHWH Elohim. Here God is presented as a caring God who is touched by the emotions of his human creation. In the statement, "it is not good that the man is alone" (2:18) God shows his caring and compassionate nature. It is easy to hear in these words God's call to Moses, "I have surely seen the affliction of my people which *are* in Egypt, and have heard their cry by reason of their taskmasters; for I know their sorrows; And I am come down to deliver them out of the hand of the Egyptians" (Exod 3:7–8a NASB; cf. 2:24; 6:5). Moreover, God gives good gifts to his creation/people. For Adam it was a wife—Eve—and a beautiful garden. As we will see in our next chapter, for Israel two of God's good gifts included protection and the land of promise, Canaan. Finally, the very giving of "law" in relation to the requirements to stay in the garden, shows a God who cares for his people and their peace of mind (2:16–17). Indeed, as we will see in the next chapter, when the law of God is flouted, the repercussions can be devastating.

Conclusion

Perhaps no other pair of chapters in Genesis offers as much instruction about the nature of who God is or about what God requires for his people

---

81. Fretheim, *Pentateuch*, 44.
82. See Watts, *Reading Law*, 91–92.
83. Von Rad, *Old Testament Theology*, 1:142–43.
84. See also Sailhamer, *Genesis Unbound*, 30.
85. Fretheim, *Pentateuch*, 49.

as do chapters 1 and 2. Today, scholars have tended, perhaps unintentionally, to downplay the clear *torah* instruction found within these texts opting rather to ask questions related to origins, myth versus history, or even modern debates related to marriage or women's rights. While these topics are indeed important, focus on such topics has caused many to miss, or at least fail to stress, the central reason of why these chapters were written in the first place and placed in a position of prominence as an introduction to *torah*. For the original implied audience, *torah* instruction was of primary concern. Therefore, how the author chose to begin the Torah should be even more of a concern for those reading it today. As we have seen, these opening chapters set the tone for the first five books by establishing who Israel's God was vis-à-vis the ANE gods, and what he expected from Israel at the foundational level of the community, namely, the family structure. While these chapters set a positive tone to the Torah, the devastating events of the following chapters lay the groundwork for why a sacrificial system was needed and what proper conduct within the God-human relationship entails. What started out as the ideal and innocent setting of the garden quickly gave way to a downward spiral of sin and devastation. It is within these subsequent narratives that Israel would not only learn more about the justice of their God and his longsuffering and compassionate nature, but also the reason for many of their laws. Indeed, when a number of specific sins, which are legislated against in the Torah, are played out in narrative format it becomes clear why God gave his Law to Israel in the first place.

3

Genesis 3–4

The Analogical Role of the Fall of Humanity

During the heyday of the historical-critical method, one of the scholarly approaches to Genesis 3 and 4 was to focus on the instructional role that etiology played. These etiological emphases included—although were not limited to—why there is pain in childbearing, why there is enmity between humans and snakes, why there are thorns and thistles, why people have to toil for food, and why death comes to all people.[1] In more recent years, one of the major debates related to these chapters is the historicity of Adam and Eve (and their family) and the fall narratives.[2] Despite these discussions, it is obvious that the account of Adam, Eve, and their sons, Cain and Abel, played an important role in instructing Israel on how to relate to their God. Indeed, the centrality of the fall to the opening of Genesis proves that this event had instructional import on a number of levels.

In light of these instructional motifs, in this chapter I will examine some of the linguistic and rhetorical connections between the fall, the Sinai event, and Israel's future in the land of Canaan. For example, Israel's breaking of the commands of God after they entered Canaan led to their expulsion from land, a similar reality visited upon Adam and Eve after they ate the forbidden fruit. Also of importance to the discussion of reading this portion of Genesis as *torah* is how the curses on Eve (i.e., barrenness)

---

1. Hartley, *Genesis*, 58. See also von Rad, *The Problem of the Hexateuch*, 169.
2. For an extended discussion on this, see Collins, *Adam and Eve* (2011).

Genesis as Torah

and Adam (i.e., toil/famine) affected every one of the patriarchs and matriarchs of Genesis and, in some cases, those in Israel in years to come.[3] In this regard, the curse of famine served to explain how Israel ended up in Egypt, which in turn served as the basis for the promise of the long trek back to Canaan (15:13–16; Exodus–Numbers). Finally, the interaction of Cain and Abel in many ways served as a harbinger to the rocky relationship that would unfold between Jacob and Esau.[4] Interestingly, their relationship would also be instructional for the international relations between the nations of Israel and Edom (e.g., Numbers 20).[5] Fortunately, unlike Cain and Abel, time allowed the animosity between Esau and Jacob to subside into a brotherly love once again,[6] a reality not always as applicable to the later relations between Edom and Israel (see Obadiah). Of course the theme of brotherly turmoil continues with Joseph and his brothers, and later with Moses and Aaron (Num 12:1–9).[7]

The Laws of Eden vis-à-vis the Laws of Sinai

As previously noted, the account of the fall plays a central role in the opening chapters of Genesis especially when read as *torah*.[8] After the presentation of God's idyllic creation and God's unhindered relationship with that creation, the very next picture is that of the fall of humanity. Why, one might ask, is the fall the very first thing presented after such a striking picture of creation and human-divine communion? Perhaps the most obvious reason can be found in the parallels between the creation of the first family (Adam and Eve and ultimately their children) and the creation of the new nation of Israel at Sinai. In this vein, the work of Seth Postell becomes central to the discussion.[9] The title of his work, "Adam as Israel," speaks volumes as

---

3. So, too, Wenham, *Story as Torah*, 28.

4. Moberly, *Theology*, 92–98; and Carr, "*Biblos geneseos*: Part 2," 337–38.

5. Greenspahn, *Brothers*, 141. For a discussion on the purported tradition history behind the text, see Bartlett, "Brotherhood," 16–20.

6. Moberly, *Theology*, 98.

7. So Morris, "Exiled," 123.

8. Fretheim, *Pentateuch*, 76; and Keiser, *Genesis 1–11*, 154.

9. Postell, *Adam as Israel* (2011). See also Erlich, "Story," 20–34 (as noted by Postell, *Adam as Israel*, 35–37).

Genesis 3–4

to how Israel may have read this account.[10] Throughout this chapter I will draw upon the work of Postell where it is applicable to my thesis.

As mentioned in my previous chapter, the creation of the tree of the knowledge of good and evil,[11] which was placed in the midst/center of the garden (2:9, 17), served an important function. For Adam and Eve, a central part of their "law" was God's commands concerning the use of this tree.[12] Moreover, because Eden has parallels with Canaan (see below),[13] the didactic purposes for Israel are immediately clear. In order to remain in the *land* of Eden, Adam and Eve needed to obey what God had commanded. For Israel, the Torah given at Sinai was meant to be kept not only so that they could dwell long in the *land* of Canaan, but so that it would go well with them.[14] Deuteronomy records numerous passages, which make this very claim (cf. Deut 4:5–6, 9, 23, 26, 40; 5:16, 29, 33; 6:2–3, 18; 8:16; 11:9; 12:25, 28; 17:20; 22:7; 25:15; 28:63; 30:5, 15, 18–19, 20; 32:47 see also *Gen. Rab.* 19:9). What is more, as I will demonstrate below, God's promise of life and his warnings of death,[15] which God gave to Adam and Eve, parallel the giving of the blessings and curses of the Sinai covenant (cf. Leviticus 26; Deuteronomy 28; 30:15–20).[16] Because Moses had warned that failure to keep God's commands/*torah* would mean death (e.g., the breaking of Sabbath; Exod 31:14[17]), he consistently encouraged Israel to choose "life" instead, a similar picture presented to Adam and Eve in the garden.[18] In light of the centrality of the keeping of the Sinai laws, the author of the

---

10. See also Emmerich, "Temptation Narrative," 18.

11. For a discussion on what the tree represented, that is, what Adam and Eve gained from eating from it, see Emmerich, "Temptation Narrative," 7–8. Clark ("Legal Background," 266–78) proposes that Adam and Eve gained "moral autonomy."

12. Moore and Peterson, *Voice, Word, and Spirit*, 7–8.

13. So, too, Hamilton, *Pentateuch*, 29.

14. See Emmerich, "Temptation Narrative," 8–9; and Sailhamer, *Genesis Unbound*, 82–83.

15. Parry ("Garden of Eden," 127) calls the tree of knowledge, the "tree of death."

16. See also Ross, *Creation and Blessing*, 127–28.

17. See Hinckley, "Garden Sanctuary," 7.

18. Sailhamer, *Pentateuch*, 101; and Sailhamer, *Genesis Unbound*, 87–88. See also Fretheim, *Pentateuch*, 51, 56.

Torah, in his compositional strategy, chose to set this analogy[19] front and center as instructional for Israel.[20]

Adam as Israel

Beyond the early rabbinic commentary on these chapters (e.g., *Gen. Rab.* 3:9; 19:9; 21:1, 9),[21] the Israel-equals-Adam perspective is in no way new to the scholarly discussion.[22] In 1965, Norbert Lohfink made many of the same connections between Genesis 2 and 3 and the situation Israel faced.[23] Also, John Van Seters intimates a similar conclusion as Lohfink, although he insists that the connections were made at a much later time period, namely, the exilic era or later.[24] Van Seters lists Lohfink's connections between Israel's experiences and those of Adam and Eve in the garden as follows:

"1. Yahweh found/created/chose Israel outside of Canaan;

2. Yahweh brought Israel into a wonderful land;

3. Yahweh gave Israel the law as covenant obligations;

4. If Israel observed the covenant law, things would be well and they would live long in the land;

5. If Israel did not observe the law, then the curse of the covenant would come on them and they would die=go into exile."[25]

One could just as easily replace the words Israel and Canaan in the above list with Adam and Eve and the Garden of Eden. The warnings are clear for Israel: keep the laws of God as established at Sinai!

One of the other key parallels is how both Israel and Adam were *placed* in their respective "gardens."[26] The word that is used is the Hebrew verb *nuach*, in the causative stem (*hiphil*), which means to "*cause* to rest." In every case where God is the subject and Adam or Israel is the object of

---

19. I use the concept of analogy as described by Klein et al., *Biblical Interpretation*, 64–65.

20. Postell, *Adam as Israel*, 74.

21. On this, see the work of Morris, "Exiled," 124–27.

22. See for example Hamilton, *Pentateuch*, 29.

23. Lohfink, "Die Erzählung vom Sündenfall," 91–92.

24. Van Seters, *Prologue*, 129.

25. Ibid., 127. See also Emmerich, "Temptation Narrative," 6

26. See similar comments by Beale, *Temple*, 69–70.

Genesis 3–4

the action of the verb, God is said to have caused Adam/Israel to *rest* in the land (Gen 2:15; Deut 3:20; 12:10; 25:19; Josh 1:13, 15; 21:44; 22:4; 23:1). Linguistically, the parallel is once again clear.

Finally, as with Adam and Eve's fall, Israel's first great fall is none other than the sin of the Golden Calf,[27] which is followed a few months later by the acceptance of the ten spies' evil report. This latter sin led to forty years of wilderness wandering. Both of these events were a foreshadowing of things to come. Eventually Israel's rebellion led to the loss of the land completely. In this regard, Eden as a parallel to Canaan becomes another important instructional feature of the fall narrative.

Eden as Canaan

The next parallel falls within the category of the good land, which both Adam and Eve, and Israel were to inherit.[28] Land plays a central role in both the life of Adam and Eve, and later, for Israel. There can be little doubt that Israel would have read Eden as an image of Canaan especially in light of the fact that Canaan is often referred to as the "garden of God" within Scripture (Gen 13:10; Isa 51:3; Ezek 36:35; Joel 2:3; cf. Num 24:5–7).[29] In this regard, the command of God to Adam and Eve to subdue Eden finds a fitting parallel with God's command to Israel to subdue Canaan.[30] Postell notes that "God's mandate to Adam and Eve to conquer the land and its inhabitant (the serpent) foreshadows God's mandate to Israel to conquer the land and its inhabitants (the Canaanites)."[31] Interestingly, the same Hebrew word for "subdue" (i.e., *kabash*) is used in both cases (Gen 1:28; Num 32:22, 29; Josh 18:1).[32] In both instances the land is good and inviting and able to sustain those who inhabit it. Unfortunately, for both Adam and Israel, the rejection of God's commands would lead them far from that good land.[33] Postell aptly notes that when evicted from the garden, Adam and Eve moved eastward

---

27. See Postell's chart on p. 37 of *Adam as Israel*.
28. See Och, "Creation and Redemption," 348.
29. Emmerich, "Temptation Narrative," 5–6; and Sailhamer, *Genesis Unbound*, 14–15, 69–77, 82–83.
30. See also comments by Fretheim, "Reclamation," 362.
31. Postell, *Adam as Israel*, 100. See also similar comments by Lohfink, *Theology*, 10–11.
32. Postell, *Adam as Israel*, 89.
33. Sailhamer, *Genesis Unbound*, 88.

away from the good land of Eden, no doubt in the direction of Babylon, but God called Abram back westward from the region of Babylon to the land of promise, that is, Canaan/Eden.[34] This is none other than a picture of what would happen later to Israel! After being exiled from Canaan to Babylon, God brought them once more from the region of Babylon to re-inhabit the land of promise.

The Serpent and the Fall

Of central importance to the discussion of the instructional aspects of the fall narrative is the role that the serpent plays.[35] Out of nowhere the author of Genesis introduces the serpent into the garden. The serpent quickly challenges the commands of God and insists that God was withholding good things from his creation.[36] In essence, the serpent becomes the prototypical "false prophet" of sorts and should have been dealt with accordingly (Deut 13:1–3).[37] Indeed, at the heart of chapter 3 is Adam and Eve's need to trust in the commands and instruction of God.[38] Will they follow God's word even though it appears that God has not told them the entirety of the "benefits" of eating from the forbidden tree? In reality, God knew best but they challenged him in this regard. For Israel, would they trust God and his commands when he declared to them at Sinai that certain things were not good? When Israel entered the land would they trust him and keep his laws even though it appeared as though being like the nations was the better choice (cf. 1 Sam 8:1–22; Ezek 20:32)?

Another point of interest is Eve's response to the serpent. When Eve told the serpent that she and Adam were not allowed to eat of the tree or

---

34. Postell, *Adam as Israel*, 88. See also Sailhamer, *Genesis Unbound*, 30, 51–52, 69, 84, 94.

35. Wolde (*Words Become Worlds*, 5) notes that in "the Canaanite, Phoenician, Egyptian and Babylonian world the serpent represents fertility, life-giving power, or life itself." See also Emmerich, "Temptation Narrative," 10–11. For a variety of perspectives on what the serpent represents, see Wolde, *Words Become Worlds*, 3–12 esp. 4–7. According to Wisdom 2:24, the serpent was none other than the devil (cf. John 8:44; 2 Cor 11:3, 14; Rev 12:9; 20:2).

36. Note that animals speak only here and in Numbers 22. Here the serpent deceives Eve whereas in Numbers Balaam's donkey clarifies the plan of God for the prophet. See Emmerich, "Temptation Narrative," 15.

37. Ibid., 16–17.

38. Fretheim, *Pentateuch*, 78; and Sailhamer, *Genesis Unbound*, 76.

even *touch* it, Eve—or perhaps Adam's instruction to his wife—had veered from what God had actually said (2:17). Eve's failure to cite clearly the commands of God when confronted by the serpent points to the dangers of not knowing exactly what God's laws are (cf. Hos 4:6) and the dangers one can encounter when adding to them, a clear Deuteronomic theme (Deut 4:2).[39] Now while some have noted the connections between Eve's remarks and the fact that touching or even looking at the uncovered Ark could bring death (2 Sam 6:7; Num 4:20),[40] here the context is a tree, not the representative presence of God. Adam's apparent improper instruction of Eve is illustrative of what happened when the king and/or the priests failed to give proper instruction of the Law to Israel (Hos 4:1–6).[41] As the "king" of Eden, it was Adam's responsibility to know and teach the Law of God, a reality no less true of the rulers of Israel (Deut 17:14–20).[42]

The Serpent Reflective of the Canaanites

If scholars are correct in noting that Adam parallels Israel, and Eden is reflective of Canaan, then it only stands to reason that the encounter of Adam and Eve with the serpent should reflect Israel's encounters with the Canaanites and/or later foreign influences.[43] In this vein, Postell notes that the voice/words of the serpent could be paralleled with similar "voices" that later confronted Israel.[44] For example, would Israel listen to the voice of the Canaanites? When the fall narrative is viewed from this perspective, the presence of the serpent in the good land of Eden makes perfect sense in an instructional manner: he is an excellent example of the "prototypical

---

39. Emmerich, "Temptation Narrative," 14.

40. Wenham, "Sanctuary Symbolism," 402–3.

41. See also comments by the rabbinic fathers as noted in Morris, "Exiled," 127.

42. Alexander, *Paradise to the Promised Land*, 119, 125–26. Hamilton (*Genesis 1–17*, 158) sees the raising of Adam from the dust of the ground as an elevation to "royal office." See also Peterson, "Egyptian Influence," 292–93.

43. See for example Holter, "Serpent," 106–12. Holter (p.108) notes the parallels between the possible metaphor of the serpent/Israel's enemies and Genesis 49 where the author uses theriomorphic language to describe Jacob's sons. Holter goes on to note the use of serpent imagery to describe Israel's enemies elsewhere in the OT (cf. Isa 14:28–32; Jer 8:17; 46:22).

44. Postell (*Adam as Israel*, 120 n1) suggests that the warning here makes it very likely that the text was geared to a pre-conquest audience, and hence is Mosaic in nature. Of course it is possible that this would have served as a fitting warning for those returning after the exile as well.

Canaanite."⁴⁵ Moreover, the later interactions of Joshua with the Gibeonites are a good example of the seduction and craftiness of the Canaanites. In the same way the serpent was cursed and humbled by crawling on the ground and eating dust, so, too, due to the Gibeonites' craftiness in deceiving Joshua, Joshua cursed and humbled them by forcing them into service for the tabernacle (Josh 9:23–27; Gen 3:14; cf. *Gen. Rab.* 20:5).⁴⁶ Is it possible that this cursing of the serpent and the Gibeonites is reflected in the promise of God to Abraham to curse those who misused him (12:3)? Some scholars certainly think so.⁴⁷ Therefore, because Adam and Eve failed to keep God's commands and exert dominion over the snake, they were cast out of the garden. Similarly, the subtle allure of the Canaanite religion and way of life would prove too seductive for the Israelites: they, too, would end up being exiled from the land, a picture that begins to be developed as early as the period of the judges.

Forbidden/Unclean Foods

One way God curtailed the interaction of Israel with the Canaanites was through the laws regulating clean and unclean foods (Leviticus 11; Deuteronomy 14). Israel had ample food from the list of clean animals without partaking of those that were unclean. The parallel with the limitations placed on Adam and Eve in the garden is important.⁴⁸ God had given Adam and his wife ample food without the need of eating from the forbidden tree. For both the first couple *and* Israel, eating prohibited food would lead to curses from God. In this regard, Genesis 3 sent a very clear message for Israel: do not think that even the smallest of sins is okay.⁴⁹ Something as simple as eating wrongly was enough to bring about harsh and severe judgment.

One of the reasons for the food limitations on the Israelites seems to be rooted in God's desire to keep them from table fellowship with Canaanites, especially in the context of religious settings (cf. Acts 10; Romans 14; Galatians 2). Interestingly, in the same way the serpent deceived Eve and by

---

45. Ibid., 104, 121, 130. See also the comments of Emmerich, "Temptation Narrative," 19.
46. Postell, *Adam as Israel*, 105–7, 123–24.
47. E.g., Holter, "Serpent," 112.
48. Sailhamer, *Pentateuch*, 109.
49. Collins, *Adam and Eve*, 62.

Genesis 3–4

extension, Adam, to eat of the tree, the "table fellowship" between Adam, Eve, and the serpent brought forth God's judgment. It is possible that an original audience would have seen in this account a warning not to eat with Canaanites. This breach of God's laws did in fact bring about the curses of the "Law" on Israel. This is particularly true of the setting in the book of Judges and later with the period prior to the exile to Babylon.[50]

The Curse on Adam and Eve

The *torah* instruction of Genesis 3 is focused not only on the warnings about breaking God's law, but also the outcome of breaking it. For Adam and Eve, the tree of life brought God's blessings whereas the tree of the knowledge of good and evil brought his curses.[51] As part of the outcome of breaking the "law" of Eden, God enacted curses upon Adam, Eve, and finally the serpent. It is the former two curses that play a dominant instructive role in the Torah.

To begin, the curse against Eve was barrenness.[52] Yes, there would be pain in childbearing, but more importantly, Eve would have trouble bearing children, that is, her womb would not always bring forth "fruit." It is no surprise that every one of the matriarchs in Genesis struggled with this very issue. Beginning with Eve we are told that she birthed a man child with the *help* of YHWH (4:1). Next, Sarah, Rebekah, and Rachel all dealt with the inability to have children. Only the intervention of God enabled them to get pregnant (18:10; 21:1–2; 25:21; 30:22). Also noteworthy is the fact that Lot's daughters, as well as Leah, and Tamar, all went to great lengths to have children (19:31–38; 29:31; 38:14–30). In every case, the matriarchal desire was indeed for their/a "man" (3:16; 30:14–16). Therefore, the curse on Eve served to explain why women could sometimes not bear children (e.g., Hannah in 1 Samuel 1; Manoah's wife in Judges 13). What is interesting is the fact that as part of the blessings of the Sinai covenant God had promised to overcome barrenness for the people of Israel if they followed and kept the Law (Exod 23:26; Deut 7:14).

---

50. This was a similar problem that the NT church had to navigate when they included the Gentiles (Acts 10; Galatians 1).

51. Emmerich, "Temptation Narrative," 9.

52. See Curley and Peterson, "Eve's Curse," 1–16. For feminist readings of 3:16, see the discussion of Stratton, *Out of Eden*, 91–96.

The curse on Adam was the land's inability to bring forth fruit due to thorns and thistles, and in many cases, through the effects of famine. Thus, much like Eve's curse, the "womb" of the earth was cursed. A slightly altered version of this curse is reiterated in the aftermath of the fall of Cain when God declares that the earth would no longer give forth its fruit due to the shed blood of Abel (4:11–12). Again it is not surprising that every one of the patriarchs dealt with famine and the inability to feed their families (12:10; 26:1; 41:54; cf. Ruth 1:1; 2 Sam 21:1). In each case, God had to intervene and help the patriarchs survive this curse. Once again, part of the curse of breaking the Sinai laws was the promise that God would send famine (Lev 26:19–20; Deut 11:17; 28:18, 23–24; 32:24), whereas the blessings of God would be to send rain in its seasons (Lev 26:4; Deut 11:14; 28:12).

In both situations, Adam and Eve became paradigmatic as to what can happen when the curses of breaking the Law of God are poured out upon people, and by extension, a nation. Sin and the curses of the Law have far-reaching effects. Indeed, sin is not isolated to one generation; it has the potential to carry forward to the following generations as well (Exod 20:5; 34:7; Num 14:18; Deut 5:9; 23:2–3, 8).[53] This is nowhere more evident than in the short account of Cain and his descendants. And as I will show in my next chapter, the progressive sinfulness of humanity in chapters 3–6 shows how sin, when it is left unchecked, has a tendency to get worse not better.

The Polemics of Genesis 3

Similar to the polemical nature of the creation narratives handled in our previous chapter, the fall in chapter 3 served to counter misconceptions prevalent in the ANE. As previously pointed out, the results of the fall, apart from the loss of the land/garden, was that both the womb of the ground (viz., the vegetation) and the womb of the woman were hindered from bringing forth their abundance. It is no surprise that these motifs find parallels in creation myths from the region, especially in Mesopotamia. One example is the Atrahasis Epic.[54] The great gods under the leadership of Enlil tried to limit the procreation of humanity by making the ground unable to bring forth its fruit.[55] When this did not stop the spread of humanity, the gods created two categories of women: those who could bear children

---

53. See a similar conclusion by Rosenberg, "Bible: Biblical Narrative," 67–68.
54. *ANET*, 104–6, esp. 106.
55. See *COS*, 1.130 p. 452. See also Kikawada and Quinn, *Before Abraham*, 42–44.

Genesis 3–4

and those who were barren. This is also the case for the earlier Sumerian myth of creation known as "Enki and Ninmah." Ninmah, the female creator goddess, created a woman who "could not give birth."[56] In both of these myths, it is the purpose of the gods to create humans who either could not procreate—to limit population—or to limit the productivity of the ground in order to create a famine-like situation to reduce the number of people.

The author of Genesis appears to be familiar with these ANE motifs but instead of assigning the blame for famine and barrenness to the capricious nature of the gods, he notes that both were the result of the fall of humanity itself. YHWH did not seek to limit procreation—something he had mandated himself (1:28; 9:1, 7; 35:11)—but rather both curses were the result of the first humans' sin. Indeed, miscarriages and loss of children among the Israelites was the result of a fallen world; yet even in this God promised to limit the effects of sin by assuring Israel that they would be blessed and this curse overridden if they would follow his commands (Exod 23:26; Deut 7:14; cf. Gen 31:38; Hos 9:14). From this perspective, the fall of Adam and Eve serves to instruct Israel on the true reason for famines and barrenness.

Others have also noted the polemical nature of the role of the serpent as both the purveyor of wisdom and the epitome of chaos/rebellion in the ANE.[57] In the former case, ancient Egyptian Coffin Texts note that the serpent dispensed knowledge to those who desired it.[58] In the Gilgamesh Epic a serpent steals a plant that Gilgamesh has in his possession that is supposed to restore his youth (*ANET*, 96). In many of the scenarios in these and other texts, wisdom and immortality are presented hand-in-hand as part of the prerogatives of the gods.[59] What is more, chaos monsters and demons pictured as serpents was a common motif in the ANE (*COS*, 1.28 p. 45; *ANET*, 62 lines 130–39; *ANET*, 326; *ANEP*, 218, plate 670; 237, plates 760–61; 215, plates 658–58, 660).[60]

In Egypt the serpent god Apep/Apophis was the "figure *par excellence* of evil and chaos."[61] And according to the Egyptian myth *The Repulsing of the Dragon and the Creation*, everyday a drawing of Apophis was to be

---

56. *COS*, 1.159, p. 518.
57. Joines, "Serpent," 4–8.
58. For the texts and discussion, see Clark, *Myth and Symbol*, 50–51.
59. Joines, "Serpent," 5–7.
60. Ibid., 8–9.
61. Ibid., 9.

Genesis as Torah

burned and stomped on with the left foot and spat upon four times (*ANET*, 6–7), an interesting parallel to the metaphorical crushing of the serpent's head in 3:15. Finally, Robert T. Rundle Clark notes that according to the *Book of the Dead* from the First Intermediate Period, at the end of time when the earth reverts to chaos and humanity returns to slime, the creator deity Atum is supposed to return to the form of a serpent.[62] Of course in Genesis God and the serpent are two distinct entities. Furthermore, in God's pronouncement of judgment on the serpent in Genesis he declares that the seed of the woman would crush the serpent's head and bring him to an end (3:15);[63] he will not be brought back to power—a similar picture reiterated in Revelation (Rev 20:2, 10).

The parallels with the biblical text are clear. To begin, the reason for the harsh pronouncement against the serpent reflected the fact that he was guilty of murder—he robbed immortality from humanity.[64] Like the chaos monsters of the ANE, the serpent desired to bring chaos to the garden through tempting Eve by pointing out that the tree would make her wise and become like God (3:5). Had God not intervened, Adam and Eve could have eaten from the tree of life and lived forever becoming in some way on par with God; a point God himself notes in 3:22. This would have created chaos for the created order.

From an instructive standpoint, the OT wisdom tradition was rooted in the fear of the Lord (Prov 1:7), which was demonstrated by keeping God's laws (Psalm 119). Eve's actions sought to circumvent the law of God. In fact, Eve's act was rebellion, as was the serpent's questioning of God's commands.[65] Eve sought to gain wisdom, autonomously, without the proper God-ordained process.[66] And the serpent placed himself in the position of God (cf. Isa 14:12–16).[67] Even something that seemed as innocuous as eating the fruit of a tree turned out to be instructive concerning a central tenet

---

62. Clark, *Myth and Symbol*, 52.

63. For a discussion on enmity and various positions identifying the "seed" of the woman in this verse, see Rosenbaum, "Israelite Homicide Law," 145–51.

64. Ibid., 150.

65. Emmerich, "Temptation Narrative," 12, 16.

66. So, too, ibid., 8–9.

67. In 1 Samuel 15:23, rebellion is likened to witchcraft/divination, which in many cases is the gaining of illicit knowledge apart from God (see 1 Samuel 28).

Genesis 3–4

in the Law of God: rebellion was an offense to God and had to be punished (Exod 23:21; 32:26–35; Num 11:32–34; Deut 9:7, 24; 13:5; 18:10; 31:27).[68]

Before leaving the topic of polemics in this portion of Genesis, one final text is worth noting, which finds affinity with our discussion immediately above. Present in Egypt at least as early as the Amarna period (fourteenth century BCE) was a Mesopotamian myth called the Adapa/Adamu myth, which is sometimes likened to the fall narrative.[69] In the text, a man named Adapa is summoned to heaven by the god Anu and is tempted by two other gods (one of which was a serpent god[70]) with eating the bread and water of life so that Adapa could live forever. Adapa rejected the offer because his god, Ea, had deceptively warned him against such an act.[71] Ironically, the eating of the forbidden food, which Adapa rejected, would have given him eternal life. Conversely, Adam and Eve's eating of the forbidden food took eternal life from them (3:22).

One cannot be certain whether or not the author of Genesis was consciously drawing a connection to this account or simply bringing to mind the motif of eating to gain immortality. Nevertheless, there is a clear parallel with Adam and Eve and the temptation to eat of the tree against God's command. As previously noted, Israel was to choose God's Law and live, the rejection of which would bring certain death. When Israel did break the commands of God, the sacrificial system and the priesthood was in place to ameliorate the effects of sin. Not surprisingly the sacrificial system is first mentioned implicitly in the fall of Adam and Eve and explicitly in the fall narrative of Cain. I will return to this topic below.

The Fall of Cain

Cain's murder of his brother Abel in Genesis 4 demonstrates perfectly the effects of unchecked sin and the reality that sin is systemic if not abrogated by proper living (4:26).[72] One of the most famous portions of the Cain

---

68. Interestingly, eating that which is forbidden and divination appear together in the laws of Lev 19:26.

69. *COS*, 1.129, p. 449; or *ANET*, 101–3.

70. See Joines, "Serpent," 2. The gods were Tammuz and Gizzida, the latter of which is the god in question and is often called Ningishzida.

71. Wenham, *Genesis 1–15*, 1, 53.

72. Jewish interpreters struggled with the apparent lack of justice for Abel. As such, some made up for this lacuna by making Abel the judge of all creation (*Test. Abr.* 12:4–9,

and Abel account is Cain's response to God when God asks him about his brother's whereabouts. Cain responds: "Am I my brother's keeper" (4:9). While this is indeed a callous response, in reality it carries a lot of theological import especially in light of the religious paradigm shift going on in Egypt in the Eighteenth Dynasty (see previous chapter for more on this period). Elsewhere I have noted this paradigm shift in the following manner:

> During the period of Hatshepsut and Thutmosis III, a religious shift was underway in which Maat (="the will of the community," which included peace, justice, morality, harmony, etc.)[73] was replaced by the pharaoh's and a person's focus on the "will of god" in what has been called a push for "personal piety" in the god–human relationship.[74] According to this worldview, "Success and failure are now no longer seen as a consequence of Maat, i.e. of social coherence and solidarity, but of direct divine intervention."[75] As a result, the individual–community relationship (i.e., "brotherhood") began to suffer.[76] No longer was the individual the "protector" of his/her fellow person but rather this responsibility was shifted to the gods.[77] At the same time, people were now accountable to the gods and to their judgment.[78]

It is not farfetched to see that Cain's response to God was illustrative of the skewed line of thinking present in Egypt in perhaps the very period that Moses and the Israelites left Egypt. Therefore, once again it is possible that the author was trying to refute the Zeitgeist of the period in which Israel had recently lived. Indeed, renowned Egyptologist Jan Assmann correctly concludes that unlike Egypt of the Eighteenth Dynasty era and the later theocracies of the Amarna period and the Twenty-first Dynasty, Israel focused its religious mindset on the triangular concept of God–Man–Community

---

15; 13:1–3). So, Levenson, *Death and Resurrection*, 76–77.

73. That is, a person's primary responsibility was to keep social harmony within the community by caring for the poor and weak. At this time, this responsibility shifted to the gods. One was not so much responsible to remain in harmony with the community as he/she was responsible to remain in harmony—through humility and obedience—with the gods. See Assmann, "State and Religion," 73.

74. Ibid., 72.

75. Ibid., 76.

76. Ibid., 80–81.

77. Ibid., 73–74. For an exemplar text from the New Kingdom, see papyrus Anastasi II, 9.2–10.1 (as noted by ibid., 73).

78. Ibid., 74, 76. Citation from Peterson, "Egyptian Influence," 298–99.

Genesis 3–4

within the confines of covenant and faith, something absent from Egyptian thinking of this period.[79] The truth is, for Israel the teaching was in fact clear: each person was not only responsible for his/her brother/sister, but they were also accountable to God especially in a covenanted community. What is more, God had every right to judge Adam, Eve, the serpent, and Cain. This was also the case during the days of the flood when God's judgment reached a global perspective.

Finally, similar to the conclusion reached concerning Adam and Eve's exile from Eden, Cain's sin caused him to be exiled from the presence of God (4:14–16). Rebellion against God's command/warning and Cain's later sin when he murdered Abel had separated him from God and the land he loved. This was no less true of Israel both during the wilderness period (Numbers 14) and during the exile to Babylon.

Teaching on Sacrifice

In my previous chapter, I developed the idea that the work of Adam and Eve in the garden reflected the priesthood in the temple. In the aftermath of the falls, a couple of instructional features naturally flow from God's actions with Adam, Eve, and Cain. First, God performed what could be classified as the first sacrifice for sin when he killed animals to cover Adam and Eve's nakedness (3:21).[80] One could argue that here we find the institution of the sacrificial system,[81] which not only explains why Cain and Abel brought sacrifices to God in chapter 4, but it helps explain the sacrificial practices of the patriarchs as well (8:20; 12:7; 13:4, 18; 22:9; 26:25; 33:20; 35:1–7). In this vein, the fact that Abel brought a blood sacrifice and Cain brought one from the ground does not necessarily answer the question of why God rejected Cain's offering:[82] the rejection of Cain's offering appears more related to his attitude (see more below). Second, the loss of animal life for the purpose of covering Adam and Eve's nakedness showed the costliness of one's sin—blood was the required payment. Third, because they functioned as the first "priests" the covering of Adam and Eve with skins (*kothnoth*; 3:21) appears to reflect the legislation that Israel's priests were required to

---

79. Assmann, "State and Religion," 78, 82.
80. So, too, Hinckley, "Garden Sanctuary," 8; and Parry, "Garden of Eden," 141–43.
81. Fretheim, "Reclamation," 364.
82. The Greek translations seem to imply that Cain's problem was that he did not prepare his sacrifice correctly. See Wevers, *Notes*, 55.

Genesis as Torah

wear tunics (*kothnoth*) to cover their nakedness (Exod 28:4, 40).[83] These accounts also demonstrate further theological instruction on the nature of God—he is holy and full of justice.

Theological Instruction on the Nature of God

Adding to our list of reflections on the nature of God from chapter 2, Genesis 3 and 4 also reveal another important characteristic of God: he judges sin. Of course this will play out consistently not only within Genesis (4:11–15; 6–9; 12:17; 19:1–29), but also throughout the remainder of the Pentateuch. For example, the accounts of the Golden Calf in Exodus 32–34 and the rebellion of the people in Numbers 11–14 reveal a pattern of rebellion in both the Sinai period and later during the wilderness wandering. In these later accounts, we see God judge Israel for a variety of sins: idolatry, licentiousness, complaining, unbelief, rejection of God-ordained leadership, giving a false report, rejecting the commands of God, and discouraging God's people. As with Adam, Eve, and Cain, in each of these later cases, God's judgment is swift and decisive. In each situation, God acts in these inceptive moments to establish justice and punish wickedness, something Israel would come to experience on a regular basis both before and after the conquest (e.g., Nadab and Abihu in Lev 10:1–5 and Achan in Josh 7:1–26).

Even within the context of judgment another attribute of God is revealed: God is one who warns of the dangers of sin (e.g., 2:17; 4:7; 20:3; 31:29), and even in failure, God shows mercy and a means of redemption (3:21; 4:15; 18:24–32; Exod 32:14; Num 21:8–9).[84] These theological truths are clearly on display in the wilderness period when Moses witnessed the very presence of God and the revelation of his attributes (Deut 34:6–7).

The account of Cain and Abel also teaches the reader that God requires a right attitude when approaching the Holy, especially when sacrificing. While a variety of reasons have been proffered as to why God rejected Cain's sacrifice, it seems just as likely that the theological truth being taught is that having a right attitude and a right heart when approaching a holy God is vitally important. Indeed, when addressing this text, Jon Levenson rightly notes "the source of the crime [is located] in the criminal himself."[85]

---

83. Sailhamer, *Pentateuch*, 109–10; Parry, "Garden of Eden," 145; and Hinckley, "Garden Sanctuary," 7.

84. See also comments by Fretheim, "Reclamation," 358–60.

85. Levenson, *Death and Resurrection*, 74.

Genesis 3–4

God warned Cain to master his emotions/attitude (4:7). This type of instruction would have been appropriate at any time period of Israel's history especially in light of the role of the priests to discern the attitudes of the worshipper. By the period of the writing prophets, the sacrificial system had become more focused on ritual rather than a changed heart (e.g., Isa 1:10–17; Micah 6:1–12; Mal 1:6–14). For this, God sent judgment upon the nation.

At the same time, R. W. L. Moberly is indeed correct that this could also depict a picture of divine election apart from any wrong doing on the part of Cain (and Esau) as seen in Paul's statements in Rom 9:10–12.[86] The apparent injustice of God's choice of Abel and rejection of Cain in many ways reflects God's apparent arbitrary choice of Israel above all the nations (Deut 14:2). The cryptic narrative of Cain and Abel displays perfectly that God's choices are often beyond comprehension.[87] Indeed, the constant overriding of primogeniture in Genesis displays this very fact.

Theophany

Closely connected to the concept of judgment is the idea of theophany. Genesis 3 reveals the first presentation of God appearing in theophanic glory. For Israel, YHWH appearing in thick clouds and in thunder and lightning was clearly evident to them on Sinai (Exod 19:16; 20:18; 34:5; Deut 4:11; 5:22; cf. Ps 77:16–20; 1 Kgs 19:11–12; Ezek 1:4–28). While many modern readers may miss what an ancient Israelite reader/hearer would have understood perfectly, some scholars are now beginning to suggest the clear instruction found in the fall narrative in this regard.[88]

For example, Jeffery Niehaus has shown in convincing fashion that the encounter between God and Adam and Eve reflects a theophany in which judgment is passed.[89] This is evident based upon a variety of linguistic features in chapter 3. First, God appeared in the "wind of the day" to confront Adam and Eve. The word for "day" (*yom*) can also mean storm (see Zeph 2:2b). Therefore, even though most see this as a reference to the early eve-

---

86. Moberly, *Theology*, 94; and Fretheim, *Pentateuch*, 46–47.

87. See Kaminsky, "Election," 143, 152; Levenson, *Death and Resurrection*, 74–75; and Brueggemann, *Genesis*, 289, 346. For a negative assessment on the presentation of divine election in Genesis, see Schwartz, *The Curse of Cain* (1997).

88. See for example, Emmerich, "Temptation Narrative," 19.

89. Niehaus, "Wind of the Storm," 263–67; and Niehaus, *God at Sinai*, 155–59.

ning (see modern translations, which tend to follow the LXX and Latin Vulgate), the grammar can also allow the phrase to be translated as the "wind of the storm," another clear reference to theophany.[90] Second, God's "walking" was not a simple stroll in the garden, but one of pacing and agitation based upon the use of the intensive iterative stem in the Hebrew for the term "to walk" (*halak*). Third, when Adam heard the "sound" of God, Adam became frightened. The term used here for "sound" is *qol*, which is also the term used for thunder, a key aspect of the Sinai theophany.[91] Fourth, God immediately passed judgment on Adam, Eve, and the serpent when he arrived. Finally, and most importantly, as part of the judgment on Adam and Eve, access to God was limited. Indeed, the garden "temple" (see chapter 2) now was guarded by cherubim and a flaming sword (3:24).

Why is the theophanic language of chapter 3 important? The answer lies in the fact that an ancient Israelite audience would have immediately been taken back to Sinai where Torah had been given. Much like Adam and Eve, Israel had been so frightened by the thundering/sound (*qol*) of God's voice that they had desired Moses to speak to YHWH on their behalf (Exod 20:18–19; Deut 5:25; 18:16).[92] In essence, they gave up their direct communication with God, as had Adam and Eve.[93] What is more, the picture of the fall explained why there was a need for the priesthood and why access to the divine was limited and to be considered holy. Yet, despite the restrictions due to the fall and humanity's loss of their freedom to walk with God in the garden, God promised Israel that if they kept his laws, God would "walk" (using the same intensive iterative stem) in their midst (Lev 26:12).[94]

Instruction on the Ten Commandments

Commandments 1–4

Before concluding this chapter it is important to note that the fall narratives also give instruction on a number of the specific laws found in the Ten Commandments. Although the first four commandments are not directly addressed, the greatest commandment not to have any other god before

---

90. Niehaus, "Wind of the Storm," 264.
91. Ibid., 264–65.
92. Ibid., 264; and Sailhamer, *Pentateuch*, 105.
93. See also Parry, "Garden of Eden," 141.
94. So, too, Damrosch, *Narrative Covenant*, 292; and Hinckley, "Garden Sanctuary," 7–9.

Genesis 3–4

YHWH is implicit in both narratives. The sin of Adam and Eve and later of Cain and his descendants, certainly is a picture of what happens when one places self and self-interest above God and neighbor.[95] At the heart of all sin is a removal of God from his rightful place (Romans 1). In this vein, the fall narratives become some of the clearest teaching for Israel on the dangers of sin and self-centeredness. What is more, Genesis 3 and 4 teach how sin damages family structures (the focus of commandments 5–10), a reality threaded throughout the patriarchal narratives.[96]

Commandments 5–10

Unlike the focus on the first four commandments noted in my previous chapter, in the fall narratives, five of the final six commandments appear in some form (adultery is not explicitly addressed). For example, Carmichael has seen in the Cain narrative the foundations for the fifth commandment of honoring one's father and mother (Exod 20:12; Deut 5:16). Cain dishonored his parents by killing their offspring Abel.[97] He also argues that Adam and Eve's taking of the forbidden fruit was the basis for the commandment not to steal (Exod 20:15; Deut 5:19).[98] He follows this by suggesting that in the legal setting of God's interrogation of Adam and Eve in the garden, the command not to bear false witness (Exod 20:16; Deut 5:20) was the result of Adam and Eve's deflecting the blame for their sin to someone other than themselves.[99] He concludes by noting that the law against coveting (Exod 20:17; Deut 5:21) also flows from YHWH's barring access to the tree of life because Adam and Eve may have ended up coveting what was now off limits.[100]

While Carmichael may see the fall narratives as the basis for these specific commandments, in reality, any number of the Pentateuchal narratives could be marshaled for such a purpose. In light of this fact, at best, all we can argue is that the fall narratives, like many others, are instructional

---

95. Moberly, *Theology*, 88; and Och, "Creation and Redemption," 335.
96. Fretheim, *Pentateuch*, 52.
97. Carmichael, *Origins of Biblical Law*, 37–38.
98. Ibid., 42.
99. Ibid., 43.
100. Ibid., 43–45. Carmichael argues that based upon the connections with Genesis 3–4, the last half of the Ten Commandments are indeed rooted in the YHWH—human relationship, not human—human relationships per se. See ibid., 45, n32.

only in that they serve as case law to demonstrate specific laws. This is nowhere more evident than in Cain's murder of Abel, a direct breach of the sixth commandment (Exod 20:13; Deut 5:17).[101]

Fratricide was one of the worst forms of murder in that it was a strike against a member of one's own family. Not surprisingly, the murderous actions of Cain against his brother flowed from his covetous actions against his brother due to God's acceptance of Abel's sacrifice. Murder became systemic in the line of Cain as seen in the actions of Lamech (4:23). And even though adultery is not on display in the fall narratives, polygamy certainly is as Lamech becomes the first explicitly noted polygamist in the Bible from the period of Shem to Terah.[102] Instructionally it is clear that the breaking of the Ten Commandments leads to a downward spiral in society as evinced in the life of Cain and his descendants. In fact, the downward spiral continues into the period of the flood, the focus of my next chapter.

Conclusion

As can be seen in the above discussion, one can find numerous parallels between the events of Genesis 3 and 4, and Israel's historical realities. Beyond those already mentioned, a number of specific laws could be connected to the actions of Adam, Eve, and Cain.[103] The falls of Adam and Eve, and later, their son Cain, demonstrate not only *torah* legislation but also general instruction about the dangers of breaking the Sinai covenant once in the land of Canaan. Moreover, there can be little doubt that the interaction of Adam and Eve with the serpent in their God-given land of Eden was meant to foreshadow Israel's encounter with the Canaanites in the Promised Land. It is also clear that these chapters in many ways had a polemical bent in light of the ANE context in which they were written. Finally, as the opening accounts of the Torah, rhetorically, the first four chapters of Genesis play a central role in establishing the character of God, his intolerance for rebellion and sin, the need for sacrifice to cover sin, and God's role as a judge. Nowhere is the latter motif more evident than in the cataclysmic events of the flood and its aftermath, the topic which dominates the next portion of Genesis.

101. Ibid., 38–39.
102. Kaiser, *Old Testament Ethics*, 183.
103. For example, Sailhamer (*The Pentateuch*, 104–5) points out that Adam was responsible for the actions of his wife according to the law on vows in Num 30:1–16.

4

Genesis 5–11

The Flood and Babel: How to Avoid the Judgment of God

The central focus of chapters 5–11 is the flood narrative and its immediate aftermath followed by the Babel event. Although most see in the flood account a parroting of flood motifs from other ANE texts, in this chapter I will move beyond this assumption and focus on specific *torah* legislation housed within the larger narrative. Here I will handle a number of themes, which appear throughout these chapters. These include: procreation (ch. 5); proper marriage (6:1–4; cf. Exod 34:16; Deut 7:3; Josh 23:12–13; Judg 3:6–7); food laws, sacrifice and capital punishment (9:1–6); and anti-Canaanite instruction (9:20–27). It is noteworthy that the first two topics in this list are central teaching points of Genesis and the larger Torah. In fact, the avoidance of mixed marriages was necessary for Israel to stay in the land of Canaan. I will conclude the chapter with an assessment of the Tower of Babel event and how the account may betray an instructional setting just prior to the conquest.

Genealogy as Fulfillment of God's Commands

In the opening four chapters of Genesis the toledoth formula (i.e., "these are the generations of . . .") appears only once (2:4). However, six more appear at key junctures in chapters 5–11 (5:1; 6:9; 10:1, 32; 11:10, 27; cf. 25:12, 19; 36:1, 9; 37:2). Why did the author decide to note so many of these

Genesis as Torah

toledoth formulae in such a short section of Genesis? David Carr suggests that the toledoth shows that Genesis serves as a "genealogical prologue" to Exodus–Deuteronomy.[1] Carr appears to be on the right track; however, perhaps a better answer is directly connected to the instructional purposes of what was required of humanity, namely, procreation.[2] In this regard, several of the toledoth appearances are directly connected to genealogies (5:1; 10:1, 32; 11:10, 27), which in turn shows the fulfillment of God's commands to Adam and Eve to be fruitful and multiply (1:26–27). Despite the problem of sin—something inevitable after the fall (6:5; 8:21)—the presence of the toledoth formulae and genealogical lists shows that God continued to bless his creation.[3] By the end of Genesis, Jacob had gone from being one lone wanderer to a family of over seventy people (46:27). By the time Exodus begins, Israel had become a great nation (Exod 1:9), a picture of true blessings as well as the fulfillment of God's promises (15:5; 22:17; 26:4; 32:12). Therefore, from an instructional perspective the numerous toledoth formulae are not simply introductory notices, they serve to show that Israel's God is one who keeps his word to bless his creation and desires his people to procreate.[4] From this vantage point the promises of life and fruitfulness found elsewhere in the Torah take on new meaning (Exod 23:25; Deut 7:12–13; 28:4).

Finally, the genealogies of chapters 5, 10, and 11 would have helped to give those in exile (either in Egypt or Babylon) a connection to the past as well as informing them about the peoples they would encounter in Canaan and the vicinity, especially as discussed in chapter 10 (see esp. 10:18–19). What is more, the tracing of Israel's line through Shem and not Ham helped Israel to understand why they were not among the cursed line of Canaan (9:18–27).[5] As they read chapters 5–11 it would have become clear that God was with the line of Seth in a special way (Deut 7:7). Men like Enoch (5:24), Lamech, Noah (5:28–31), and Shem (10:21–31; 11:10–26) stand out as being blessed by God. Therefore, even before Abraham was called out of Ur, Israel's distant ancestors had a special relationship with God that

---

1. Carr, "*Biblos geneseos*: Part 1," 172. See also Carr, "*Biblos geneseos*: Part 2," 327–47.
2. Polin, "Jewish Law," 37; and Klein et al., *Biblical Interpretation*, 437.
3. So, too, Clines, *Theme*, 66–69. Clines points out that the notations about death in the genealogies show that the curse is active as well.
4. Ibid., 45.
5. Cassuto, *Genesis: Part II*, 149.

was passed on to Israel through Abraham, Isaac, Jacob, and his sons (Deut 4:37).

The Multiple *Torah* Instructions from the Flood Narrative

To begin, the instruction in the flood narrative, while encompassing all peoples, still falls within the larger *torah* instruction for Israel.[6] Moreover, it is important to note that the flood account was recorded as a part of Israel's sacred history as a means of relating what happened in the distant past. It is impossible to isolate the didactic aspects of the flood narrative to one or two points. On the contrary, multiple levels of instruction appear in the account both at the individual law level as well as at the level of larger motifs. Due to this fact, this section will be devoted to unpacking the different ways Israel may have understood this well-known account, an event that is attested in a variety of ANE myths, especially from Mesopotamia.

The Flood as Polemic

One cannot determine with certainty whether or not Israel was familiar with the actual myths of Atrahasis, Gilgamesh, or the Sumerian Eridu Genesis; however, one can state with a high degree of confidence that at some point in their lives they would have been familiar with the event itself. As such, much like I have noted in previous chapters concerning creation and the fall, the account of Noah served in a polemical fashion to rectify ancient misconceptions of what happened during the flood and why.

For example, in the Atrahasis Epic, the gods desired to destroy humanity because of the noise that they made. In other words, humanity was not punished for sin, but was innocent. In the Genesis account it becomes clear at the opening of chapter 6 that humanity's sinful behaviors were the cause of the flood. Forbidden relationships, evil intent, and violence marked the downward spiral of humanity after the falls of Adam, Eve, and Cain.

Other factors to consider when comparing the flood accounts of the ANE and the Bible are: the length of the flood (7 days versus 40/over 150 days); the site/mountain where the ark landed; what happened when the main character offered a sacrifice after the flood (the gods behave like flies versus God's acceptance of Noah's sacrifice); and the fate of the main

---

6. See Crüsemann, *Torah*, 3.

character (eternal life is granted versus a progeny for Noah). Despite the narratival differences, it is in fact the cause of the flood according to the biblical text that seems to be the most instructive: God punishes people for sin and rebellion, not because he is capricious. And as just noted, the central cause for the flood appears to have been violence, rampant evil in general, and indiscriminate marriage practices.

When Israel would have read this account they would not only have received proper instruction on what happened during the flood of the distant past, but they also would have learned that God does not allow sin to go unchecked. Although God may not destroy the earth again by a flood (9:15), as Genesis unfolds it becomes clear that God would do "surgical" judgment when needed in order to limit the effects of sin (e.g., Babel, Sodom and the cities of the plain, Er and Onan, etc.). Depending on what generation was reading the book of Genesis, similar surgical judgments against them as a nation would have immediately come to mind. In the exodus generation alone, events like the Golden Calf fiasco (Exodus 32–34), the murmuring for meat (Numbers 11), the rebellion of Miriam and Aaron (Numbers 12), the evil report of the ten spies (Numbers 13–14), the challenge of Korah, Dathan, and Abiram (Numbers 16), and the sin of Baal of Peor (Numbers 25) gave clear evidence that God would not allow sin to go unchecked, especially if it was in direct violation of the Sinai covenant. One of the primary ways that Israel sinned against the covenant was in their intermarriage with foreign/Canaanite women.

Instruction on Intermarriage

The meaning of the opening four verses of Genesis 6 have been discussed *ad nauseam* and certainly will not be the central focus of my discussion here. More ink has been spilled over the identification of the daughters of men (the line of Cain or humanity in general) and the sons of God (fallen angels, demons, rulers, sons of Seth etc.) than perhaps any other topic in Genesis. Despite the stalemate in the scholarly discussion, when this portion of the flood narrative and the destruction of the world are viewed in light of *torah*, an analogical application can be made.

At the heart of the narrative seems to be the issue of inappropriate marriage unions (polygamy, angels and humans, demons and humans etc.; cf. Matt 24:37; Luke 17:26). The results of these marriage unions led to violence and the destruction of the human race. In this vein, it is indeed possible that the "sons of God" served as an analogy for the children of Israel themselves (Exod 4:22–23; Deut 14:1; Ps 82:6–7). Instructionally, the account smacks of similar *torah* instruction about mixed or inappropriate marriages for Israel (Exod 34:12–16; Deut 7:3; cf. Josh 23:12; Judg 3:6; 1 Kgs 11:1–8; Ezra 9–10).[7] Similarly, Wenham notes that "Gen 6:1-4 may well be condemning cult prostitution and sacred marriage rites."[8] God's design for marriage had been established in Genesis 2. Interestingly, God brought Eve to Adam as an acceptable spouse in the same way God gave Israel multiple tribes from which to find spouses.

As one of the main reasons for God's judgment on the earth in Noah's day, the issue of indiscriminate marriage was meant to carry theological weight for Israel. While many in Israel may have thought that mixed marriages were of no consequence (see Judg 3:6; Ezra 9–10; Neh 13:23–28), the truth of history showed otherwise. In the period of the judges, assimilation through marriage brought the near destruction of Israel. And Solomon's many wives caused one of Israel's greatest kings to be brought to the brink of spiritual ruin (1 Kgs 11:1–13). In the postexilic period, fear of assimilation with the surrounding nations caused both Ezra and Nehemiah to act decisively to maintain proper marriage relationships within the newly re-founded nation of Israel (Ezra 9–10; Neh 13:23–28). Thus, the message of these opening lines of chapter 6 would have resonated in any period as a warning: first, to those prior to entering the land of Canaan; second, to those already in the land; third, to those in exile in Babylon; or fourth, to those in the postexilic resettlement.

The Flood as a Picture of Judgment on Israel

As previously noted, the flood account focuses on God's judgment due to unchecked sin, namely, intermarriage, violence, and evil intent. Not surprisingly, early Jewish interpreters identified the sexual sins of the people (e.g., adultery), along with idolatry and robbery, as the cause of the flood (b. *Sanh*. 57a and 108a).[9] As a result of humanity's rebellion, God enacted his justice and judgment, a similar picture, which I noted in the accounts of the falls of Adam, Eve, and Cain.[10] For Israel, the parallels to the wilderness

---

7. Wenham, *Story as Torah*, 27.
8. Wenham, "Sanctuary Symbolism," 403.
9. So Polin, "Jewish Law," 40.
10. For parallels between Noah and Adam as the progenitors of a new civilization,

Genesis as Torah

wandering and/or the exile are evident. On numerous occasions Israel's rebellion was the impetus behind the judgment of God, in some cases with the threat of almost total annihilation. For example, the sin of the Golden Calf certainly comes to mind (Exodus 32–34) as the primary example of Israel's spiritual rebellion, which almost cost them their very existence (Exod 32:10) and God's accompanying presence (Exod 33:1–3). Also, Numbers 14 records God's response to the people's acceptance of the ten spies' evil report. God desired to destroy them and start anew with Moses (Num 14:11–12).

The wickedness of Israel's heart and their constant rebellion boils to the surface within these and other narratives and brings about the divine wrath of YHWH. Nevertheless, similar to Noah's preaching/intercession in his day (2 Pet 2:5), it was only the intercession of Moses that stayed God's hand (Exod 33:12–17). In Noah's day, the wickedness of the people's hearts was the catalyst that brought about the flood. However, God relented from destroying the earth again with a flood because of the pervasive wickedness of human hearts (Gen 6:5; 8:21),[11] a similar image reflected in the consistent evil inclinations of Israel both before and after the wilderness wandering (Deut 31:27).[12] At the heart of this teaching a picture emerges of a God who can bring his people through the darkest of times due to his judgment and still reestablish a covenant that is everlasting. Justice must be served, but mercy abides as well.

Also of importance is the way the motif of the remnant plays out in Noah's generation. God chose to save a remnant of the world, that is, the eight persons aboard the ark (6:18; 7:1). The issue of God's selectivity in saving a remnant has at least two *torah* connections and one prophetic parallel. First, even before the end of Genesis we see the preservation of Jacob's family in the Nile delta. Even though there were countless families affected by the famine in the days of Joseph, God chose to save Jacob and his family. In this regard, Egypt became a metaphorical "ark" for preserving the righteous remnant, which would emerge from the time of trials (i.e., famine) and develop into a great nation (cf. Exod 1:9; Genesis 10). Second, during the wilderness wandering YHWH preserved a "remnant" in the

---

see Carr, "*Biblos geneseos*: Part 2," 331–33.

11. Moberly, *Theology*, 112–14, 117. Moberly suggests that the "evil thought clause" of 8:21 is a later addition because it breaks up the poetic bicola. He renders the verse as "I will never again curse the ground because of humankind//nor will I ever again destroy every living creature as I have done" (p.113).

12. Fretheim, *Pentateuch*, 56.

wilderness, that is, Joshua, Caleb, and the second generation of Israelites. Everyone else perished including Miriam, Aaron, and Moses. Third, the message of the prophets focused on the preservation of the remnant in the Babylonian exile.[13] Death and destruction rained down upon Israel in the days of the Assyrian (722 BCE) and Babylonian exiles (586 BCE); yet, in the midst of this God preserved a remnant and brought them out from the period of trials.

It therefore should not be surprising that both the flood and the wilderness wandering find affinity in the period of the testing, namely forty days. The forty days of watery judgment (7:4, 12, 17)—followed by over 150 days of waiting (7:24; 8:3)—brought a rapid end to all life due to rebellion and sin in Noah's day.[14] For the wilderness generation, their punishment was connected to the forty days the spies spent reconnoitering the land: this translated into one year of wandering for every day the spies were in Canaan (Num 14:34); hence the forty years of testing in the wilderness. Safety had been assured in the Promised Land had Israel obeyed; however, as a result of disobedience, forty years of judgment followed.

Instruction on the Sinai Event

The detailed instructions for the construction of the ark were instructive for the nation on how to be obedient to the details given by God at Sinai.[15] This is particularly true when one considers the detailed instructions for the Ark of the Covenant, the tabernacle, and its furnishings. The instructions to Noah were not simply for the reader to understand the specifics of the construction of the ark and the period leading up to the flood; on the contrary, like the later instructions for the tabernacle and its furnishings, both served as instruction *for* Israel.[16]

In this vein, David Damrosch suggests that there are a number of parallels between the Priestly version of the flood account and later portions of the Pentateuch. For him Sinai "is a new Ararat;" Noah's obedience in building the ark parallels Moses' obedience to God in building the tabernacle

---

13. Isa 1:9; 10:20–22; 11:11, 16; 37:31–32; Jer 15:11; 23:3; 31:7; Ezek 6:8; 11:13; 14:22; Joel 2:32 [3:5 Heb]; Amos 5:15; Micah 2:12; 5:3 [5:2 Heb]; 5:7–8 [5:6–7 Heb]; Zeph 2:7–9; Hag 1:12, 14; Zech 8:6, 12.

14. The total length of the flood was roughly one year.

15. Sailhamer, *Pentateuch*, 63.

16. Ibid.

(Gen 6:22; Exod 39:42); the "wandering" of Noah on the flood waters reflects the wilderness wandering; Noah's sending out of birds to "search out" the land—one bringing back a "growing thing"—mirrors Moses sending out of spies to search out the land who in turn brought back "growing things" (Gen 8:11; Num 13:23–25); and the destruction of the old world followed by a recreation finds a fitting parallel with the loss of the first "evil" generation of Israel in the forty-year wandering only to have a new generation/creation emerge after the period of trial (Numbers 1; 26).[17]

The Post-Flood Events as *Torah* for Israel

In preparation for the flood, God instructed Noah to bring seven pairs of clean animals and one pair of all the other animals onto the ark (7:2). One can see already *torah* instruction in this requirement, which will take on more detail in Leviticus and Deuteronomy (Leviticus 11; Deuteronomy 14). After the flood, Noah took from each of these clean animals and made a whole burnt offering to God (8:20). The centrality of sacrifice, as noted in our previous chapter, will take on pedantic detail in the Levitical law, especially in Leviticus 1–7.

Within the Noahic covenant we also find several specific laws reiterated and/or expanded later in the Torah (cf. b. *Sanh.* 59a). One in particular is the prohibition of eating animals without properly draining the blood (9:4; Lev 7:26; 17:10–15; 19:26; Deut 12:16; 15:23). We also find that capital punishment is instituted for murder because humans are created in the image of God (9:5–6). In the Torah, God expands the death penalty to include a variety of infractions that in some way violated God's created order and/or the stipulations of the Sinai covenant. These included, but are not limited to, bestiality (Exod 22:19; Lev 20:15–16), homosexual acts (Lev 20:13; cf. Lev 18:22), adultery (Lev 20:10), rape of a betrothed woman (Deut 22:25–27), incest (Lev 20:12), working on the Sabbath (Exod 31:14; Num 15:32–36), blasphemy (Lev 24:16), false prophecy (Deut 13:1–10), divination/witchcraft (Exod 22:18; Lev 20:27), rebelling against or striking one's parent (Exod 21:15; Deut 21:18–21), kidnapping (Exod 21:16; Deut 24:7), and bearing false witness (Deut 19:15–21). Rabbi and biblical scholar Milton Polin goes one step further and argues that with the exception of

---

17. Damrosch, *Narrative Covenant*, 292–94.

monotheism, the Noahic laws in fact were the basis for all other ANE legislation (Assyrian, Hittite, and Hammurabi).[18]

Also, 9:18–27 makes a clear polemic against Canaan and some of the sexual proclivities with which they are later identified. This latter reality is further noted in 13:13, the account of Sodom and Gomorrah (ch. 19), and Shechem's rape of Dinah (ch. 34). Indeed, if the sin of Ham was sexual in nature,[19] then it is possible that this event may have been part of the impetus behind the sexual laws of Leviticus 18 and 20 (see more on this in my next chapter). Finally, the focus on Canaan and not Ham per se serves to instruct Israel on why Canaan was cursed and needed to be driven from the land. While Ham may have thought that the effects of his sin were limited to himself, in essence sin had far-reaching effects on his family line, especially that of his son Canaan. From a *torah* perspective, this same teaching is clear in God's words about holding sinful people accountable to the fourth generation (Exod 20:5; 34:7; Num 14:18; Deut 5:9) but blessing those who love him (Exod 20:6; 34:7; Deut 5:10). For YHWH, keeping the laws as found in the Sinai covenant was of vital importance. Long before the Sinai event, God gave instruction through the Noahic covenant, and later the Abrahamic covenant, on the importance of covenant and how to keep from breaking it.

The Importance of Covenant

As will be developed more fully in the next chapter, the idea of covenant appears the clearest for the first time here in the flood narrative. The Noahic covenant (6:18; 9:1–17) foreshadows not only the unilateral Abrahamic covenant (15:18), but also the Mosaic covenant. Covenants brought a level of protection for those involved. For the post-flood world, God had promised not to destroy the entire earth by a flood again. At the same time, those associated with a covenant—especially those made with God (i.e., Israel)—were required to abide by certain laws. Indeed, more was required of them. Curses could be enacted to punish the breach of a covenant (Leviticus 26; Deuteronomy 28).

From the institution of the Noahic covenant, Israel learned that before their unique covenant at Sinai, Israel's God was a covenant-making God

---

18. Polin, "Jewish Law," 38.

19. See my discussion in Peterson, *The Sin of Sodom*, 45–47. Note also Polin, "Jewish Law," 40.

Genesis as Torah

who promised to preserve life (Gen 6:19-20; 7:3). Covenant also served as the means for God to bring redemption to his people and to return his people to the Promised Land, which had been lost when Adam and Eve were driven from Eden.[20] However, along with all of the benefits of the covenant came responsibility.

One of these requirements was the need for individuals to associate themselves with the covenants by God-ordained signs. The rainbow was the sign of the Noahic covenant (9:13-17) and required nothing per se of the inhabitants of the earth but recognition of what it stood for—God's promise to humanity not to destroy the earth ever again by a flood.[21] On the other hand, circumcision was the sign of the Abrahamic covenant (17:10-11), and Sabbath was the sign of the Mosaic/Sinai covenant (Exod 31:15-17). Both of these signs were to be kept by those associated with these covenants. Failure to do so could bring death or being cut off from Israel. Therefore, through this early covenant, Israel learned valuable instructions on why covenant was important. Finally, the implied Edenic covenant, which was broken by the pre-flood generation, taught Israel what happened to people who violated God's covenantal commands especially the natural order of creation as established in Genesis 1 and 2 (viz., procreation, heterosexual marriage, and the importance of the family unit).[22]

Noah and Moses Paralleled

Before leaving the topic of the flood narrative, it is important to note how the author of this material desired to make connections between the life of Noah and that of Moses, Israel's greatest law giver. From the beginning of the flood narrative, hints within the account point to the reality that whoever recorded the final form of Genesis sought to highlight Moses as a key figure in the Torah, a point I have made throughout the previous chapters. This is made evident as early as the third verse in the introduction to the flood narrative. In 6:3, the author notes that the days of humanity would be 120 years. Now while a number of interpretations for this cryptic phrase have been proffered, it seems most likely that this refers to the limiting of a person's life to 120 years. If this is the case, then Moses lived the exact

---

20. Sailhamer, *Genesis Unbound*, 84-85.
21. Carr, "*Biblos geneseos*: Part 2," 335.
22. See my discussion on this in Peterson, "Genesis 2."

amount of time promised by God (Deut 34:7).²³ Therefore, in the period after the flood, Moses exemplified the limits of God's blessing vis-à-vis life expectancy.

Next, it is interesting that the language used of Noah, namely, that he was a righteous man in his day, finds a fitting parallel with Moses who was the paragon of humility and righteousness (Num 12:3). Moberly suggests that further parallels between Moses and Noah can be found in the Golden Calf incident where Moses becomes an intercessor for a "stiff-necked" people when God desired to destroy the entire nation.²⁴ Similarly, Noah was the one to intercede for his generation (cf. 2 Pet 2:5). Moberly aptly concludes,

> If both Israel and the world show themselves to be faithless at the outset and to be continuously faithless ("evil in thought" and "stiff-necked"), then their continued existence is similarly to be understood in terms of the merciful forbearance of God towards those who do not deserve it: Life for both Israel and the world is a gift of grace—recognition of which should elicit a gratitude that renounces faithlessness.²⁵

It is the demonstration of God's grace and mercy in the account of the flood that helped to flesh out the picture of who YHWH was and the attributes of the God Israel served.

Theological Instruction on the Nature of God

As I have been noting in each chapter, the Genesis narratives betray a number of God's attributes. Similar to our discussion in the previous chapter, the flood narrative and the Babel account show that God is judge; yet at the same time he exhibits mercy to a remnant and remembers the righteous (8:1; cf. 19:29; 30:22; Exod 2:24; 6:5; Num 10:9).²⁶ Also, in the opening of the flood narrative we find for the first time in the Torah a clear teaching on the reality that God can be grieved (*'atsab*) in his spirit when faced with the sinfulness of humanity (6:6). The emotions of God that would become most instructive for Israel, especially when God was confronted with Is-

---

23. So, too, the conclusion of Greenstein, "Biblical Law," 92.
24. Moberly, *Theology*, 118–20.
25. Ibid., 120.
26. Clines, *Theme*, 62.

Genesis as Torah

rael's sin would be God's anger (*'aph*; cf. Exod 4:14; Num 11:1, 10; 12:9; 22:22; 25:3–4; 32:10, 13–14; Deut 4:25; 6:15; 7:14; 9:18–19; 13:17; 29:20, 23–24, 27–28; 31:17, 29; 32:16, 21–22) and his jealousy (*qana'*; cf. Num 25:11; Deut 29:20 [29:19 Heb]; 32:16, 21).

Instruction on the Ten Commandments

Two clear case-law examples of the breaking of the Ten Commandments can be found at the end of the flood narrative and within the Babel account. The men of Babel flouted the first commandment by putting themselves above God's commands. The actions of the men at Babel clearly displayed the reality that their desires trumped the laws of God especially when they directly disobeyed God's commands to spread out and populate the land (cf. 9:1; 11:4).[27] One could argue that they put themselves in the place of God. As a result of their sin, God forced them to spread out by confusing their language (11:8–9). Instructionally, it is clear that God would not allow disobedience to go unpunished. Israel must follow the commands of God in detail in order to receive God's full blessings.

The second clear breach of a commandment appears at the end of the flood account. Ham's actions against his father when Noah was naked in his tent were a clear violation of the fifth commandment.[28] On the one hand, Ham mocked his father by telling his brothers about their father's vulnerable state (9:22). On the other hand, Shem and Japheth honored their father by shielding their sight when covering their father with a sheet (9:23). The fifth commandment is also known as the commandment with a promise, namely, by honoring one's parents, God promised long life in the land. Relatively speaking, Ham's actions affected his son, Canaan, and generations after him and resulted in the loss of the land of Canaan by his descendants.

Instruction from the Tower of Babel

In the Babel account it is possible to identify a number of teaching points applicable to a variety of Israel's historical situations. First, some see the desire of the men of Babel to remain in Babylon/Shinar as a picture of the

---

27. Cassuto, *Genesis: Part II*, 243.

28. Luther, *Genesis I*, 173; and Cassuto, *Genesis: Part II*, 152.

Genesis 5–11

Judean exiles who did not want to return to Judah after the Babylonian exile ended. Thus the Babel event served as a polemic against remaining in Babylon if in fact the text is dated to the exile.[29] Similarly, as we will see in our next chapter, some see Abraham's call out of Ur as yet another call to the exiles to leave Babylon and return to Judah.[30] Of course it is also possible that these two accounts served as encouragement for the first generation to leave Egypt (Exod 13:17; Num 14:3–4; Deut 17:16).

Second, if the setting for Genesis is on the Plains of Moab as described by the end of Numbers, then Babel also looks forward to the conquest of Canaan, and specifically, the fall of Jericho. An Israelite could easily have taken away from the story that they should not fear walled cities (i.e., Jericho; cf. Deut 1:26–30): God could bring about their demise by something as simple as confounding the language of the people. Ironically Jericho was destroyed without Israel raising a hand against the walls. Like Babel, God brought Jericho to an end.

Third, for those of the first generation coming out of Egypt, when the author noted that the people at Babel made bricks, the toilsome work of making bricks for the store cities of the pharaoh while they were in slavery in Egypt would have been brought to the fore (Gen 11:3; Exod 5:7).[31] By remembering their past in slavery and servitude, this account would have caused them to recognize their need for YHWH's leading and protection. As such, they would have been encouraged to offer thanksgiving to God for all he had done for them (Lev 7:12–15; 22:29).

Fourth, when the people of Babel refused to spread out, God judged them for their rebellion. The instruction for Israel, which is visible in this detail of the story, is ultimately manifest in the command of God to occupy the land of Canaan (Deut 9:3–5; 11:23–25; Josh 3:10; 13:6). Unfortunately, Israel desired to stay centralized either at Gilgal and its locale or in the small areas they had success in conquering (Josh 15:63; 17:14–18; Judg 1:19–33). They had failed to spread out and occupy the land in its totality according to the word of the Lord (Josh 13:1; cf. Deut 6:18; 8:1). Because of their rebellion, God judged Israel (Num 33:52–55; Josh 23:13; Judg 2:3). Thus, the rebellion of the inhabitants of Babel against such a simple command of God is mirrored in Israel's rebellion against the simple command of God to

---

29. Briggs and Lohr, *Theological Introduction*, 45–46; and Wenham, "Sanctuary Symbolism," 403.

30. Hepner, *Legal Friction*, 103.

31. So, too, Briggs and Lohr, *Theological Introduction*, 38.

go in and possess the land both before the wilderness wandering (Numbers 13–14) and later when they refused to complete the task.

Fifth, whereas those at Babel desired to blend the human and the divine by trying to reach heaven, at Sinai, God reversed this concept by coming down and living in Israel's midst thus blending the holy and the profane/earthly.[32] In order for this to happen though, the Sinai stipulations needed to be adhered to rigidly.

Finally, one could argue that the account of Babel also served as an ongoing polemic against city life (cf. Gen 4:17; 13:12–13; chs. 14, 19, 34; cf. Num 13:28). It is noteworthy that the construction of the first city was actually attributed to Cain, the first murderer (4:17).[33] And immediately after the Babel account the reader is told that Abraham was called out of the great city of Ur. Of course it is not surprising that the cities of the plain, Sodom in particular, are noted as places of rebellion and wickedness.[34] While Israel would eventually settle in cities they did not build (Deut 6:10–11), the low-grade polemic in these and other texts seems to indicate the author's distaste for city life in general.

God Promotes His People

One of the reasons for the construction of the Tower of Babel was so that the inhabitants could make a name for themselves (11:4). People within the Bible who sought to promote themselves ended up being judged in some way. For example, the "men of a name" in Gen 6:4 met their end in the flood. And the lives of Saul and Absalom, who made monuments to themselves so they would be remembered (1 Sam 15:12; 2 Sam 18:18), both ended in tragedy and in ways mirror the motives of the men at the Tower of Babel. This is no less the case for Egypt's pharaohs who often built magnificent self-named cities, of which Israel was forced to be a part (Exod 1:11).

Another instructive feature of the Babel account is the possibility that the men of Babel were actually building a mountain/high place on which to worship their gods. Many identify the Tower of Babel as a ziggurat. These were man-made mountains used for cultic purposes. For the Israelites this was taboo. High places and mountains were not the place to worship God

---

32. Carr, "*Biblos geneseos*: Part 2," 340.
33. Peterson, *The Sin of Sodom*, 25.
34. See White, "Same Sex Orientation," 20.

Genesis 5–11

(Lev 26:30; Num 33:52; Deut 12:2; 1 Kgs 3:3; 12:32; 13:2; etc.); this was to be done at the site where God would place his name (Deut 12:5–6).

Conclusion

The theological and didactic richness of the flood and Babel accounts is self-evident in light of the foregoing discussion. While it is true that these accounts would have filled in much of Israel's prehistory, it is also the case that this portion of Genesis still recorded many Torah laws in "case-law" format and as general instruction. By the end of the opening eleven chapters it becomes evident that disobedience removes God's blessing and brings upon the earth/a nation the curses of God.[35] It is also clear that many times God judged people based upon his laws without necessarily warning them of coming judgment. In this vein, with the exception of the cryptic text in 2 Pet 2:5, the flood generation appears to have been oblivious to their breach of God's laws, even though they were responsible for them (Matt 24:38–39). And the text does not record that God warned the men of Babel concerning their rebellion but he still acted and passed judgment based upon his earlier commands to Noah (9:1).[36] This concept showed Israel that the breaking of law—what had already been declared to them—would bring God's judgment, sometimes in ways that they were not forewarned about. In some cases, this was simply due to the fact that the presence of a holy God dwelt in their midst (Exod 19:22–24; 33:3; Deut 4:23–24). The wilderness generation experienced the reality of this type of judgment on more than one occasion.

Despite the need for God's judgment against sin, God also had a plan to redeem his creation (3:15). While a number of key figures had been instrumental in carrying this promise forward up to this point, it was none other than Israel's earliest progenitor, Abraham, who would be blessed with the specific promises and blessings in this regard. Furthermore, as a foundational figure in Israel's history, Abraham's life was marked by numerous instructional events.

---

35. Keiser, *Genesis 1–11*, 156.
36. Stahl, *Law and Liminality*, 14.

5

Genesis 12–25

Abraham as an Example of Righteous Behavior

When speaking of the patriarchal narratives in general, von Rad notes that central to all of these narratives is the role that the family plays. He says "it is the framework of all human activity, politics and economics as well as religion."[1] While I have already developed the importance of the family vis-à-vis the Torah in my discussion of Genesis 2, its significance indeed continues in the Abraham cycle. To be sure, in this regard the life of Abraham is instructive both in positive and negative ways. Yet, despite the questionable decisions of Abraham vis-à-vis his family, his election and example of the righteous life was something with which Israel should have resonated. Of particular importance to the patriarchal narratives are the numerous accounts where proper sexual ethics within the family and society at large play a key role. For example, in what follows I will suggest that Genesis 19 serves as a narrative commentary on the sexual laws of Leviticus 18 and 20. As such, the purpose of chapter 19 along with a number of other chapters was to warn Israel of the dangers of associating with the Canaanites and their sexual proclivities. As we will see, Lot's life and family dynamics is certainly instructive in this regard.

Closely connected to a proper sexual ethic is the instructional purpose of the command to men and women to be fruitful and multiply (1:28;

---

1. Von Rad, *Genesis*, 34–35. See also Briggs and Lohr, *Theological Introduction*, 29–31.

25:12, 19). In the broader narrative, this *torah* command was something that the pharaoh had tried to undo regarding Israel in Exodus 1.[2] Another narrative, which I will examine, is that of 12:10–20. Because this text is a microcosm of the exodus event, it played a direct didactic role in the life of Israel.[3] Finally, throughout this chapter I will also address some of the specific Torah legislation where Genesis displays case-law applications such as that seen in the situation of child sacrifice depicted in Genesis 22 (cf. Exod 22:28; 34:20). As we will see, the historical and geographical setting from which Abraham emerged helps to explain the instructional purposes of this particular text.

The Setting for the Narrative of Abraham

Before beginning our analysis of chapters 12–25, it is important to note the best historical setting within which the account of the life of Abraham would have made the most sense. Establishing this fact will help address how *torah* instruction is being used in the narrative. Many note that anachronistic language in the calling of Abraham from Ur *of the Chaldees*, which is in the region of Babylon, reflects an exilic setting for the writing of the text. As such, Abraham's call would have encouraged an exilic audience to return to Canaan. While this is possible, it could also be argued that the language of the text has merely been updated and that it had an earlier function. For example, this account may rhetorically serve to show the reversal of Adam and Eve's movement to the east after the fall (see previous chapter). Furthermore, as I will develop in more detail below, Abraham's immediate descent into Egypt and return noted in 12:10–20 best reflects the Egyptian exodus context. Therefore, in many ways the premise that the patriarchal narratives fit best within the postexilic period, at least from a didactic perspective, does not seem a settled fact. In this vein, Moberly correctly points out that even the names of people and places (e.g., Ishmael, Bethel, Israel) reflect the theophoric name of El not YHWH, perhaps pointing to an earlier setting.[4] Indeed, the parallels between the biblical names for God (i.e., El and its derivatives) and those used at Ugarit, a site dating to an earlier period, strengthen Moberly's claim.[5] It also does not make

---

2. So, too, Och, "Creation and Redemption," 343.
3. Greifenhagen, *Egypt*, 30, 44.
4. Moberly, *Theology*, 135. See also comments in n16.
5. See Gemser, "Religion of the Patriarchs," 40–42.

Genesis as Torah

sense that if the accounts of Genesis were fabrications from a later period, as some posit, that the patriarchs would display behavior counter to the Torah, unless, of course, they actually lived in a period prior to the giving of the law when such behaviors were more "acceptable."

In this regard, it is important to note the clear break with the cultic practices of the patriarchs as instructed later by Moses in the Law.[6] Whereas the patriarchs in some instances worshipped beside trees (12:6–7; 13:18; 21:33) and built pillars (28:18, 22; 31:45; 35:14), later teaching moved away from these practices (Exod 23:24; 34:13; Lev 26:1; Deut 16:21–22).[7] Yet even here we must be careful not to overanalyze the apparent conflicts. For example, it is possible that the erecting of a pillar by Jacob (28:18) could be explained based upon the three uses of pillars (Heb. *matseboth*) in an ANE context: commemorative, cultic, and legal. Jacob's action seems to fall under the first category.

According to scholars other practices contrary to the Mosaic legislation include, sacrifices by the patriarchs, no attempts to take the land of Canaan by force (although God did tell Abraham that the time of the Amorite was not yet full; Gen 15:16), and the author's silence on issues of holiness, etc.[8] However, once again I would urge caution on these rigid assumptions especially on the issue of holiness. The book of Genesis does present the need for holy living before God as indicated by God's need to judge sin and unholy behavior as evidenced by the flood, the judgment on Pharaoh and Abimelech, and the destruction of Sodom. One could also add that the author's presentation of Joseph's holy lifestyle in Potiphar's home was instructive for a later audience.

Now to be fair, there can be little doubt that the religion of the patriarchs was indeed different than that of later Mosaic Yahwism, what Moberly

---

6. See discussion by Wenham, "Religion," 157–88 esp. the list on 163–64. For the classic discussion on the religion of the fathers, see Alt, *Der Gott der Väter* (1929) and in English, Alt, *Essays on Old Testament History and Religion*, 3–77.

7. Moberly, *Old Testament of the Old Testament*, 92.

8. So Moberly, *Theology*, 135; Brett, *Genesis*, 27; Wenham, "Religion," 184–85; and Gemser, "God in Genesis," and "Religion of the Patriarchs," 12–29, 30–61 respectively. Gemser ("God in Genesis," 27) notes the difference in presentations between the God of Genesis and of Exodus—one kinder and gentler the other more capricious and unapproachable. However, this is perhaps true only in perception. As I have demonstrated thus far, in reality, the theological teaching on the nature of God in Genesis reflects a very consistent picture with the God of Exodus. On the issue of patriarchal pacifism, see Schmid, *Moses Story*, 82–83.

has labeled the "Old Testament of the Old Testament."[9] Nevertheless, that does not mean that one cannot see in these same narratives an obvious desire of the author to present teaching reflected in the Mosaic legislation and germane to the period of the exodus. Indeed, as noted in my opening chapter, the reason the author included certain facets of the patriarchal stories may in fact be telling of his desire to teach specific truths from the Torah. This becomes apparent when one views how the author chose to begin the account of Abraham.

The Call of Abraham vis-à-vis the Exodus of Israel

The beginning verses of chapter 12 record the call of Abraham to go to the Promised Land even though Abraham begins making his trek to Canaan in chapter 11 (11:31). The recollection of Abraham's time in Haran is fitting in that Jacob, the progenitor of Israel,[10] was also called out of Haran to return back to Canaan, the land of promise (31:3, 13). Moreover, YHWH's call of Abraham from Ur of the Chaldees noted in 15:7 by the phrase, "I am YHWH who brought you out from Ur of the Chaladeans," is echoed in the language found in the opening of the Decalogue when God says, "I am YHWH your God who brought you out of Egypt" (Exod 20:2).[11] One could argue that the obedience of both Abraham and Jacob served as an example for Israel when they were called out of Egypt to return to *their* Promised Land.[12] And the centrality of remaining in the land of Canaan will play out later with the last wishes of both Jacob and Joseph both of whom desired to be buried in the land promised to Abraham (47:29-31; 49:29-32; 50:5, 24-25). Therefore, God's promises to Abraham had a life well beyond the patriarch; they applied to Israel as well, especially in the period of the exodus.

The Promises to Abraham and by Extension to Israel

God's tripartite promise to Abraham dealing with land, progeny, and blessings (12:1-3) sets the tone for the remainder of the book of Genesis as well

---

9. See discussion by Moberly, *Old Testament of the Old Testament*, 105-46. For a critique of Moberly's perspective, see Schmid, *Moses Story*, 113-14.

10. See Rogerson, et al., *Genesis and Exodus*, 109-10.

11. Moberly, *Theology*, 138.

12. So, too, Brodie, *Genesis*, 44.

Genesis as Torah

as the OT. Of particular interest is the promise of blessing—for Israel and for the nations—which plays itself out in the remainder of the Torah as well as the rest of the Bible. More pointedly, the blessing of the nations through Abraham prepares the nation of Israel for the inclusion of those beyond their borders (cf. Isa 2:2–4; 42:6; 49:6; 60:3; Acts 3:25; Rom 4:13; Gal 3:8, 16).[13] To a degree, the inclusion of a mixed multitude joining Israel when they left Egypt (Exod 12:38) and the later addition of Rahab, her family, and the Gibeonites, finds its roots here in 12:3. The Balaam oracle also displays a clear rendering of Gen 12:3 in Num 24:9. As of the period of the exodus generation, the promises of progeny and blessing had come to fruition: Abraham's descendants had become a great nation and they had received God's blessings of rescue from captivity as well as a covenant with YHWH. The promise of land would ultimately fall to the second generation after the exodus.

Yet despite the lack of fulfillment of the land promise, it is important to remember that land is one of the central motifs of Genesis even though the complete fulfillment of the land promise would not come to pass until the period of the conquest and later under the reign of David. The continual reiteration of the land promise reassured Israel that the land was in fact theirs by divine gift (12:1; 13:14–17; 15:7; 17:8). And similar to the loss of the garden by Adam and Eve, the land of Canaan could be lost by those who God felt abused the privilege of living there (15:16; Lev 18:25–30). If Israel rejected God's laws, as had the Canaanites, they, too, would be removed and the land given to someone else (cf. Jer 27:5–6).[14]

Even though Abraham never saw the promise of land come to fruition, he did gain a foothold in the land when he purchased a small piece of Canaan for a burial place for Sarah (23:3–20; cf. 25:9–10).[15] In Abraham's act of purchasing the plot of land from the sons of Heth, Israel would have understood their connection to the land. The importance of being buried together as a family would have helped them understand the need to return to the land, as can be seen in the requests of Jacob and Joseph to be buried in Canaan (47:29–31; 49:29–32; 50:25).

We also see the importance of remaining in the land of promise when Abraham gave a stern warning to his servant not to allow Isaac to leave

---

13. See von Rad, *Genesis*, 160–61.

14. Sailhamer, *Genesis Unbound*, 91–93.

15. On ANE negotiation practices vis-à-vis Genesis 23, see Tucker, "Legal Background," 77–84.

Canaan to find a wife (24:5–8). This was instructional on the importance of remaining in the land that God had given Israel even though in Abraham's day the promise was generations away from fulfillment (15:13–16; Heb 11:9). From this perspective it is understandable why God refused to allow Israel to return to Egypt after the exodus event. Both Abraham's and Israel's exodus to the Promised Land was not meant to be a temporary thing; it was to be permanent. Yet even in the land of promise, God's people were not exempt from the hardships associated with the curse of Genesis 3. In the midst of normal everyday life, difficulties could emerge, which could threaten continued existence in the land for the righteous followers of God. One of these was the threat of famine (12:10; 26:1; 41:54).

The Threat of Famine

The threat of famine immediately confronted Abraham after arriving in Canaan (12:10). Without inquiring of God, Abraham decided to move to the land of Egypt, a move that brought upon him not just a temporary reprieve from the famine, but also the correction of God and the rebuke of Pharaoh. Instead of trusting God for provision, as would his son Isaac later (26:1–5), Abraham tried to remedy the situation on his own (12:11–20). For Israel the instruction was clear: while the land promise was assured (13:15–17; 15:1, 18; 17:8 etc.), that did not mean that life within the land was going to be without its challenges. On the contrary, they would have to fight to conquer the land (Judg 3:2); it was not going to be given to them on a silver platter: they would have to trust in their God. And much like Abraham's attempt to "fix" the problems of his life as evinced by the fiasco in Egypt and later with Hagar (16:1–16), when Israel tried to remedy difficult situations on their own, chaos ensued (e.g., Num 14:40–45).

It is important to keep in mind that famine came upon the patriarchs for no other reason than the fact that they lived in a fallen world (3:16–19; 12:10; 26:1; 42:5; 47:13). Israel needed to learn that because the world is "broken," as a result of the fall, they must trust in God completely as the patriarchs often did. Interestingly, when confronted with a lack of food and water—common occurrences during a famine—Israel had opted to murmur and complain thus bringing upon themselves God's wrath (cf. Exod 15:23–25; 16:3–29; Numbers 11). And later audiences could easily have related to the privations associated with siege and exile.[16] In the midst

---

16. Fretheim, *Pentateuch*, 95.

of this instruction, 12:10–20 also foreshadowed the exodus of Abraham's descendants from Egypt.

Abraham's Journey to Egypt and Return Foreshadows the Exodus

It is not new to see in Abraham's descent to Egypt and his return to Canaan a parallel with the future trek of Jacob to Egypt and the exodus of Israel back to Canaan.[17] There are a number of parallels:

1. Both Abraham and Jacob move from Haran to Canaan at the command of God (12:1; 31:3).

2. Both Jacob and Abraham are confronted with famine in Canaan and go to Egypt: Abraham against God's will (12:10–20), Jacob in obedience to it (46:2–4).

3. Both are blessed with good things from a pharaoh: Jacob with the land of Goshen, Abraham with a bride price for Sarah (12:16; 45:17–20).

4. Abraham and Israel are mistreated by a pharaoh: Abraham's wife is taken and Israel is forced into slavery (12:15, 19; Exod 1:9–22).

5. God intervenes and sends plagues upon the pharaoh to save God's people (12:17; Exod 9:14).

6. Abraham and Israel despoil the Egyptians before they leave (12:16–20; Exod 12:35–36).[18]

7. Both are driven out of Egypt by a pharaoh (12:20; Exod 12:30–33).

8. Others go with them when they leave: Abraham takes Egyptian servants (e.g., Hagar; cf. *Gen. Rab.* 45:1; *Pirqe R. El.* 26.190; *Tg.Ps.-J.* on Gen 16:1; 1QGenApoc 20, 31–32[19]) and a mixed multitude follows Israel (Exod 12:38).[20]

9. Both make the trek back to Canaan (13:1; Num 13:2).

---

17. E.g., Schmid, *Moses Story*, 57–58.
18. So, too, Blenkinsopp, *Abraham*, 51.
19. Ibid., 92.
20. Hepner, *Legal Friction*, 112.

10. And both receive a promise of the land of Canaan at Bethel (13:3, 14–17; 28:13–14).[21]

The reason for the recording of this event in the life of Abraham was due in part to the fact that it was instructional for Israel on a number of levels.

1. It taught Israel that their forefather went through similar experiences as they had and God had delivered him.
2. It showed that God works on behalf of his people.
3. It taught Israel that Canaan was God's intended homeland for them.
4. In many ways, the experiences of Abraham in this text parallel the wilderness wandering: in the same way Abraham failed to stay in Canaan due to fear of famine, so, too, Israel had lost the ability to enter Canaan because they feared the people/giants—this caused both to go elsewhere (Abraham went to Egypt and Israel desired to return to Egypt).
5. This account taught Israel that they should not rely on their own devices for protection, but rather that they should rely on God to protect them from their enemies or oppressors.
6. Implicitly it showed that ill-gotten gains can lead to devastation for those around you. This becomes more apparent in chapter 13 when Abraham and Lot had to separate due to excess livestock (cf. Gen 36:6–8). The text makes it clear that Pharaoh had given them many things on account of Sarah (12:16; 13:2).
7. As is commonly suggested, the end of chapter 12 could be viewed as a subtle polemic against kingship. The Pharaoh does what kings do; they take your daughters (1 Samuel 8)!
8. Along with the accounts of chapters 20 and 26, Abraham's fiasco in Egypt in chapter 12 taught Israel the reality that the laws of God applied to everyone, even rulers like Pharaoh and Abimelech. No one was above the laws of God, especially the laws reiterated at Sinai.

Another way of viewing this and other Abraham narratives is from the perspective of case law.

---

21. So Schmid, *Moses Story*, 101–4.

Genesis as Torah

Examples of Case Law in Genesis 12 and 20

Chapters 12 and 20 reveal a number of specific examples of case law. For example, Pharaoh's and Abimelech's taking of Sarah reflects a narrative picture of the command against adultery, or attempted adultery (Exod 20:14; Deut 5:18).[22] It also shows what can happen when legislation is not in place that prohibits the marrying of one's sister (Lev 18:9, 11; 20:17; Deut 27:22).

Carmichael suggests that chapters 12 and 20 are the impetus behind a number of Torah laws. For example he argues that these chapters inform the Torah legislation of how to treat women captured during war (Deut 21:10-14).[23] However, Carmichael's suggestion does not seem plausible seeing how the legislation in Deuteronomy 21 is referring to single women or at least widows who were captured in the context of war. In neither of these cases in Genesis is this the reality. Carmichael also asserts that these accounts are the underpinning for the law forbidding the divorce and remarriage of the same woman in Deut 24:1-4.[24] He suggests that the story was slightly changed and the inspiration for the law somewhat clouded in order to protect the reputation of Israel's greatest patriarch, Abraham.[25] This later case-law suggestion is more probable than his former proposal, although still questionable.

From a didactic perspective, the account of Pharaoh and Sarah also shows that God holds people accountable for sin even though culturally they may think certain conduct is okay. The actions of Pharaoh, especially in taking multiple wives, are in fact against the law of creation which promotes monogamous marriage (Genesis 2).[26] God's laws on sexuality and marriage trump culture. This is particularly the case with Abraham's pawning off of Sarah as his sister and in turn gaining materially from the transaction. Adultery and coveting in any form was against the Law (Exod 20:14, 17; Lev 20:10; Deut 5:18, 21; 22:22).[27]

---

22. See also Bruckner, *Implied Law*, 13.

23. Carmichael, *Women, Law, and the Genesis Traditions*, 23. See also Daube, *Exodus Pattern*, 65.

24. Carmichael, *Women, Law, and the Genesis Traditions*, 10-21.

25. Ibid., 21; Carmichael, *Laws of Deuteronomy*, 203-7.

26. Bruckner, *Implied Law*, 191.

27. See also Carmichael, *Law and Narrative*, 215-16, 254-55; Carmichael, *Women, Law and the Genesis Traditions*, 10, 23, 43-44; Carmichael, *Laws of Deuteronomy*, 203-7; and Carmichael, *Origins of Biblical Law* (1992).

Even though Pharaoh and Abimelech entered into relationships with Sarah innocently, they still were held accountable because of God's protection of his people.[28] And although God acquitted both Abimelech and Pharaoh—as God did for Sarah in these two cases—the more focused instruction is that polygamy is not God's plan for marriage. Thus, sexual ethics, or the breach thereof, becomes a central focus here in the narrative. To be sure, it is one of the most prevalent themes in the book of Genesis. Indeed, the Abraham narratives have a number of case-law examples from which Israel could learn what improper sexual relations looked like and how to avoid them.

Sexual Ethics in the Abraham Narrative: Some Case-Law Examples

Throughout chapters 12–25 a number of the narratives reflect instruction on proper sexual ethics, which are noted later in the laws of Sinai. In fact, sexual impropriety, which is attested both before and after the flood (6:1–4; 9:20–27), appears to have been a central reason for God's destruction of the world. It is obvious that God cared deeply about the nations' and Israel's sexual lives, that is, what they did in their "bedrooms." Put simply, sexual sins brought the curse of God upon people. In some cases, sexual sin could bring death to an entire people group as witnessed in the Sodom account and later when Abimelech took Sarah (20:7). However, many times God sent a warning before he passed the sentence of death. For Abimelech the curse of barrenness came upon the women of his nation to alert him that something was amiss (20:17–18). And in the parallel text of chapter 12, plagues came upon Pharaoh and his people. The keeping of one's self from sexual offences was so important that marriage was the first major institution recorded in Genesis immediately after the creation event itself. The message: sexual desires are to be fulfilled within the confines of marriage.

The next place where teaching about sexual ethics appears is in the cryptic note concerning the men of Sodom in 13:13. When the author notes that they were "sinners against God," he most likely had sexual deviance in mind.[29] This conclusion is reinforced when we understand that the two other places where this phrase appears are in the accounts of Abimelech with Sarah (20:6) and Joseph with Potiphar's wife (39:9). In both of these

---

28. Albertz, *Israelite Religion*, 1:34, 36.
29. Peterson, *The Sin of Sodom*, 34–36.

cases, sexual impropriety, that is adultery, is the focus. Not surprisingly, the Babylonian Talmud draws the same connection between 13:13 and 39:9 (b. Sanh. 109a).

Chapter 16 records the scheme of Sarah and Abraham to use Sarah's Egyptian handmaiden, Hagar, to fulfill God's promise to Abraham that he would have a child. Even though there may have been precedent for this type of action in other ANE laws (e.g., Nuzi), the reality was that God did not need the help of Abraham and Sarah to fulfill his promise. If anything, their actions caused much grief for Abraham (21:9-14), and later for the Israelites (37:25-36) when Ishmael's descendants vied for the land (Judges 8, esp. v. 24). While one could argue that the account of Hagar and Abraham explained for Israel the origins of the Ishmaelites,[30] a greater instructional feature of the account was that God did not condone polygamy nor did he need the help of people to fulfill his promises, the details of which God could bring to fruition according to his own timetable. Moreover, these types of familial arrangements brought chaos to the family unit. These sexual scenarios could very well have been the reason for the penning of the sexual laws of Leviticus 18 and 20. This certainly appears to be the case for the events that took place at Sodom and within the cities of the plain.

The sexual proclivities of the Sodomites take center stage in chapter 18 and more pointedly, in chapter 19. While a number of theories have been put forward as to what sin the men of Sodom committed (e.g., rape, social injustice, domination using sex, same-sex practices etc.), the truth is that a number of sexual laws were broken both by the men of Sodom and by Lot and his daughters. Because I have handled this topic in detail elsewhere, here I will only summarize my conclusions.[31]

The indictment against Sodom is not explicitly stated as the breaking of a particular law but it does implicitly portray the perspective that the natural laws of God were in some way abrogated. The men of Sodom were guilty of breaking not just social laws (i.e., inhospitality; cf. Exod 22:21; Lev 19:33; Deut 10:19; 24:17; Ezek 16:49; what Bruckner calls "the rejection of God, who appears in the form of vulnerable humanity"[32]) but mainly sexual laws established by God at creation. Therefore, when taken as a whole, chapter 19 serves as an ideal case-law example of what happens

---

30. So Dozeman, "Hagar Story," 25-26.

31. See Peterson, *The Sin of Sodom*; and Peterson, "The Sin of Sodom Revisited," 17-31. For a fuller bibliography see these sources.

32. Bruckner, *Implied Law*, 220-21.

when a city and its environs decide to flout the sexual ethic established by God in Genesis 1 and 2. Interestingly, procreation and the threat to it, is a central motif within chapters 16–21 (cf. 16:1–16; 17:2–6, 15–21; 18:9–14; 19:31–38; 20:17–18; 21:1–8). It is also evident that Genesis 19 is a narrative example and antecedent of many of the key sexual laws of Leviticus 18 and 20.[33] Generally speaking, these Levitical chapters handle a variety of sexual sins such as incest, adultery, bestiality, and same-sex acts.

When Genesis 19 is viewed from this perspective, the *torah* instruction is clear. The men of Sodom desired not only to practice same-sex acts (something against God's creation model, especially his plan of procreation); at least for some of them, they also were ready to be unfaithful to their wives in doing so. This is an obvious form of adultery even if the ancients thought otherwise. Similarly, when Lot offered his betrothed virgin daughters to a hostile mob, he was willing to allow a form of adultery to take place (Deut 22:23–24). Moreover, the actions of Lot's daughters after their departure from Sodom present a clear picture of incest, the results of which, directly affected Israel (19:30–38). The two sons born through these incestuous relationships became the progenitors of the nations of Moab and Ammon, two neighbors of Israel that were a constant thorn in the side of Israel (see Judges 3; 10–12). Also, some have noted that Lot's actions with his daughters appears to have a direct connection to the laws against bastard children and the Ammonites and Moabites as found in Deut 23:2–3.[34] Much like the possible incestuous relationship between Ham and Noah and the ensuing cursing of Canaan, the account of Lot and his daughters serves, in part, to inform the nation of Israel why these surrounding nations were not to be intermingled with and allowed into fellowship with Israel (Deut 23:3).

Further *torah* instruction related to this chapter is the graphic picture of what happens when a city becomes sexually corrupt in this manner: God judges severely. In fact, God is the judge of the entire earth, not just Israel. He judges sin wherever he finds it if humanity's sin is in danger of corrupting society beyond measure (cf. Gen 6:1–7; 18:25). In this regard, communal versus individual responsibility as well as communal merit (i.e., the acts

---

33. Ibid., 219–20. See also Carmichael, *Law, Legend, and Incest*, 53–55. Embry ("The 'Naked Narrative,'" 429–31) sees 19:30–38 as instruction against incest, which helped inform the incest laws of Leviticus 18 and 20.

34. Carmichael, *Women, Law, and the Genesis Traditions*, 54–56; and Carmichael, *Law and Narrative*, 228–31. See also comments by von Rad, *The Problem of the Hexateuch*, 169.

Genesis as Torah

of righteous people can cause a deferment of punishment on the wicked) plays out in the narrative of 18:20–32 (cf. Deut 24:16).[35] The presence of ten righteous people could have saved Sodom! Furthermore, the fact that the author notes that God told Abraham about the sinfulness of Sodom and its destruction specifically so that Abraham could tell his household and family (18:19) highlights the instructional aspects of the text for later generations, namely, the children of Israel. Also, within the context of chapter 18, the intercessory actions of Abraham (18:23–32) reflect the life of Moses as intercessor and the importance of this spiritual discipline for the people of Israel.

Other instructional benefits of this narrative are related to the dangers of sexual sin vis-à-vis family unity. Entire families become dysfunctional when God's sexual ethic is set aside. As was true of Israel's later history, God brought severe judgment and exile on Israel for sexual sins.[36] Indeed, these types of sexual sins would bring about the defilement of the land, which in turn would cause Israel to be spewed out of the Promised Land (Lev 18:27–30; cf. Jer 16:18). In his vein, Frederick Gaiser rightly notes,

> The Sodom story may have had special reference to Israel's perception of sexual chaos in Canaan. It may function as a microcosmic example of a macrocosmic experience—Israel portrays itself as a 'sojourner' in Canaan, subject to attack by the local inhabitants, with whom Israel associates inappropriate practices of sexuality and violence; the result is divine judgment by which God identifies and protects his own people.[37]

Finally, the account of Abraham's attempt to find a wife for his son Isaac is an explicit anti-Canaanite polemic no doubt rooted in Abraham's disdain for the pagan sexual degradation of the Canaanites. Abraham's prohibition of Isaac marrying a Canaanite (24:1–4, 37) bespeaks the later legal prohibition for Israel not to marry into the Canaanite clans (Deut 7:3–4).[38]

---

35. Daube, *Studies in Biblical Law*, 155–58.

36. Note for example, the sin of going after a neighbor's wife (Ezek 18:6, 11, 15; 22:11; 33:26) and adultery in general (Jer 5:8; 13:27); sexual abominations (all-inclusive; cf. Jer 13:27; Ezek 16:22, 43, 47, 58; 6:9 [implicit]; 18:12–13; 22:11; 23:36; 33:26); incest with one's daughter-in-law and sister (Ezek 22:11); and harlotry and adultery (Hos 4:13–14).

37. Gaiser, "Homosexuality," 163.

38. Some early Jewish interpreters suggested that Laban's request to delay Rebekah's departure (24:55) reflected the ancient law of a twelve month betrothal period (b. *Ketub.* 57b.). So Polin, "Jewish Law," 40.

Indeed, the entirety of chapter 24 taught endogamous marriage. As noted above, God honored this practice for Israel as exemplified by the divine oversight in choosing Rebekah for Isaac (24:12–14, 50).

Instruction on the Nature of God in the Sodom Narrative

Chapter 19 also shows that God is a just judge who does not judge people without proper juridical procedures.[39] The two "men"/angels who came to determine the nature of Sodom's sin was in keeping with the requirements of the Law (Deut 19:15).[40] Two witnesses to a crime were needed in order to bring about capital punishment. This of course is exactly what happened in Sodom. God followed the Law perfectly when he brought about punishment on the city of Sodom. What is more, the account teaches that God can, and will, use cosmological events to bring about judgment. This is in fact one of the means noted within the Law by which God judges his people in an agrarian setting (e.g., Lev 26:18–19; Deut 28:23–24; cf. 1 Kgs 17:1). God's destruction of the cities of the plain of the Jordan and his making it a wasteland[41] serves as a warning to Israel. Later we will see that part of God's judgment on his land for sin is that God will make the land of Israel, Jerusalem in particular, a wasteland and a haunt of jackals (Jer 9:11; 10:22; 14:1–6; cf. Isa 13:19–22; 34:13–15; Jer 49:33; 51:37; Micah 1:3).

Lessons from the Life of Lot

Drawing *torah* instruction from the actions of Lot is not new. Jewish interpreters suggested that the reason Lot moved to Sodom was in order to practice blasphemy and lewdness (*Gen. Rab.* 41:7; *Rashi* commentary on 13:10).[42] Apart from the lessons on sexual ethics noted above, the experiences and actions of Lot also highlight a number of important instructions for the children of Israel. First, in the aftermath of Abraham and Lot's exo-

---

39. Bruckner, *Implied Law*, 142–57. For a detailed presentation of the juridical proceedings, which unfold in the Sodom narrative, see ibid., 124–70, esp. 157–58 for a summary.

40. Some see the destruction of Sodom as a picture of the tenth plague on Egypt, see Hepner, *Legal Friction*, 171–82.

41. Bruckner, *Implied Law*, 168–69.

42. As noted by Polin, "Jewish Law," 40.

dus from Egypt, Lot made several poor choices.[43] When he chose the best land, he did not honor his elders, in this case his father figure, Abraham, which was a breach of the fifth commandment. Second, Lot pitched his tent towards Sodom. In doing so he raised his family within the social context of the evil influences of a godless society. For Israel, the danger of allowing Canaanites to dwell in their midst and to influence them is palpable in the account. Third, Lot was willing to offer his betrothed virgin daughters to a hostile mob, foreigners/Canaanites at that, a direct violation of Deut 22:23–24. Fourth, Lot and his family experienced the blessings of being associated with Abraham. For Israel, they, too, were to be a blessing to the nations, not a curse. Fifth, never does the author of Genesis note that Lot built an altar to God, whereas Abraham does so, on a regular basis (12:8; 13:18). Israel was to follow the example of Abraham in putting God first in their lives. Lot's life and actions in many ways served as a negative example to Israel; however, it is worth noting that Hagar, a foreigner, actually had more affinity with Abraham and Israel in her worship of God than did Lot.

Hagar as Israel

The instructive aspect of Hagar's life has not been missed by scholars. To begin, Sarah's oppression (16:6) and later expulsion of Hagar (21:8–21) is a direct violation of later Sinai legislation prohibiting the harsh treatment of foreigners (Exod 22:20–22; see *Gen. Rab.* 45:6; cf. Deut 21:14). This in turn has led some scholars to see in Sarah's affliction of Hagar a fitting parallel for Egypt's later affliction of Israel,[44] a point equally applicable to Abraham's mistreatment of her as well.[45] Thus, some have noted that Abraham and Sarah's negative treatment of Hagar in chapter 16 explains God's prophetic pronouncement in 15:13–16, namely, that Abraham's descendants would be enslaved 400 years. From this perspective, the oppression of Israel was therefore due to Abraham and Sarah's mistreatment of Hagar![46] Ironically,

---

43. Blenkinsopp, *Abraham*, 51.

44. See Trible, *Texts of Terror*, 13, 21, 28; Dozeman, "Hagar Story," 28–29; Shinan and Zakovitch, "Midrash on Scripture," 270; Hepner, *Legal Friction*, 215; Tsevat, *Meaning*, 69–70; and Greifenhagen, *Egypt*, 32 nn23–24. See also Daube, *Exodus Pattern*, 26–27.

45. Rosenberg, "Bible: Biblical Narrative," 68.

46. So Shinan and Zakovitch, "Midrash on Scripture," 270; and Hepner, *Legal Friction*, 189–91.

Sarah asked God to be the judge between her and Abraham (16:5), yet she was the one doing the oppressing.[47]

Further still, do the actions of Sarah and Abraham in some way explain why Joseph, the fourth generation from Sarah, suffered hardship in Egypt (cf. Exod 20:5; 34:7; Deut 5:9)?[48] There are obvious connections between the two events. In both cases, God saw the affliction perpetrated against both Hagar and Israel (16:11; Exod 3:7). Thomas Dozeman also points out that the expulsion of Hagar from the house of Sarah, and later, Israel from Egypt, allowed both to be released from the grips of slavery.[49] And Hagar's journey to the wilderness of Shur (16:7) finds an immediate parallel with the first stop of Israel after their crossing of the Red Sea (Exod 15:22).[50] In both cases, the wilderness experience was one of uncertainty and ultimate trust in God.

Hagar as Moses

In keeping with the author's subtle presentation of biographical material, which presents Moses as the key figure in the life of Israel, one could argue that Hagar's and Moses' experiences parallel one another.[51] On this Dozeman notes the following parallels: apart from both running to the wilderness to flee oppression/hardship,

> (1) each encounters the messenger of God in the wilderness (Hagar in Gen 16:7 and Moses in Exod 3:2); (2) each is commanded to return to the threatening situation from which they fled (Hagar in Gen 16:7–14 and Moses in Exod 3:10); . . . (3) each receives a word of promise and leaves the wilderness with a special name for God (Hagar names God as El Roi in Gen 16:13; and Moses receives the name Yahweh). . . . [and (4)] Sarah demands the expulsion of Hagar and Ishmael from the camp (Gen 21:10), while Pharaoh drives out Moses from his house (Exod 10:11) and the Egyptians drive out Israel from their land (Exod 12:39).[52]

---

47. Hepner, *Legal Friction*, 195.
48. Ibid., 192, 204.
49. Dozeman, "Hagar Story," 30.
50. Ibid., 37.
51. So Dozeman, *Pentateuch*, 236.
52. Dozeman, "Hagar Story," 30.

Genesis as Torah

Dozeman continues by noting that both Hagar and Moses led others (Ishmael and Israel) into the wilderness and in turn needed to cry out to God for provisions to save those who were with them from privation of water (21:15–16; Exod 15:24).[53] In the end, both were liberators of their "people" (Ishmael from Abraham and Sarah, and Israel from Egypt) and were directly connected to the founding of two nations: Hagar's son Ishmael became the father of the Ishmaelites and Moses helped establish the nation of Israel through the covenant with God.[54] In this regard, the covenant with God is the key feature, which allows the reader to draw a distinction between both nations.

Covenant and Prophecy

Covenant

Covenant plays a central role in the book of Genesis. In chapters 15 and 17 God not only makes a unilateral covenant with Abraham, he also institutes circumcision as the sign of the covenant, and by extension, the way a man could be identified as an *Israelite* male (17:14; Exod 12:48).[55] While the Noahic covenant taught basic laws germane to all peoples (see previous chapter), the Abrahamic covenant became instructional mainly for those within Israel both early in their history (Gen 34:15; Exod 4:24–26; Josh 5:3–7) and later during the monarchic period. For example, it is difficult not to see parallels between the unilateral and everlasting Abrahamic covenant and the Davidic covenant of 2 Samuel 7.[56] George Mendenhall (1916–2016) called the former the "prophecy" and the latter the "fulfillment."[57] What is more, the Abrahamic covenant is the basis upon which the Sinai covenant is developed (Exod 32:13; 33:1; cf. Exod 2:24; 6:4–5, 8; 12:25; 13:5, 11); the Sinai covenant thus became the specifics for Israel's "vocational" status as God's light to the world (Deut 4:6; Exod 19:5).[58]

53. Ibid., 31–32.
54. Ibid., 33.
55. Polin, "Jewish Law," 37.
56. Moore and Peterson, *Voice, Word, and Spirit*, 98; Rosenberg, "Bible: Biblical Narrative," 66; and Clements, *Abraham and David*, 54–60. Clements (p.55) questions the direction of influence based upon the scholarly assumption that the Abrahamic covenant may have been recorded *after* the Davidic covenant.
57. Mendenhall, "Covenant Forms," 72.
58. Fretheim, "Reclamation," 360–61.

The *torah* instruction in chapter 17 was vital for Israel if they intended to please God and keep his Passover (Exod 12:43–50). Moreover, God's covenant with Abraham taught Israel of their value before God and their association with their forefathers. When God declared that he would be with Abraham (21:22; cf. Gen 24:1; 26:12–14; 30:27–30, 43), this paralleled God's blessings upon Israel (Deut 28:1–14).[59] Of course being associated with the family of Abraham in any time period would be important, especially in the troubling times of the sojourn in Egypt and during the exilic and postexilic periods when Israel's very identity was in jeopardy (Nehemiah 13) as was their ties to the land.[60]

In a similar vein, the treaty between Abimelech and Abraham (see also Abimelech and Isaac—26:30–31; Laban and Jacob—31:47–55) becomes instructional for the importance and procedures of treaty making between people. While the average Israelite no doubt would have been familiar with treaties of the ANE, the process of treaty making in Genesis would have helped them appreciate the gravity of the treaty/covenant made at Sinai. And the land grant made by God to Abraham in Genesis 13 and the covenant of chapter 15 would definitely have helped Israel to appreciate their rights and claims to the land of Canaan, something that God had prophetically declared multiple times in Genesis.

Prophecy

The prophetic pronouncements of God appear throughout the narrative of Abraham's life. This is in keeping with God's direct communication with Abraham, much like he did with Moses (see also 20:7). Apart from the promises and prophetic pronouncements given directly to Abraham about his own future (e.g., the birth of a son; 15:4; 18:10, 14), chapter 15 is especially important for Israel because it proved to them that they were not only promised the land and progeny but also that they would be successful if they followed God's laws.

Furthermore, God had declared that he would judge the nation that oppressed Abraham's family (viz., Egypt; 15:14). Israel could be comforted by the fact that those who oppressed them would be judged by God for their actions (cf. Ezekiel 38–39; Habakkuk 2; Joel 3:2 [Heb 4:2]; Amos 1–2). The fulfillment of God's prophetic words (e.g., Gen 21:1) also pointed to the

---

59. Moberly, *Old Testament of the Old Testament*, 98.
60. Syrén, *Forsaken First-Born*, 41; and Clements, *Abraham and David*, 23.

Genesis as Torah

reality that God could be trusted to fulfill his promise to bring Israel into the land of Canaan or to return them to the land after the exile.

Instruction on the Ten Commandments

Commandments 1 and 2

In keeping with instruction on the Ten Commandments in my previous chapters, the Abraham narrative also offers instruction on a number of the key commandments, specifically those related to choosing YHWH/God as the only deity to serve. Abraham's call out of Ur, and later Haran, forced him to choose between a life of polytheism and monotheism. Not once is the reader confronted with the issue of idolatry in the Abraham account. Abraham's life offered a fine example not only of one who followed God, but one who embraced monotheism. For those living in exile or leaving Egypt this would have been an important message to accept and to which to cling.

Commandment 5

The fifth commandment is one of the central teachings on the Ten Commandments in the Abraham narratives. Honoring one's parents is vital to the proper functioning of the family unit—a key aspect of the patriarchal narratives. As previously noted, Lot disrespected his father figure, Abraham, when he took the best of the land around the Jordan (13:11). Conversely, later, Isaac respected and honored his father Abraham to the point of being willing to lay down his life on Abraham's altar to God (22:9).

Commandment 7

Also of importance is the seventh commandment against adultery. While Pharaoh and Abimelech may not have known Sarah was already married, the accounts of chapters 12 and 20 teach of the dangers of taking someone else's wife. In both instances, we see case studies on God's response to someone who even attempts to commit adultery (Deut 22:22; cf. Matt 5:28).[61] Both rulers took Sarah because they coveted her as a wife (a breach

---

61. So Carmichael, *Law and Narrative*, 209–10, 214–16. Carmichael (p.216) draws a connection between the distinct language in both verses, namely, the phrase "a man's wife" (*be'ulath bā'al*; cf. Gen 20:3; Deut 22:22).

of the tenth commandment) even though the text intimates that they already had numerous wives. Finally, as noted above, apart from the near humbling of Lot's betrothed daughters, the actions of the men of Sodom constituted adultery (attempted) against their wives.

Commandment 9

The actions of Abraham first with Pharaoh and later with Abimelech could be interpreted as a breach of the ninth commandment not to bear false witness. Sarah's mistreatment of Hagar also meets the definition of bearing false testimony, especially when she petitioned Abraham against Hagar (16:5–6; Deut 19:15–21). In this latter case, both Abraham and Sarah had failed to trust in the words of God, another instructional aspect of this particular narrative. Despite this infraction, the Abraham narratives still offered Israel many examples of how to have faith and trust in their God even from the most unlikely people.

Instruction on How to Trust in God

While any number of instructional examples in the Abraham cycle could be given pointing to the way Abraham (and others) trusted God, it is the account of chapter 21 that taught Israel how to rely on God in the midst of dire circumstances. The disheartening sight of Hagar and Ishmael in the wilderness without water served as a precursor to the similar events of Israel in the wilderness when they, too, lacked water (Exod 15:22–27; 17:1–6; Num 20:2–11). In the case of Hagar, she wept before God and God heard her cries and provided (21:16–21). Furthermore, she and Ishmael were blessed by God in the midst of their dire circumstances. Israel was no less accountable to behave properly before their God as they trusted in him to provide in the midst of need and privation. What is more, Hagar, an outsider, demonstrated trust in God in a similar way Rahab would later trust in the God of Israel and be saved (Joshua 2; 6). Israel had no excuse when this type of instruction was related to them. Yet, even if this may have been too subtle for them to connect the proverbial dots, Abraham's trust in his God in the near sacrifice of Isaac certainly would not have been lost on an Israelite reader.

Genesis as Torah

Torah Instruction from the Near Sacrifice of Isaac

The picture of Abraham's near sacrifice of Isaac is indeed troubling for modern sensibilities. It was equally troubling for readers of the past as well (e.g., Luther and Kant).[62] The *torah* instruction in this text, however, defies the ethical tensions and leads to a fuller appreciation of its inclusion and purpose within the Torah. Moberly correctly notes the instructive nature of this text. This includes: the role of testing within the life of the covenanted; the identification of the site where Israel would eventually worship, namely, Jerusalem (perhaps reflective of a later editing?); and finally, the instruction that God does not require child sacrifice.[63] Based upon the usage of the phrase, "go, yourself" (*lek leka*), which marks the beginning of the narratives in 12:1 and 22:2, it is clear that Genesis 22 was meant to be read in tandem with chapter 12 and Abraham's call.[64] As Moberly notes, the instruction is clear: Abraham was to relinquish his past, as required by God in chapter 12, and now, his future, namely, Isaac the son of the promise.[65] For Israel reading this narrative in any historical context would have been instructive. They would have heard the resounding message to trust YHWH for the here and now, and in turn, to trust that God had full control of any of their bleak circumstances (e.g., the wilderness wandering or the exile).

Also of importance is the idea of God "testing" (*nissah*) Abraham. Again, Moberly aptly notes that the use of the verb *nasah* had more than the idea of what today might be considered a trial/test. On the contrary, within the Torah, especially in Deuteronomy, *nasah* is used to denote a humbling experience (Deut 8:2), which in turns brings about a desired response—the fear of the Lord.[66] Israel had failed to fear God in their most crucial moment prior to entering the land of Canaan when they listened to the evil report of ten of the spies (Numbers 13; Deuteronomy 8). Ironically, their fear was that their children would be "sacrificed" to the giants/people of the land (Num 14:3); instead, God allowed their children to inherit Canaan, whereas they died in the wilderness.

The contrast is unambiguous. On the one hand, Abraham had taken his beloved son and placed him into the hands of his God in total trust. The

---

62. Moberly, *Theology*, 181–84.
63. Ibid., 184–89. See also comments by Wenham, "Religion," 184.
64. Ibid., 186.
65. Ibid.
66. Ibid., 186–87.

cryptic statement of Abraham to his servants intimates as much: "stay here while I and the lad go yonder to worship and we will return to you" (22:5). It is not surprising that some have seen in this statement the complete trust of Abraham in his God either to provide a way out of the divine request or to raise Isaac from the dead. On the other hand, the Israelites had hidden behind their children and had refused to place them metaphorically into the hand of God. As just noted, it would be their children who would eventually inherit the Promised Land.

The verb *nasah* is also used in conjunction with the giving of the Ten Commandments. In Exod 20:20, Moses informs Israel that God had come to "prove"/"test"/"humble" them by giving them the Law and by using the wilderness wandering experience to "humble" them (Deut 8:16).[67] The trying of both Abraham and Israel's faith through the near-sacrifice of Isaac and the giving of the Law was meant to teach Israel, as it did Abraham, something about who YHWH was. Abraham would have been all too familiar with the requirements of child sacrifice of the ancient world, especially in the region in Babylon from which he came. The test of Genesis 22 thus became a means of instructing Abraham on the nature of the God who had called him out of Ur. Abraham's God did not require child sacrifice! For Israel, the instruction was no less poignant. YHWH did not require their firstborn, rather they were to redeem their children with a ram (Exod 13:13, 15; 34:20; Num 18:15). Furthermore, the narrative taught a proper response to the call/testing of YHWH. As Moberly notes, "Abraham's response to God models what Israel's response should be. It is not that Abraham becomes an observer of *torah*, but that the language of *torah* has been used to make sense of Abraham and to intimate that there is an analogy between Abraham's response to God and that which is expected from Israel."[68]

Finally, there is a clear indication that the site of Moriah is none other than the site of Jerusalem. Now while it is true that Abraham was familiar with Salem, the city of peace (cf. Gen 14:18), it is perhaps best to see the site where Abraham attempted to offer Isaac as north of the ancient city on what later would become the temple mount. Indeed, David purchased the northern approaches to the city as a place of sacrifice to stay the plague, which was descending upon Jerusalem in his day (2 Sam 24:16–25). While it is possible that this text reflects a later editing/compilation, namely, as

---

67. Ibid., 186.
68. Ibid., 187.

Genesis as Torah

"an etiology for the Jerusalem temple,"[69] it is also possible that this text was prophetic by identifying where YHWH would one day choose to place his name (Deut 12:5, 11, 21; 14:23, 24; 16:2, 6, 11; 26:2).

Miscellaneous Laws

Before completing our examination of the Abraham narratives, I would like to point out a number of miscellaneous laws that appear in these accounts. In Genesis 14, Abraham's attack[70] on the kings of the east and his rescue of Lot and the people of Sodom shows that God was with him despite the numerical odds.[71] For Israel, God had promised to give them victory as well in Canaan and that they would despoil the Egyptians (15:14) and the Canaanites. Those who opt for a later dating of the text see in Abraham's great victory a "model" for those returning after the exile to establish their lives in a destroyed Jerusalem.[72] Also, the law of tithing is first instituted by Abraham when he tithed to Melchizedek, the priest of God (14:20).[73]

Some have also noted the similarities between the animals used by Abraham (at the command of God) in chapter 15 and what constituted acceptable whole burnt offerings/sacrifices noted in Leviticus 1. As such, some conclude that this chapter is a later rendering of these requirements.[74] Although this assertion is in keeping with my thesis, in reality only the terms for goat (*'ez*; 15:9; Lev 1:10) and turtledove (*tor*; 15:9; Lev 1:14) appear in both chapters. The terms used in Genesis 15 for the three-year-old heifer (*'eglah*) and the pigeon (*gozal*) are not present in Leviticus 1. At best this shows that God is consistent in requiring certain *types* of animals for sacrifice but nothing more.

---

69. Ibid., 189.

70. Contra Westermann (*Genesis 12–36*, 79), who says that there is no "war in the patriarchal stories" because of the family structural dynamic of the period; Abraham actually joined forces with some of the local clans when he went to war with the kings of the east (14:24).

71. Many scholars question the veracity of this account for this very reason, see for example Blenkinsopp, *Abraham*, 54–55.

72. So ibid., 56.

73. Wenham ("Religion," 160) notes the problem of Abraham apparently worshiping at a Canaanite shrine. However, 14:18 only notes that Melchizedek "brought out" (*yatsa'*) bread and wine to Abraham. No mention of a shrine is made.

74. Hepner, *Legal Friction*, 124, 139.

Next, the response of Abimelech and his men to the threat of God concerning Abimelech's taking of Sarah (20:7–8) was one of fear. Abimelech and his people were so scared that they gave Abraham 1000 pieces of silver as retribution (20:16). If these non-god-fearers responded with such humility and fear, how much more should the Israelites have feared God when they broke the Law? Indeed, Israel should have learned not only about the dangers of sexual sin (see above discussion), but they should also have taken note of how quickly Abimelech and his people repented for their *accidental* sin and their level of contriteness.

Finally, the birth of Isaac brought joy and laughter—the meaning of Isaac's name—to Abraham and Sarah (21:1–6). Carmichael sees in this instance the impetus for the law on marriage and military service in Deut 24:5.[75] Men were to stay home for one year after getting married in order to insure that a child would be born from the union in case a woman's husband died in battle without an heir. This connection is tangential at best.

Conclusion

As can be seen from these last few miscellaneous laws and instruction, any number of connections could be made between the life of Abraham and later *torah* teaching. As I have noted throughout, Abraham's life, while flawed in many ways, still was primarily about teaching Israel how to trust and serve their God in a righteous manner. Central to the righteous life, was instruction on how to maintain godly sexual ethics, how to enter and remain in the covenant, and how to trust in God in the midst of testing and daily trials.

As the Abraham cycle comes to a close in chapter 25, the reader is introduced to his two grandsons, who would become the progenitors of two nations. The account of Jacob and Esau's early life sets the stage for Israel's later conflicts with Edom (Num 20:14–21). This account, along with what follows, gives a history of why there was animosity between the brothers.[76] It is to this topic and its *torah* teaching that I now turn my focus.

---

75. Carmichael, *Laws of Deuteronomy*, 207–9.
76. Fretheim, *Pentateuch*, 93.

6

Genesis 26–36

"Israel" as an Example for Israel

In this chapter I will examine the implicit and explicit *torah* instruction present in the accounts of the lives of Isaac and his two sons, Jacob and Esau.[1] Although Isaac is the next patriarch after Abraham, in reality the Jacob narrative takes center stage within this trio of patriarchs in offering instruction for Israel.[2] For example, the Jacob narrative teaches about the central role of Bethel as a holy site (ch. 28; cf. 1 Sam 7:16; 10:3), the beginnings of the Edom—Israel conflict, the laws of tithing (28:22), why one man should not marry two sisters (chs. 29–30; cf. Lev 18:18; Deut 21:15–17), the importance of the Transjordan in Israel's inheritance rights (ch. 32), food restrictions (32:32), the laws on virgins (ch. 34; cf. Deuteronomy 22); and the role of Shechem as a covenanted partner (ch. 34; cf. Joshua 8; 24).

It is clear that the instructive force of the life of Jacob is no less valid than for the life of Abraham as we saw in the previous chapter. This pedagogical import becomes apparent in 26:5. Here we find that Abraham's keeping of the commands, charge, statutes, and laws (i.e., the Torah) of God points to the author's desire to present the life of Abraham as the ideal

---

1. Miscall ("Jacob and Joseph Story," 28–40 esp. 31–39) notes the numerous intertextual analogies between the lives of Jacob and Joseph. These analogies, he notes, help to enrich and add emphasis to each (29).

2. For the sake of smoothness in chapter divisions I have started the Jacob cycle at chapter 26 even though it technically starts in 25:19.

for all Israel to follow, including his son and grandsons.[3] Indeed, Moberly correctly points out that in 26:4b–5 "what appears to be going on . . . is a *recontextualizing* of the Abraham material so that it can function as religiously authoritative for Israel" (italics original).[4] Earlier critical scholars tended to see the language of 26:4b–5 as the work of a later hand,[5] perhaps the Deuteronomist.[6] Yet, is it not possible that the lesson for the implied audience was to show continuity between their ancestor and them? And is it not also possible that God did reveal to Abraham specific laws by which he should live (cf. m. *Qidd.* 4:14; b. *Yoma* 28b)?[7] I would argue that an affirmative response to these queries is in order. As we move forward, I will attempt to draw the same conclusion based upon the lives of Isaac and Jacob, and to a degree, Esau.

Instruction from the Life of Isaac

Although the author of Genesis spends only a fraction of the time on the life of Isaac compared to Abraham, Jacob, and Joseph, his life still exemplifies what obedience to Israel's God looks like. From the opening lines of chapter 26, God reaffirms his promise of land, protection, and progeny (26:3–4, 24; cf. 28:15; 46:4[8]), promises that had been key components of Abraham's experience. It is obvious that the author wished to juxtapose Abraham's early experiences with those of Isaac's early adulthood. This is made clear by the repetition of the motif of famine. Where Abraham had chosen on his own to go to Egypt in the time of famine (12:10), Isaac chose to follow the word of God when confronted with the same hardship (26:1–2). As a result, God blessed him one hundred fold and made him prosperous (26:12–14) despite opposition from the local inhabitants (26:15–22). In this case, Israel should have followed the example of Isaac, not Abraham. Nevertheless, when it came to fearing the local inhabitants, Isaac had behaved just like his father by pawning off his wife as his sister (26:6–11; cf. 12:13; 20:2), something an Israelite should never do.

---

3. Moberly, *Theology*, 138.
4. Ibid., 139.
5. Von Rad, *Genesis*, 270–71.
6. See for example the comments of Westermann, *Genesis 12–36*, 424–25.
7. See a similar conclusion by Bruckner, *Implied Law*, 32.
8. Fretheim, *Pentateuch*, 98–99.

Genesis as Torah

As with Abraham's dealings with Abimelech (21:32), some see Isaac's making of a covenant with Abimelech (26:28) a violation of Mosaic laws (Exod 23:32–33; 34:12; Deut 7:2–3).[9] This is no less true of Jacob's implied covenant with the Shechemites (see more below). While this could be construed as problematic, one must bear in mind that this is prior to the giving of the Law. Furthermore, the instructive aspect of the text should not be overlooked. God blessed Isaac in spite of the oppressive actions of the inhabitants of the land. Interestingly, the local inhabitants—much like the Shechemites with Jacob (34:23)—recognized God's blessings on Isaac and sought to take advantage of that fact (26:28; cf. 12:3).

Yet even in the act of covenant making, the author appears to offer a subtle rebuke of Isaac's actions. His son, Esau, married two of the "local" girls and they became a "grief" to Isaac and Rebekah (26:34–35). It is possible that the close covenanted relationship between Isaac and the locals paved the way for these marriages, a similar reality, which happened to Lot at Sodom. Carmichael suggests that the distress caused by Esau's wives (27:46) showed a level of rebellion in Esau that may have been part of the reason for the forming of the rebellious-son law of Deut 21:18–21.[10] Whatever the case may be, it is clear that covenants and intermarriage, no matter how innocent, were to be rejected by Israel when they entered the land of Canaan (Exod 23:32–33; 34:11–16; Deut 7:2–5) and/or when they returned from exile (Ezra 9–10; Nehemiah 13).

Next, while some have seen in Isaac's act of blessing Jacob a foreshadowing of the Aaronic blessing of Num 6:24–26,[11] one can easily glean more practical instruction from Isaac's life. For example, Isaac's actions at the end of his life serve the purpose of teaching Israel what happens when a father and a mother split their affections for their children and show favoritism.[12] This motif will reappear in the life of Jacob with his son Joseph. Both of these scenarios had devastating effects on the patriarchs' families. However, the actual reason for the inclusion of this particular account in the life of Isaac has a number of instructive features, one of which is a case study of the right and wrong way to keep the fifth commandment, a point I will return to momentarily.

---

9. Hepner, *Legal Friction*, 315–19.
10. Carmichael, *Law and Narrative*, 146–50.
11. So, too, Briggs and Lohr, *Theological Introduction*, 34.
12. See Visotzky, *The Genesis of Ethics*, 136–40.

Genesis 26–36

Finally, Isaac's instructions to Jacob in 28:1–5 offers yet another instructional moment for Israel regarding intermarriage. Even though some have suggested that the patriarchal religion allowed intermarriage with the local population,[13] this is clearly not the case for Abraham, Isaac and Jacob. Jacob was not to take a wife from the Canaanites (cf. Exod 34:16; cf. Judg 3:6; Ezra 9–10; 1 Kgs 11:1–10).[14] In this, Jacob was obedient to his father's commands. Esau's response was to try and alleviate some of the tensions between him and his parents by marrying a daughter of Ishmael as a third wife (28:6–9). Even though Esau may have exhibited some positive qualities in honoring his father (e.g., when Isaac asked for venison—see more below), a reader could not help but see the warnings of why Israel should not mix with the surrounding nations: Abraham, and now Isaac, had declared it was off limits for those covenanted with God. Even though Moberly suggests that the author of Genesis does not assign the fear of unfaithfulness to God as the reason why the patriarchs were so selective in marriage,[15] the text indeed intimates as much as a likely reason for their selectivity. Not only is Esau's choice of wives stressed as being not good, later, Judah's choice of a Canaanite wife and perhaps a Canaanite wife for his son[16] led to a very negative outcome (see also my discussion in chapter 4 on 6:1–4).

Instruction on the Ten Commandments

Commandments 1 and 2

Although some scholars have concluded that there is no explicit teaching on the first commandment in Genesis 1—Exodus 18, Jacob's command in 35:2–4 clearly addresses this very thing.[17] In fact, instruction on the first two commandments is perhaps nowhere clearer in the patriarchal narra-

---

13. See for example the comments of Gemser, "Religion of the Patriarchs," 39.

14. While Blenkinsopp (*Pentateuch*, 105) and Westermann (*Genesis 12–36*, 446) suggest that the focus on endogamous marriage in this text reflects an exilic or postexilic period for the author, there is nothing that would preclude one from applying this to an earlier period as well.

15. Moberly, *Theology*, 135; and Moberly, *Old Testament of the Old Testament*, 90–91.

16. So Golka, "Genesis 37–50," 159; and Speiser, *Genesis*, 300. While one cannot be certain, the fact that Tamar's lineage is not noted (i.e., something along the lines of "Tamar the daughter of X") does imply that she may have been a daughter of a Canaanite.

17. Patrick, "Structure," 105–18; and Bruckner, *Implied Law*, 221–22.

Genesis as Torah

tives than when Jacob told his family to put away their foreign gods.[18] Some scholars have also suggested that Gen 35:1–4 may point forward to Exod 22:20 and the prohibitions against sacrificing to other gods.[19]

Another text offering instruction on the first two commandments is Rachel's stealing of Laban's household gods (31:19, 34–35), no doubt some of the very same gods that Jacob sought to remove from his midst before arriving at Bethel (35:2–3). Various reasons could be proffered as to why Rachel took her father's gods. For example, Hepner suggests that Rachel stole Laban's gods to keep him from enacting the legal proceeding noted in Exod 22:8—the bringing of a case against someone before the judges/gods.[20] By taking Laban's gods, Rachel was protecting Jacob against such an act.[21] Of course it is also possible that Rachel was simply an idolater. That Laban worshipped a different god than Jacob seems to be implied by the note that Jacob and Laban's covenant was sworn to by an oath before the God of Abraham and the god of Nahor: the text states that *they* (i.e., these *elohim*/gods) would judge between Jacob and Laban (31:53).[22]

Whatever the reason was for Rachel's actions, the author appears to be offering a polemic against false gods. This is evident when the author chose to note that Rachel *sat* upon the teraphim while she was menstruating (31:35). Whether she was lying about being on her cycle is not clearly stated in the text. Nevertheless, what could be worse than for a woman to sit upon a deity during her menstrual cycle (Lev 15:20)?[23] For the people of Israel, in any period, these events become instructive. YHWH is the only true God; idols are not to be tolerated; they are no more than rubbish to be associated with uncleanness.

Commandment 5

The events of chapter 27 present one of the clearest case studies of why the fifth commandment is important. Unexpectedly, Esau and Jacob switch roles. Esau becomes exemplary of how to respect one's father and Jacob reaps the consequences of not doing so. This switching of roles, so to speak,

---

18. Patrick, "Structure," 113.
19. Carmichael, *Origins of Biblical Law*, 167–69.
20. Note also the explanation of Speiser in "The Biblical Idea of History," 213.
21. Hepner, *Legal Friction*, 472, 474.
22. Brett, *Genesis*, 25.
23. So, too, Hepner, *Legal Friction*, 479.

Genesis 26–36

appears twice in the life of Abraham (first with Pharaoh and then with Abimelech) and once with Isaac and Abimelech (26:10). Both of these earlier patriarchs were not a positive role model for Israel in these particular cases.

In Isaac's dying days, Esau responded to his father's request for venison with obedient submission (27:1-4). Esau's willingness is demonstrated by his response to his father's summons with the phrase "here am I" (27:1). This is the recurring response of obedient people in Genesis (22:7, 11; 31:11; 37:13; 46:2). Conversely, Jacob took advantage of his father—at his mother's bidding (27:6-13)—and tricked Isaac into blessing him (27:19-29). Even though Esau desired to take revenge on his brother, he refrained because of his respect for his father (27:41).[24] Not surprisingly, the fifth commandment's promise of dwelling long in the land (Exod 20:12) appears to have been experienced by Esau as opposed to Jacob. Esau stayed in the vicinity of his homeland, Canaan, but Jacob ended up an exile in Haran for twenty years (31:38, 41) and later he lived another seventeen years in Egypt where he died (47:9, 28).[25] Interestingly, both Abraham and Isaac are said to have lived long and good lives (25:8; 35:29); however, Jacob himself states to the pharaoh that the days of his life had been "few and hard" (47:9).[26] There can be no question that Jacob had lived a hard life due to his deceptions (31:25-55; 32:4—33:16, 25-33; 34:1-5, 30; 35:16-20; 37:26-33).[27]

The fifth commandment finds another fitting demonstration in the actions of Jacob's sons Levi and Simeon (cf. *Test. Levi* 6:7).[28] Not only did they bring dishonor upon their father when they killed the Shechemites, unlike Esau with Isaac, they also dishonored Jacob by taking vengeance upon their brother Joseph while Jacob was still alive (see more in the next chapter). As a result, they, too, were scattered/"exiled" in the land of Israel (49:5-7).

---

24. See also Kaiser, *Old Testament Ethics*, 82.

25. Rosenberg ("Bible: Biblical Narrative," 68) also notes the harshness of Jacob's life in "exile."

26. So Sarna, *Genesis*, 397.

27. See comments by Noble, "Esau, Tamar, and Joseph," 243.

28. According to this Intertestamental text, Levi acknowledges that they sinned against their father.

Genesis as Torah

Commandment 6

Simeon and Levi's actions against the Shechemites were a clear violation of the command not to murder (34:25-26); although some suggest that Jacob may have viewed them as "soldiers" and their actions, an act of war.[29] Similarly, Esau's desire to kill his brother, and later Laban's desire to kill Jacob, certainly help explain the need for the sixth commandment and the legislation of Exod 21:12-14, which deals with laws against premeditated murder (cf. 27:41-45; 31:29; 32:1—33:16).[30] Although *thoughts* of murdering someone may have been acceptable to those living in the period prior to the NT, John makes it clear that the thought is as bad as the actual act (1 John 3:15).

Commandment 7

By having sexual relations with Bilhah, Jacob's wife/concubine (35:22), Reuben broke not only the fifth commandment by not honoring his father, but he also violated the seventh commandment instructing against adultery (Exod 20:14; Deut 5:18). Furthermore, Reuben's actions reflect the incest prohibitions of Lev 18:8, 20:10-11, and Deut 22:30.[31] It is worth noting that the author of Jubilees also recognized that the acts of Reuben were the impetus for these incest laws (*Jub.* 33:10-20).

The incest laws in particular were meant to protect families that lived in close proximity, which was the norm in Bedouin settings. In Reuben's case, his actions brought a curse (49:4) and were the reason Jacob overrode the inheritance rights as required in Deut 21:15-17, a fact implied in Gen 49:3-4.[32] Here we have a case-law example of when such an inheritance law may be overridden. Instructionally, these were the types of sexual sins that caused the Canaanites to be spewed from the land. As I will point out in more detail below, the assimilation of Jacob's sons to the ways of the

---

29. Mathews, *Genesis 11:27—50:26*, 617.

30. Carmichael, *Origins of Biblical Law*, 98-106. Carmichael adds Jacob's encounter with the "man" at Peniel (32:24-32) but nothing here indicates that the "man" desired to kill Jacob or vice versa.

31. Carmichael, *Women, Law, and the Genesis Traditions*, 49; and Carmichael, *Law and Narrative*, 221-23.

32. See Carmichael, *Laws of Deuteronomy*, 170-71; Carmichael, *Law and Narrative*, 142-45; and Carmichael, *Law, Legend, and Incest*, 59.

Canaanites may in fact have been one of the reasons why God sent them to Egypt (46:2–3).

Commandments 8 and 9

The commandment against stealing plays out in chapters 27, 31, and 34. Although Jacob had negotiated the trade of Esau's birthright for a pot of stew (25:29–34), Jacob's actions in tricking and then lying to his father certainly allowed him to steal that which was not rightfully his (27:36). And Rachel's removal of her father's gods falls into the category of theft (31:19). Interestingly, the same verb (*ganab* "to steal") is used both here in describing Rachel's act and in the commandment against stealing in Exod 20:15 (cf. Deut 5:19).

What may have appeared to be a simple vindictive act could have cost Rachel her life (31:32). This was a similar situation that Joseph's brothers encountered when Joseph's cup was "stolen" by Benjamin (44:9). Both Jacob and Benjamin's brothers pronounced the death sentence on the guilty culprit without realizing the possible consequences. Of course, this, too, would have been instructional for Israel: do not pronounce judgments in haste. Jephthah and Saul certainly could have learned from this account (Judg 11:31; 1 Sam 14:24).

In the case of the Shechemite fiasco, the murder of the Shechemites (i.e., the males) led to the stealing of their wives, children, and material wealth (34:29). The author makes sure to note that these actions were not God-honoring especially when both Levi and Simeon lost their inheritance rights on account of it (49:5–6) and received a curse from their father (49:7).

Finally, although bearing false witness is the technical designation for the ninth commandment, closely associated with it is the idea of lying and deception. Not only did Jacob lie to his father when he stole the blessing of Esau, but Rachel lied to her father when questioned about his missing gods (31:35). Jacob also deceived Esau when he did not follow him on to Seir as he had promised (33:14). Not surprisingly, in every one of these cases, tragedy followed the event after the person lied. For Jacob it was experienced through exile to Haran, where he was taken advantage of by his father-in-law, and then later he had to endure the rape of his daughter Dinah because he had settled among the Shechemites (33:18–19; 34:1–2). One can see in this latter action of Jacob a parallel with Lot pitching his tent towards Sodom and the disaster that ensued with his family (13:12; 19:26, 30–38).

Genesis as Torah

For Israel the message once again rang loud and clear: intermingling with Canaanites would lead to disaster for one's family and for the nation.

Jacob and Esau as Israel and Edom

God declared the eponymous nature of Jacob and Esau before their birth (25:22–23, 30; cf. 36:1, 8, 19, 43). The inclusion of this tidbit of information tips the author's hand regarding his instructional intentions on several points. From this vantage point it is clear that part of the purpose of the Jacob/Esau narrative was to show how Jacob became Israel and gained hegemony over Esau as well as how Edom got its name (25:30; 27:40).[33] Some have even seen in the actions of Esau "political satire" against the Edomites.[34] This does have some merit in that the separation of Esau from Jacob noted in 36:7–8 recalls the earlier separation of Lot and Abraham (13:6).[35] Both pairs separated due to an overabundance of livestock.[36] After the separation, although still cared for by God (Deut 2:1–23; 23:7), both Lot and Esau ended up as outsiders and the fathers of three countries that would both border and invade Israel from time to time. It is clear that God blessed Esau because of his connection with Abraham. On this point, scholars have rightly noted that the genealogy of Esau shows the fulfillment of God's word that Esau would also become a nation (25:23).[37]

As the Jacob-Esau account unfolds the reader is also informed about the locality within which both Edom and Israel would one day reside: Edom occupied the region of Mt. Seir (32:3; 33:14; 36:8–9; Deut 2:4–5), whereas Israel's inheritance was in Canaan (12:7; 13:17; 15:7, 18; 24:7; 26:3; 28:4, 13). Even though both would overstep their territorial bounds throughout their history, God's declaration to Abraham, Isaac, and Jacob that Canaan was theirs would not be overridden unless God so declared. In this vein, Ezekiel's rebuke of Edom for their trespassing on Israel's inheritance (35:1–15)[38] as well as Obadiah's intercession on Israel's behalf against Edom becomes prototypical of the centuries-old struggle first prophesied by God

---

33. Daube, *Studies in Biblical Law*, 199–200; and von Rad, *The Problem of the Hexateuch*, 169.

34. So Blenkinsopp, *Pentateuch*, 104.

35. Miscall, "Jacob and Joseph Story," 36.

36. Blenkinsopp, *Abraham*, 52.

37. Blenkinsopp, *Pentateuch*, 106–7.

38. See Peterson, *Ezekiel in Context*, 266–70.

in Genesis 25. Nevertheless, from the Torah perspective, the reconciliation of Jacob and Esau perhaps is best linked to the command in Deut 23:8 [Heb] not to abhor an Edomite,[39] after all, they still were brothers.

Instruction from the Life of Jacob

Many have seen in the life of Jacob "Israel personified."[40] The stubbornness and bargaining nature of Jacob is a fitting parallel to the later Israelites. As the life of Jacob unfolds in Genesis, it becomes clear that God had to take him through a series of difficult circumstances in order to make Jacob into the man of God he was supposed to be. YHWH's actions with Israel are no less true in this regard. For example, Jacob's sojourn and "oppression" in Haran foreshadows both the Babylonian sojourn and return, and the exodus of Israel from Egypt.[41] Indeed, Jacob's and Israel's experiences have a number of parallels. These include:

1. Jacob's family left Canaan and went to Egypt small in number and came out as a nation with great possessions. So, too, Jacob left Canaan as one man but returned from Haran with great abundance and a family of great size.[42]

2. Both Israel and Jacob thrived despite the attempts of the pharaohs and Laban to cheat them out of their duly earned wages (31:9, 16; Exod 3:22; 12:36).

3. Both Jacob and Israel lost favor with those who ruled over them (31:1–2, 5; Exod 1:8–16).

4. Both were oppressed in harsh conditions (31:28–31; Exod 1:11; 3:7; 5:6–19).

5. God intervened to protect his people because he saw their affliction (31:12, 42; Exod 3:7; 4:31).[43]

---

39. Syrén, *Forsaken First-Born*, 109. See also Carmichael, *Laws of Deuteronomy*, 202–3.

40. Briggs and Lohr, *Theological Introduction*, 22.

41. So, too, Hepner, *Legal Friction*, 377.

42. Blenkinsopp, *Pentateuch*, 105; and Daube, *Exodus Pattern*, 63, 70. Daube (p.71) notes that the rabbis saw the same parallels between Jacob and Laban and Israel and pharaoh.

43. Daube, *Exodus Pattern*, 67.

Genesis as Torah

6. In both cases, the oppressor pursued after them (31:23; Exod 14:8–10).
7. Both Israel and Jacob made a break with their past by entering covenants: Israel with YHWH and Jacob with Laban (31:44–55; Exod 19:5).
8. Both Jacob and Israel were confronted with a hostile inhabitant(s) before reaching Canaan (32:1–20; Num 21:23–35).
9. And both end up settling in Canaan.

The Jacob/Israel connections are further bolstered by the parallels between Jacob and Moses. Obviously the author wanted the exodus generation to glean instruction from the Jacob account. The parallels between Moses and Jacob include:

1. Both left their homelands due to someone seeking their life (27:41–45; Exod 2:15).
2. Both worked as shepherds (29:15; Exod 3:1).
3. In the same way Jacob worked for his wife and gained children, so, too, Moses worked for his wife Zipporah and gained two sons, Gershom and Eliezer (Exod 2:22; 18:3–4).
4. God told Jacob and Moses to return to their people from their land of sojourn/exile (31:3, 11–13; Exod 3:6–22).

These type-scenes would have helped the Israelite reader to focus on their own past and what God had done for them. God was with both their ancestors and them: God was unchanging in this regard. In such moments, Israel could easily have recalled their period of dedication at Sinai. This was no less the case for Jacob who returned to Bethel in an effort to renew his pledge to the God of his fathers.

Instruction from Jacob's Bethel Experience

One cannot overstate the spiritual importance of Bethel to the patriarchs, and later for Israel. However, what had begun as a place of positive supernatural experiences between God, the patriarchs, and those of the united monarchy (12:8; 13:3–4; 1 Sam 7:16; 10:3) turned into a place of derision during the divided monarchy (1 Kgs 12:29–32; 2 Kgs 23:4, 15; Jer 48:13; Amos 3:14; 4:4; 5:5–6; 7:10–13). Depending on the date of the writing of Genesis, the Bethel account taught Israel, once again, about their divine right to the land (28:13; 35:11–12) and what god truly was to be associated with Bethel. It was not Baal as in the days of Hosea and Amos it was in fact YHWH, the God of heaven and earth. What is more, Jacob, the progenitor of Israel, had declared there that YHWH would be his God—a similar reality for Israel at Sinai. Finally, although Abraham had initiated the practice of tithing when he tithed to Melchizedek (14:20), it was at Bethel that Jacob, not God, initiated the practice of tithing to God (28:22), a practice that later would be foundational for supporting God's priests and the poor of Israel (Lev 27:30–32; Num 18:24–28; Deut 12:6, 11; 14:22–29; 26:12).

Jacob's Bethel experiences also taught Israel that the destiny of Jacob/Israel was inextricably linked to the plans of God, if they would but yield to God's plan (28:11–22; 35:1–15). In his first encounter with God at Bethel, Jacob had witnessed the bridging of heaven and earth when YHWH prophesied about Jacob's future. The nation of Israel certainly could resonate with their forefather's experience in this regard. They, too, had witnessed the bridging of heaven and earth at Sinai. Moreover, from the very inception of the conflict between YHWH and pharaoh through the plagues, Israel began to understand the true nature of the God they served. This was nowhere clearer than in the Sinai event, which, like Jacob's Bethel experience, included a covenant of sorts.

Prior to arriving at the site during Jacob's second trek to Bethel, Jacob called for the removal of all the foreign gods/idols to which his family still clung (35:2; Josh 24:14, 23), some of which may very well have come from the recent looting of Shechem (34:27; *Tg. Ps-J.*).[44] The type-scene is very close to Israel's second generation's declaration of devotion to YHWH at Shechem under the watchful eye of Joshua (Josh 24:1–27). Furthermore, Jacob and his family's changing/washing of their garments recalls the moment at Sinai just before Israel agreed to the Sinai covenant (35:2; Exod 19:10; cf. Lev. 13:34; 14:8–9). Here we see the close connections between God's blessing and covenant keeping, as well as the dangers of the "ritual impurity of idolatry."[45] Jacob's camp, as with the camp of Israel, was to be clean when approaching the holy presence of God (Exod 19:10; 30:19–21) especially after a period of looting and war (Num 31:19–20, 24; cf. *Tg. Ps.-J.*).[46]

---

44. Mathews, *Genesis 11:27—50:26*, 617.
45. Polin, "Jewish Law," 39.
46. Mathews, *Genesis 11:27—50:26*, 617.

Genesis as Torah

Instruction from Jacob's Life While in Haran

It is self-evident that the overall narrative relating Jacob's marriage to Laban's daughters and the accounts of the births of the children that issued from those unions served as a prehistory of the tribes of Israel, namely, where they came from as well as some of the key family dynamics (29:31—30:24).[47] As I will demonstrate in the next chapter, the events of chapter 29 set the stage for the family chaos, which will dominate much of the remainder of the book of Genesis.

However, beyond mere historical content, Jacob's time in Haran is rife with events and experiences, which are later regulated with specific legislation in the Torah. Perhaps the most glaring legal issue is Jacob's marriage to two sisters—Rachel and Leah—a situation which is forbidden in the later Levitical law (Lev 18:18). Adding to this family disorder was Rachel and Leah's giving of their handmaids—Zilpah and Bilhah—to Jacob in order to have more children. This is the second time in the book of Genesis that the author has shown how ANE adoption practices through the use of a handmaiden (30:3-4, 9; cf. 16:1-4) were not necessarily part of the plan of God for Israel. God was to be trusted: he could open and close wombs as he saw fit (29:31; 30:22; cf. 1 Sam 1:19). Those reading the account of Jacob would have quickly realized the importance of the Levitical regulation. Such actions brought dysfunction to a family that could affect it for generations.

One of the ways dysfunction is exhibited when a man marries two women is the inevitable situation of one wife being loved more than the other—a reality that is clearly stated in the Jacob narrative (29:30; cf. 1 Sam 1:5). In this case, once again the Law corrected this circumstance by requiring a man with two wives to administer conjugal rights to both, even if one was disliked (29:32; 30:15-16, 20; cf. 31:50; Exod 21:10).

Closely connected to this concept is the issue of inheritance rights for the children who were born into this dysfunctional situation. The Law made it clear that the inheritance rights of the children of the unloved wife could not be abrogated in favor of the children of the loved wife (Deut 21:15-17). One can easily understand why this was important especially in light of the circumstances that would unfold in the lives of Jacob's children. Joseph, the eldest of Rachel, ended up being given the inheritance of the firstborn even though he was younger than Leah's oldest child, Reuben (48:22; I will return to this in the next chapter).[48]

---

47. Fretheim, *Pentateuch*, 87.
48. Carmichael, *Women, Law, and the Genesis Traditions*, 24, 31-32.

Genesis 26–36

Next, some have suggested that Jacob's desire to be released from serving Laban was the impetus for the law dealing with the release of an indebted person in his seventh year (29:18–30; Deut 15:9–12).[49] While this is possible, we must keep in mind that Jacob ended up spending *twenty* years with Laban, not seven. Closely related to this law are the laws related to the property rights of an employer of indentured servants. In this vein, Hepner and Carmichael posit that Laban's desire to retain custody of his daughters as well as his grandchildren recalls the laws of Hebrew slaves noted in Exod 21:4–6 (cf. Deut 15:18).[50] Carmichael also propounds that the Jacob and Laban account in 27:41—31:55 lies behind the laws of female captives of war (Deut 21:10–14).[51] However, Hepner's and Carmichael's links are tenuous at best.[52] While there are tangential connections, it is important to keep in mind that Jacob was a hired laborer who made wages. He was not an indentured servant. Furthermore, Jacob and Laban were not only blood relation, Jacob was in a full marriage relationship with Rachel and Leah. Jacob is never portrayed as a slave even though he may have been treated like one at times (cf. Gen 31:43; Exod 21:4).[53]

David Daube (1909–1999) is no doubt closer to the reality of what case law looks like in this section of Genesis when he notes the parallels between Gen 31:39 and Exod 22:10–11 (Heb 22:9–10).[54] In the latter text, the reader is informed about what is required of a hired shepherd vis-à-vis the owner of an animal/flock. Restitution was not required if the animal wandered away, died, or was injured. In this case, Jacob went above and beyond the requirements of the law in order to make sure Laban suffered no loss while he was taking care of Laban's sheep.

---

49. Carmichael, *Law and Narrative*, 21.

50. Hepner, *Legal Friction*, 379–80. Hepner (p.393) suggests that the Laban and Jacob account favors the Deuteronomic laws because Laban allows Jacob to "go free" with a double portion (two wives). See also Carmichael, *Origins of Biblical Law*, 79–87. Carmichael (87–97) also propounds that the law dealing with concubines in Exod 21:7–11 owes its origins to the Jacob–Laban account.

51. Carmichael, *Law and Narrative*, 139–42.

52. Carmichael points to the use of the phrase, "beautiful in form" found in both Gen 29:17 and Deut 21:11. While this is an interesting connection, it may simply point to similarity in authorship.

53. Carmichael (*Origins of Biblical Law*, 80–81 n5) acknowledges this fact but chooses to argue that there is some overlap between the two.

54. See also Daube, *Studies in Biblical Law*, 13–14, 64 n5; and Carmichael, *Origins of Biblical Law*, 153–58.

Genesis as Torah

Many specific laws could be drawn from Jacob's sojourn in Haran, yet none are more important than the promise of God to bless those associated with Abraham and his descendants. As we have seen consistently in the lives of the patriarchs, the promise of God to bless the nations through Abraham and his descendants came to fruition once again in the life of Jacob. Indeed, it was Laban who recognized that God had blessed him on account of Jacob (30:27). Israel was to be the head and not the tail when God blessed them (Deut 28:13). Others would recognize this fact as had Laban.

Instruction from Jacob's Life on the Way to Canaan

Jacob's first stop after his parting from Laban was Mahanaim ("two camps") in the Transjordan. Other than a brief notation about meeting angels there, nothing is developed beyond this fact other than the note about how the site got its name. This brief note, however, carries a lot of weight when one considers the importance of the site throughout Israel's history. The same site was a priestly city of refuge (Josh 21:38); the place where Saul's son, Ishbosheth, was crowned king after the death of his father (2 Sam 2:8-9); the location where David stayed during Absalom's attempted coup (2 Sam 17:24; 19:32 [v.33 Heb]); and the capital of an administrative district during the days of Solomon (1 Kgs 4:14).[55] For Israel, the site had a special, and holy, significance mainly because of the events that Genesis records from the life of Jacob. This account also gave Israel an attachment to this region of the Transjordan. The tribes of Reuben, Gad, and the half tribe of Manasseh would eventually settle here.

Within the narrative describing Jacob's return to Canaan from "exile" a number of instructive features appear. Besides the obvious didactic parallel between Jacob's and Israel's exodus and return (see above list), the proverbial low hanging fruit is the Jewish prohibition of not eating the muscle of the thigh (32:32) even though the Law makes no mention of it in Leviticus 11, Deut 14:3-21, or any other place in the Bible for that matter.[56] Also, Jacob's confrontation with Esau prior to entering Canaan foreshadowed Israel's confrontation with Edom prior to entering the Promised Land (Numbers 20).

---

55. Sarna, *Genesis*, 223.
56. Stahl, *Law and Liminality*, 78; see also Polin, "Jewish Law," 37.

One could also draw a parallel between the hardships and spiritual struggles of the wilderness generation prior to entering Canaan and Jacob's struggles with God/a man as he returned to the land of Canaan (32:24–31). In this regard, some have even seen in Jacob's intimate struggle with the "man" (cf. Hos 12:4; Hosea identifies him as an angel[57]), a picture of the Sinai covenant and Israel's ongoing struggle, and intimacy with her God.[58] It is also noteworthy that in the same way Jacob encountered angels and later a "man," so, too, Joshua encountered the angel of the Lord prior to the conquest of Canaan (32:1–2; Josh 5:13–15). Sailhamer believes this may be due to the fact that Canaan was equated with the land of Eden/the garden of God, which was also guarded by cherubim after Adam and Eve's sin (see my chapter 3).[59]

To be sure, these are all valid instructive features in their own way. But it is just as important to note that Jacob's meeting/reckoning with Esau foreshadowed Israel's encounter with their destiny in Canaan after forty years of wandering. Jacob's response to this challenge was to give a "peace offering" to Esau. Now while some have argued that Jacob was giving back that which he had stolen from Esau through the lost birthright and blessing,[60] in essence, Jacob's gifts to Esau were not only a wise action, it proved that God had blessed him exceedingly. In this vein, von Rad may be correct to see in Jacob's shrewd act of reconciliation (32:13–21) aspects of the wisdom tradition (i.e., Prov 17:14).[61]

In the same way Jacob prepared himself to enter Canaan and "made himself right" by offering gifts to Esau, so, too, Israel had prepared themselves prior to entering Canaan by enacting the rite of circumcision and by celebrating Passover (Josh 5:3–8, 11). By doing these things, they were not only making themselves right before God, they were also associating themselves with the Abrahamic covenant and in a sense offering themselves as "gifts" to God.

Jacob's preparation for meeting Esau was not only marked by fear and his self-reliance to thwart Esau's wrath (32:7–8, 13–21; 33:1–3, 8), he also entreated God for deliverance (32:9–12). One should be cautious in judging

---

57. Sarna (*Genesis*, 404) identifies the "man" as the "celestial patron of Esau-Edom."
58. Stahl, *Law and Liminality*, 85.
59. Sailhamer, *Genesis Unbound*, 52.
60. For a list of scholars holding this view, see Noble, "Esau, Tamar, and Joseph," 237 n19. See also Carr, "*Biblos geneseos*: Part 2," 338.
61. Von Rad, *Genesis*, 319.

the propriety of Jacob's actions vis-à-vis his trust in God. Throughout Israel's history, many times the nation and its kings walked the same fine line between self-reliance and trust in their God (2 Kings 18–20). David certainly walked that tightrope as a God-fearing warrior (cf. 1 Sam 21:10–15; Psalm 34). For the wilderness generation, their fears of confronting the Canaanites must have been palpable. It is no wonder why God reassured them that he was with them (Num 14:9; 21:34; Deut 1:21, 29; 3:2, 22; 31:8; Josh 8:1; 10:8, 11–14). They were to trust in him to help them fight their battles (Deut 1:30; 3:2; 20:4; Josh 6:2–5; 10:25), but they still needed to do their part (Exod 17:8–13; Num 31:1–5; Josh 8:1–4).

Finally, along with the etiological accounts of the naming of Mahanaim, Peniel, Succoth, and of the dietary restriction noted above (32:32), one of the other key instructive features of this account was the changing of Jacob's name to Israel (32:28; cf. 35:10). This was more than a simple changing of a man's name; for Jacob's offspring it was to be their name as a country—a name, which would unify them as a nation once and for all.

Instruction from Jacob's Life in Canaan

Next to the Sodom narrative, the events of chapter 34 present one of the clearest examples of case law in the book of Genesis. In this situation, however, the events clearly demonstrate not only what not to do, but why legislation needed to be in place to deal with similar situations in the future. As we will see, later laws actual appear to rectify the injustice and atrocity perpetrated against the Shechemites by Levi and Simeon.

The circumstances of the first part of chapter 34 have been played out thousands of times throughout history: boy meets girl; boy falls in love with the girl; boy takes unfair advantage of the girl; boy desires/is forced to marry the girl. Unfortunately it did not end with a marriage that lasted. No, Levi and Simeon, Dinah's two older brothers, decided to take matters into their own hands and massacre the entire male population of Shechem after they had foisted a false solution on the men of the city in order to remedy Shechem's rape of Dinah. Their solution: let all the males be circumcised and the marriage will go forward.

Interpreters of this text have struggled with the injustices and the harsh reaction of Levi and Simeon. Early Jewish interpreters suggested that Levi and Simeon were justified in their execution of the male population due to the fact that the Shechemites had failed to punish Shechem for what he had done to Dinah, especially as was required by the Law (*Gen. Rab.* 80:6; cf. Exod 22:15–16 [Heb]; Deut 22:28–29; *Test. Levi* 5:3).[62] While this is possible, in reality the laws in question in Deuteronomy 22 and Exodus 22 required the one who had intercourse with a non-betrothed damsel to marry her if her father would allow it. The death penalty was not the punishment. Jacob and his sons apparently arranged a marriage agreement because the text tells us that Simeon and Levi removed Dinah from Shechem's house *after* they murdered him (34:26).[63]

Three responses could be given to this dilemma. First, some have posited that portions of the account of chapter 34 are an anachronistic anti-Samaritan polemic added to the book during the postexilic period.[64] As such, the severe actions of Jacob's sons were justified based upon later problems with intermarriage in the postexilic era (Ezra 9:11–12). Second, the actions of Levi and Simeon may simply have been an overreaction to Shechem's act, hence the reason Jacob was upset with what they had done (34:30), after all, Abraham's descendants were to be a blessing to the nations (12:3). Third, and as touched on above, the author of the material may have purposely included this story to show why the canonically later laws of Exodus and Deuteronomy were needed as a corrective to the injustice perpetrated against the Shechemites. In this way, the actions of Levi and Simeon would not be repeated.

In this vein, three later laws seem to speak directly to this case. First, only if a woman was betrothed to be married could the death penalty be instituted for raping someone (Exod 22:15–16 [Heb]; Deut 22:28–29).[65] Forcing a non-betrothed woman to have intercourse required the guilty party to marry and take care of her for the rest of his life (cf. 2 Sam 13:11–16). Second, the fact that Hamor, the father of Shechem (as well as all the other males), was killed for the sins of his son may be the reason for the institution of the law of Deut 24:16.[66] A father was not to be punished for the sins of his son and vice versa. Third, some have suggested that the actions of

---

62. Polin, "Jewish Law," 41.

63. Amit (*Hidden Polemics*, 195) suggests that Shechem was holding Dinah "captive."

64. See Rofé, "Defilement of Virgins," 369–75; and Na'aman, "'Conquest of Canaan,'" 276.

65. Carmichael, *Law and Narrative*, 218–20; and Carmichael, *Origins of Biblical Law*, 158–61.

66. Ibid., 232. Carmichael (*Women, Law, and the Genesis Traditions*, 44–47) also has suggested that Dinah's rape was the basis of adultery laws of Deut 22:23–27. This is unlikely.

Genesis as Torah

Jacob's sons lay behind the law forbidding the mistreatment of strangers (34:29; Exod 22:21–24; Lev 19:33–34).[67] Each of these laws would have been important teaching points for Israel.

Instructionally, the proverbial elephant in the room is the fact that the account gives the reader a clear view of why intermarriage with Canaanites was against the commands of God (34:9; Exod 34:16; Deut 7:3; cf. Judg 3:6; Ezra 9:12).[68] That this is a central focus of the author is made clear by the anachronistic note that Shechem had "done a disgraceful thing in Israel" (37:7 NASB).[69] In this regard, Carmichael suggests that the story is reflected figuratively in the law prohibiting the use of an ox and ass together when plowing (Deut 22:10); after all, Hamor's name means "ass" and one could view Israel/Jacob as the ox (cf. Gen 49:6).[70] Thus, for Carmichael, the account of Shechem and Dinah was a parabolic prohibition against mixed marriages and assimilation (34:23). While Carmichael's suggestion may be possible, a clearer point of instruction would be that even in the case of an Israelite woman's rape by a Canaanite, marriage was not the solution.[71]

Finally, while some may argue that the fate of the Shechemites was similar to the fate of the Canaanites in Joshua's day, the fact remains that the sins of the Amorites had not yet come to the point of all out punishment (15:16). As such, Jacob and his sons were to dwell peaceably with the locals; yet, stay separate from them. It is possible that the problems of violence, mixed marriages, and general spiritual laxness may in fact have been the primary reason why God removed Israel to Egypt until they could become a great nation (46:2–4). Indeed, the mysterious and unknowable plans of God are another aspect of the nature of Israel's God.

---

67. Carmichael, *Origins of Biblical Law*, 170–73.

68. Amit, *Hidden Polemics*, 189–211; and Hepner, *Legal Friction*, 506–9. Amit (196–211) also suggests it served as a polemic written by the putative "Holiness School" against marriage and association with those at Samaria at the beginning of the Second Temple period (cf. *Test. Levi* 5:1—7:3; Sir 50:25–26).

69. Amit, *Hidden Polemics*, 195, 203.

70. Carmichael, *Women, Law, and the Genesis Traditions*, 34–36; Carmichael, *Laws of Deuteronomy*, 159–63; and Carmichael, *Law and Narrative*, 193–97. Carmichael (*Origins of Biblical Law*, 164–67) also propounds that the account of Dinah lies behind the law on bestiality in Exod 22:19 because of the meaning of the name of Hamor. This is at best an interpretive stretch.

71. Amit, *Hidden Polemics*, 193; and Na'aman, "Conquest of Canaan," 276. While Amit and Na'aman place this prohibition in the postexilic period, the instruction would fit at any time for Israel in the Promised Land.

Genesis 26–36

With these concerns being noted, one final legal issue appears to be in play in this text, namely, the importance of covenant and keeping one's word. Now to be sure, the author is using the account of Dinah to teach a variety of legislative points, specifically, the very important truth about why the Law rejected intermarriage with the Canaanites; however, when a covenant did take place, regardless of the party, Israel was not to break covenants sworn in the name of their God (Lev 19:12; Deut 6:13; 10:20; Josh 2:12). Even though the text is silent about the swearing of a covenant between Jacob and the Shechemites, one can be assured that if Jacob and Laban entered into a covenant by invoking their gods (31:53), Shechem and Jacob certainly would of as well. And Joshua's trips to the region of Shechem for religious reasons during the conquest supports the fact that some type of covenant had been instituted between Israel and Shechem (Josh 8:30–33; 24:1–25) or that a remnant of the Shechemites may have been integrated into the nation of Israel (34:29; cf. Num 26:31[72]). Finally, as with Joshua's interaction with the Gibeonites, once a covenant was sworn to, Israel was to keep its word unless otherwise instructed by God himself. Interestingly, the connection between the Gibeonites and Shechemites is strengthened by the identification of both as Hivites (34:2; Josh 9:7; 11:19).[73]

As a result of Levi and Simeon's actions, Jacob became somewhat of a fugitive in the land of Canaan (34:30)—apparently surviving annihilation by being protected by God (35:5). Moreover, it is possible that the breach of covenant between the Shechemites and the family of Judah was the very reason for the ensuing hardships of Jacob, which included: the loss of Rachel (35:16–19); Reuben's tryst with Bilhah (35:2–3); the loss of Joseph (37:31–35); the loss of his grandsons Er and Onan (38:1–10); and the later famine in the land (41:54–57). The breaking of covenants certainly brings to mind Saul's breach of the covenant with the Gibeonites that resulted in famine (2 Sam 21:1–14; Joshua 9). And Zedekiah's breach of his covenant with Nebuchadnezzar certainly did not end well for Judah (Ezekiel 17).[74]

---

72. Noth (*Numbers*, 207) posits that Shechem had been incorporated into the tribe of Manasseh. See also Budd, *Numbers*, 293.

73. Amit, *Hidden Polemics*, 200–201. See also Na'aman, "'Conquest of Canaan,'" 276.

74. Peterson, *Ezekiel in Context*, 169–70, 182–84; Hillers, *Covenant*, 44; Mendenhall, "Puppy and Lettuce," 30 n16; and Frankena, *Kanttekeningen*, 13.

Genesis as Torah

Theological Instruction on the Nature of God

Within the Jacob narrative one is confronted with a God who not only encounters his people (26:2–5; 28:12–17; 29:31; 30:17, 22; 31:3, 11–13, 24; 32:1–2, 24–29), he also works behind the scenes to bring about his plans, even when his people try to do things on their own. In this vein, not only did Rebekah and Jacob plot to force the fulfillment of God's word to Rebekah that Jacob would have the ascendency over Esau (25:23), but Jacob's breeding scheme for Laban's flocks (30:37–42) as well as his attempts to appease Esau when he returned to Canaan (32:3–7) certainly fit this picture.

The reader is also reminded of the importance of God looking upon his people as opposed to hiding his face from them (cf. 4:14; 16:6, 8; 35:1, 7; 36:6; 43:3, 5; 44:23, 26).[75] Jacob's wrestling with the "man" and the subsequent naming of the site as Peniel ("face of God"; 32:30) followed by the likening of Esau's acceptance of Jacob with seeing the face of God and being accepted (33:10) are important facets of this motif. In light of this fact, when reading these texts a reader would be immediately drawn to the Aaronic blessing (Num 6:24–26).

Conclusion

The struggles between Jacob and Esau come to a fitting conclusion with the genealogy of Esau in chapter 36. While Edom will play a role in Israel's life in the wilderness wandering period (Numbers 20), Esau's name will not appear again until Moses' final words in Deuteronomy 2. Throughout this block, Jacob's interactions with Esau, Laban, and the Shechemites has offered a number of important examples of case law and why several of the later laws were required to govern Israel's interactions with both the Edomites and the Canaanites. I also noted a number of the important factors related to the cult site of Bethel and the importance of covenant making. In this vein, Jacob's troubles in the land of Canaan were just starting with the fiasco at Shechem. From this point on, Jacob's family struggles take center stage as Joseph becomes the focus of the narrative. As we will see in the next chapter, *torah* instruction continues as the dysfunction of Jacob's family bubbles to the surface in the struggle for supremacy and position in the clan. This is all the result of Jacob's older sons' jealousy due to Jacob's favoritism of his beloved son Joseph.

---

75. See Balentine, *Hidden God*, 45–79; and Peterson, *Ezekiel in Context*, 98–102.

7

Genesis 37–50

The Life of Joseph: How to Live in Exile

The account of Joseph's life certainly plays a central role in the book of Genesis. Spanning fourteen chapters, the story of Joseph covers a similar amount of space as that of the account of Abraham. Even Jacob's life story, which crosses over with that of his son Joseph, at best covers about the same number of chapters as Joseph's life. Yet even in the case of the Jacob narrative, many of the stories are loosely linked chronologically spanning twenty years in Haran. On the other hand, Joseph's story tends to be more of a continuous narrative of his life with a special focus on his interactions with his brothers (chs. 42–47). It is clear that those responsible for the final form of Genesis wanted to highlight very specific details of Joseph's life. Joseph's interaction with his brothers, both in Canaan and in Egypt, is rife with teaching moments and instruction for the nation of Israel, especially for those who perhaps knew the account prior to their exodus from Egypt.[1]

Of course Joseph's story could also be instructional for those of the Babylonian exile. This is evident based upon the tantalizing parallels between the experiences of Joseph and Jehoiachin. Both were released from prison; both had their prison garments changed to fine clothing, and both

---

1. Some have suggested that the Joseph account fits best within the Persian period when the descendants of both Joseph and Judah were important rulers. See for example Golka, "Genesis 37–50," 160, 171–73. Golka's assertion is based mainly upon a late dating of Ezekiel 40–48, Daniel, and portions of Zechariah, which is questionable at best. See also Brett, *Genesis*, 25, 113–14, 137.

Genesis as Torah

were promoted to living in the presence of the king/pharaoh (41:14, 40–44; cf. 2 Kgs 25:27–30).[2] It is perhaps for this reason that the account survived and became a dominant part of Genesis. Yet, as I will demonstrate in this penultimate chapter, beyond this general instruction one can also find a number of very specific Torah laws on display in the Joseph narrative. I will begin by discussing the general instruction and conclude the chapter by examining a few of the specific case-law examples.

General Instruction

As Wisdom Instruction

Because of the obvious instructional/didactic bent of the Joseph narrative,[3] scholars are not adverse to the idea of connecting good portions of the account to later instructional material. In this vein, von Rad famously argued that this block of Genesis reflected the wisdom tradition.[4] Now while concepts of wise living can be gleaned from the account, caution must be taken in assigning the entire account to the wisdom tradition.[5] Yet even with this caveat, it is clear that within this narrative we find the motif of the "fear of the LORD," a central tenet of wisdom thinking (Prov 1:7); Joseph feared his God in a healthy way. This healthy fear kept him from a variety of transgressions. For example, he refused to be vindictive with his brothers (42:18; 50:21),[6] although he did test them. However, even in the midst of this testing we see Joseph's insights into the mind of God; what the brothers had intended for evil, God had intended for good (cf. 45:5–8;

---

2. Postell, *Adam as Israel*, 158.

3. So Coats, "Joseph Story," 290.

4. Von Rad, "Joseph Narrative," 75–81 or von Rad, *The Problem of the Hexateuch*, 292–300. See also von Rad, "The Story of Joseph," 19–35 esp. 25; von Rad, *Old Testament Theology*, 172; and von Rad, *Genesis*, 435–40. So, too, the conclusion of Coats, "Joseph Story," 28–97; and Coats, *From Canaan to Egypt*, 78–79, 90. Coats (295 and 78 respectively) and von Rad (*Genesis*, 435) suggest the Solomonic era as the period for the origins of the account. For a refutation of von Rad's position and dating, see Golka, "Genesis 37–50," 164–65, and his sources cited there.

5. Note also the critique of von Rad by Crenshaw, "Method," 135–37, and the caution of Fox, "Wisdom in the Joseph Story," 30–36. Fox (38–40) suggests that the book of Daniel, especially chapters 2, 4, and 5, is a better parallel to the Joseph account.

6. Moberly, *Theology*, 235.

Genesis 37–50

50:19–20).[7] It is clear that much of Joseph's wisdom came from God, not Joseph's earthly learning per se.

Another central tenet of the wisdom tradition is sexual purity in the midst of temptation (Proverbs 5–6). When faced with the temptation to sin by having sexual relations with another man's wife—a foreigner at that— Joseph rebuffed the advances of Potiphar's wife. To be sure, these wisdom connections are important, but then again, the general teaching of *torah*, especially the general ANE law against adultery as reflected in the seventh commandment (Exod 20:14; see more below), seems just as appropriate of a place to look for such instruction. And even though von Rad argued that the Joseph account would have functioned well as instruction for young men being groomed for service in the royal court, many of the wise actions of Joseph would have been just as instructive for a general audience in Israel, none more so than Joseph's reliance on God in all facets of his life.

As History

Another important feature about these chapters is that they explain how Israel ended up in Egypt.[8] Therefore, they serve as a backdrop to the book of Exodus.[9] God's prophecy to Abraham in 15:13–16 had begun to come to fruition with the life and work of Joseph. If the sojourn in Egypt was 300 or more years, the history of how Israel became a nation and ended up in Egypt—ultimately in slavery—needed to be related. The Joseph account does this very thing.

In many ways, Joseph's story connects the exodus generation to the land of Canaan as well. This was the land of their forefathers and the land of their burial. In other words, it explained why those of the exodus generation and/or the exilic period were returning to a land they had never seen before (49:29–33; 50:24–25).

One could also argue that the Joseph account completed the "history" of the book of Genesis by bringing it full circle. In this regard, some have seen in the Joseph account a picture of the Eden narrative: like the Garden

---

7. Ibid., 239–40.

8. See Coats, *From Canaan to Egypt*, 54, 77, 92; Schmid, *Moses Story*, 50; and Redford, *Story of Joseph*, 27.

9. Fretheim, *Pentateuch*, 87; and Coats, *From Canaan to Egypt*, 54.

of Eden, Egypt became a place of protection, plenty, and rest from the famine plaguing the world.[10]

Why Israel had to stay in Egypt beyond the seven-year famine is not stated. As I have noted before, Jacob's time in Egypt may have been meant to protect him and his family so that they could become a great nation thus fulfilling the prophetic word of God that Abraham would have a progeny.[11] Perhaps YHWH was protecting them from comingling with the Canaanites and losing their identity, as seen with Judah's and Dinah's lives. The sojourn not only protected and isolated them from the Egyptians, who apparently detested shepherds (46:32–34), it also allowed them to become a great nation capable of occupying the promised land of Canaan (46:2–4).[12] However, once the pharaoh threatened to diminish the nation of Israel through infanticide (Exod 1:8–22), YHWH acted on behalf of his people to bring to fruition the prophetic words he had spoken to Abraham.

As Prophecy

In light of this prophetic bent, the Joseph account gives a glimpse into Israel's future struggles and realities.[13] The clearest picture of this is in chapter 49. This chapter serves as an overview for what the tribes would become in the future, that is, what they *had become* at the time of the exodus and wilderness wandering. For example, the cursing of Simeon caused the tribe to be scattered in Judah/Israel. The fulfillment of this prophetic word actually begins in the period of the wilderness wandering when Simeon in particular sinned with Baal of Peor.

Also, the entire period of testing with which Joseph tests his brothers to see if they had truly changed foreshadows the testing of Israel in the wilderness. Would they follow God because of a changed heart or were they merely doing what they thought was required while retaining a wrong motive? Although the brothers assumed Joseph was treating them kindly for the sake of their father (50:15), in reality he was acting out of the goodness of his heart, without malice; he was being a vessel for his God in order to save them (45:5–8; 50:20). In a similar vein, God had served as a means of saving his people both from certain death at the hands of pharaoh and

---

10. See Sigmon, "Between Eden and Egypt," 315–20.
11. Coats, *From Canaan to Egypt*, 91; and Clines, *Theme*, 29.
12. See similar comments by Greifenhagen, *Egypt*, 39–41.
13. See also Neusner, *Genesis and Judaism*, 1, 9, 171–88.

from the perils of the wilderness out of the goodness of who God was and in fulfillment of his promises (15:16).

Summary

It is clear that a number of instructional motifs can be drawn from the Joseph account. However, apart from these broader motifs a number of recurring themes reflect not only legislation laid down in the Mosaic Law, but also typological instruction found within the parallels between the life of Joseph and the nation of Israel. The election and special status of both was of paramount importance for the author.[14] Moreover, the actions of Joseph and his brothers demonstrate the pros and cons of breaking some of the specific laws recoded later in the Torah. This is particularly the case when one views the Joseph account through the lens of *torah* instruction found within the Ten Commandments.

Instruction on the Ten Commandments

Commandments 1–4

The first four commandments, which one could argue are the most important for Israel's existence, find no explicit references within the Joseph account. Nevertheless, what is the reader to make of Joseph's marriage to Asenath, the daughter of the priest of On (41:45)? Did Joseph worship or pay homage to the gods of Egypt?[15] These types of questions so troubled the rabbis that they reinterpreted the text to present Potiphar as a "chief" or "master" (*Tgs. Onq., Neof., Ps.-J.*) and Asenath as his daughter as opposed to her being the daughter of the priest of On (*Gen. Rab.* 89:2). Another tradition presents Asenath as the daughter of Dinah and Shechem thus allowing more Israelite "blood"—as opposed to Egyptian blood—to flow through Ephraim and Manasseh's veins (*Tg. Ps-J.; Pirqe R. El.* 36.272; 38.287–88).[16] While the biblical author is silent on these questions, interestingly, similar questions could be asked about the early life of Moses before he fled to Midian as well as his time with his father-in-law, the *priest* of Midian (Exod 2:16; 3:1; 18:1). Despite these concerns, the account of Joseph is clear in its

---

14. Kaminsky, "Election," 144–45.
15. See also Gunkel, *Genesis*, 421.
16. Mathews, *Genesis 11:27—50:26*, 764.

teaching that Joseph honored and served the God of his fathers and was blessed for it. Even though the first four commandments find little to no direct references in the Joseph account, that is not the case when it comes to commandments 5–10.

Commandment 5

One of the most lucid pictures of what happens when one fails to honor his/her father or mother plays out in the lives of Jacob's sons. While it is true that Jacob's favoritism towards Joseph had created the environment that would later give rise to his family's dysfunction (37:3–4),[17] no amount of family turmoil could condone Joseph's brothers' treatment of their father. Not only had they lied to their father—the breaking of another commandment—but they did so with no remorse for their father's emotional pain and turmoil (37:34–35). As I will demonstrate below, actions such as these do not go unpunished. The failure to honor one's parents had far-reaching consequences for Joseph's brothers especially for Judah. Whereas Judah had been a key part of depriving Jacob of his son Joseph, in chapter 38 we find out that he in turn lost two sons (38:7–10). Judah's marriage to a Canaanite (38:1–2)—another form of dishonoring his parents (24:3, 37; 28:1–8)—had set the stage for the loss of these two sons.[18]

Despite the deplorable actions of Jacob's sons during his life, in his death they redeemed themselves—to a degree—by honoring the final wishes of their father to bury him in Canaan (49:29–33; 50:12–13). Honoring the deceased is not a phenomenon unique to the ancient Israelites, but it did carry with it more importance than what most people today would consider appropriate. Not only was the mourning period for Jacob extensive (over seventy-seven days; 50:3, 10), Joseph and his brothers also travelled a great distance to fulfill their father's dying wish of being buried with his forefathers.[19]

In ancient societies, being gathered to one's fathers (25:8; 49:29; Judg 2:10; 2 Kgs 22:20; 2 Chr 34:28) was more than a simple burial, it had spiritual import. People believed that proper burial with one's ancestors allowed

---

17. See Kaminsky, "Election," 139.

18. Carmichael, *Women, Law, and the Genesis Traditions*, 57–58; and Carmichael, *Origins of Biblical Law*, 235.

19. Greifenhagen (*Egypt*, 43–44) notes that the circuitous route that Jacob's body takes foreshadows the exodus event.

for a connection between the living and the dead.[20] As such, the worst curse that could happen to a person in death was to be left unburied to become food for the animals and birds (cf. Lev 26:30; Deut 28:26; 1 Sam 17:44; 2 Sam 21:10; Jer 8:1–3; 15:3; 34:20; Ezek 6:5–7; 29:5; 32:4; 33:27; 39:4, 17–20). Thus, the extensive preparations and great journey of Jacob's sons had a redemptive quality to it in light of their dishonoring actions earlier in life.

Commandment 6

The sixth commandment dealing with murder was narrowly averted when Joseph was captured by his brothers. This was due in part to Rueben's quick actions and Judah's greed to make some money by selling Joseph. Nevertheless, although they did not kill their brother (Exod 21:12, 14), an action punishable by death, they did, nonetheless, commit another capital offense in their kidnapping and sale of their brother to the Ishmaelites (Exod 21:16; Deut 24:7).[21] Here we see how a canonically later text/law sheds light on the Genesis narrative and vice versa. Circumstances like that of Joseph and his brothers in chapter 37 may in fact help explain why kidnapping was a capital offense. There is no question that they knew that they were in the wrong and deserved punishment (42:21–22; 44:16). However, Joseph's refusal to take revenge on his brothers envisions the teaching that vengeance belongs to God (Lev 19:18; Deut 32:35; cf. Ps 94:1; Rom 12:19; Heb 10:30).[22]

Commandment 7

Case-law examples of the commandment not to commit adultery appear in the parallel texts of chapters 38 and 39. Many scholars have seen the incongruity of chapter 38 vis-à-vis the Joseph narrative and have posited that it was added as a means of showing the preeminence of the tribe of Judah.[23] Similarly, a number of historical critics, source theorists in par-

---

20. See the work of Peterson, *Ezekiel in Context*, 232–47; Fensham, "Curse of the Dry Bones," 59–60; Gevirtz, "Curse Motifs," 171–90, esp. 171–72; Richardson, "Death and Dismemberment," 200; Brichto, "Kin, Cult, Land, and Afterlife," 1–54, esp. 8–11, 48; Stavrakopoulou, "Ezekiel's Use and Abuse of Corpses," 1–16 esp. 3; Chesson, "Remembering and Forgetting," 109–39, esp. 120–23; and Gnoli and Vernant eds., *La mort, les morts dans les sociétés anciennes* (1982).

21. Carmichael, *Origins of Biblical Law*, 109–12.

22. Jacobs, "Conceptual Dynamics," 316.

23. Speiser, *Genesis*, 300; and Noth, *Pentateuchal Traditions*, 42.

Genesis as Torah

ticular, have struggled with the apparent intrusion of the account of Judah and Tamar into the Joseph story.[24] However, despite the chronological tensions[25] it fits perfectly with *torah* teaching within this portion of Genesis.[26] These two chapters appear to be juxtaposed for the purpose of teaching two key points. The first is retribution for deception (*Gen. Rab.* 84:11–12; 85:9, 11; 87:6). Judah received punishment from God for his actions against his younger brother Joseph. Where he deprived Jacob of his beloved son, Judah was deprived of his two oldest sons. The second area of instruction deals with proper sexual ethics and morals;[27] it is these latter two points that I wish to explore here, especially since the instruction on sexual ethics intersects with the seventh commandment.

To begin, Carmichael sees within Joseph's plans to prepare for the coming famine reflections of the law of tithing (Gen 41:34; Deut 14:22–29).[28] Tithing would be used throughout Israel's history to care for the priests, the poor, and the needy. This is certainly morally commendable. On the other hand, Aaron Wildavsky has argued that the moral instruction for Israel in both accounts is that sinful actions should never be used to further God's plan. Judah sinned when he refused to fulfill the levirate laws in order to save his son[29] and Joseph sinned when he took the land of the Egyptians and enslaved them in order to "save" them—actions that should never happen in Israel.[30] Similarly, some scholars have noted that the Jo-

---

24. On this point see the discussion of Golka, "Genesis 37–50," 153–77; and Speiser, *Genesis*, 299. Note also the assessment of Schmidt, *Literarische Studien zur Josephsgeschichte*, 127; Longacre, *Joseph*, 26; and Westermann, *Genesis 37–50*, 49–50. Typical of the assumptions of higher critics, Dietrich ("Joseph," 35–36) does not even list chapters 38 and 49 as being part of the Joseph cycle. This is a similar approach of Galling, "Joseph," 859; and Vawter, *On Genesis*, 390.

25. See Redford, *Joseph*, 17–18. Redford points out that because Jubilees inserts chapter 38 between 42 and 43 it shows that chapter 38 had no set position in the text tradition. However, what Redford fails to note is the fact that Jubilees consistently has a different order for the chapters of the Jacob and Joseph accounts.

26. On the importance of the role of chapter 38 in the larger narrative, see Kaminsky, "Election," 140–41; Alter, *Biblical Narrative*, 1–12; and Levenson, *Death and Resurrection*, 157–64. Noble ("Esau, Tamar, and Joseph," 234–43) connects it to both the Joseph and Jacob-Esau accounts. Wright ("Genesis 38," 523–29) argues for the unity of the texts based upon ancient mythological connections, a thesis that is tenuous at best.

27. So, too, Kaminsky, "Election," 141; and Wildavsky, "Survival," 41. For a sociological approach, see also Niditch, "The Wronged Woman," 143–49.

28. Carmichael, *Law and Narrative*, 74–78.

29. See also Redford, *Story of Joseph*, 16.

30. So Wildavsky, "Survival," 37–48.

seph account served as a polemic against high taxation under the kings,[31] especially as early as the period of Solomon (47:14–26; 1 Kgs 12:4). While I can agree that Judah's actions in chapter 38 were sinful, the text never gives a negative assessment of Joseph's actions. On the contrary, the author notes that God was with Joseph to preserve life, even making him a "father" to pharaoh (45:5–8). It seems unlikely that if Joseph's actions were sinful that God would make him a model for pharaoh to follow. Although these scholarly assessments of Joseph and Judah's life may be insightful, I feel that the moral teaching is more pronounced in the overt sexual instruction in both of these chapters (i.e., chs. 38 and 39).

In chapter 38, the text records that after his wife died (38:12) Judah went out and had sexual relations with a prostitute, who was none other than Tamar his daughter-in-law. While the ancients may have believed that employing the services of prostitutes was permissible,[32] in God's eyes it was an obvious violation of the spirit of the seventh commandment and the Levitical law (Lev 19:29). In essence, the seventh commandment taught sexual purity, especially within marriage. Conversely, Joseph, when confronted with committing adultery with Potiphar's wife in chapter 39 (cf. Exod 20:13), refused because of his fear of the Lord (39:9).[33] Slaves may have been the property of their owners, even for sexual purposes, but Joseph's devotion to God outweighed the overtures of his master's wife. In this vein, Sailhamer notes that in an ironic twist, whereas the women of the patriarchs were taken by pharaoh and Abimelech, now a "patriarch" was set upon by a woman/wife of a foreign leader.[34] The difference was that Joseph remained faithful to God and did not make the situation worse for the foreigner. And even though God protected him (39:21–23), Joseph bore the brunt of rebuffing the sexual advances of Potiphar's wife by suffering the injustice of being thrown in prison.

A couple of key pedagogical factors arise from the events of chapters 38 and 39. First, Judah, who was supposed to be a leader in his family, paid the price for refusing to fulfill the laws of the levirate when he withheld

---

31. Coats, "Joseph Story," 286, 293; and Crenshaw, "Method in Determining Wisdom," 137.

32. See Niditch, "The Wronged Woman," 147.

33. So, too, Kaiser, *Old Testament Ethics*, 82. See also comments by Greenberg, "Reflections," 2. And contra Coats (*From Canaan to Egypt*, 89), who argues that Joseph's actions reflected his respect for his master, as opposed to an act rooted in "theological moralism."

34. Sailhamer, *Pentateuch*, 211.

his son Shelah from Tamar. Second, even with the full spiritual support of his entire family while living in Canaan, Judah chose to break the natural moral commands of God.[35] When one views the life of Joseph as depicted in chapter 39 an opposite picture emerges. First, Joseph, the eleventh son of Jacob, became a leader in his family *because* he honored God and followed God's commands. While some have suggested that Judah's actions at the end of chapter 38 reflect the heart of a changed man ready for leadership as seen later in 44:14–34,[36] in reality, apart from the prophecy of Jacob in 49.8–10, Judah still fell far short of the ideal set by Joseph. Second, even though Joseph was a slave in a foreign land with no family and spiritual support, he still honored his God and was blessed for it (cf. Daniel 1–3). Furthermore, the keeping of God's sexual laws reflects the proper way to respond to the presence of the Spirit of God in an individual's life. The author makes it clear that the Spirit's presence with Joseph was evident especially to the pharaoh (cf. Gen 41:38; Deut 30:6–10).[37]

Instructionally, the message is clear: in the midst of exile in a foreign land, whether Egypt or Babylon, God honors those who honor his Law. In some cases, even those who remain in the land of promise may not receive God's blessings if they do not keep the Law (Ezek 33:24–29). Interestingly, when Israel entered Canaan it was a man from Judah, Achan, who suffered loss due to a failure to keep God's commands; whereas a Canaanite, Rahab, found favor in God's eyes (Josh 6:23–25; 7:1, 16–26; James 2:25; Heb 11:31). Of course the parallels between Tamar, who acted like a prostitute, and Rahab, a real one, are self-evident. Both women ended up being blessed by God even to the point of being a part of the direct lineage of Messiah (Matt 1:2, 5).[38]

Commandments 9 and 10

Apart from Potiphar's wife bearing false witness against Joseph (39:17),[39] and Joseph's accusations against his brothers (42:9–16),[40] an example of the

---

35. Although 38:1 says that Judah left his brothers, he still would have been able to have contact with them if he desired as is evident by the end of the Joseph account.
36. Golka, "Genesis 37–50," 162.
37. Sailhamer, *Pentateuch*, 211.
38. Carson, *Matthew*, 65.
39. Kaiser, *Old Testament Ethics*, 82.
40. Jacobs, "Conceptual Dynamics," 324.

commandment not to bear false witness appears in the opening chapter of the Joseph account. When faced with covering up their sale of Joseph to the Ishmaelites/Midianites, all his brothers swore to the fact that a wild beast had killed Joseph (37:31–32). In this situation, Jacob's sons broke the ninth commandment, showed their contempt for Jacob (cf. 37:31–35; Exod 21:17),[41] and gave a false report (cf. 37:18–20; Exod 23:1).[42] It would not be until later that they would be forced to own up to their deception (44:16). Even though Reuben had tried to rescue Joseph from the hand of his brothers, he ended up being swept up in the deception thus breaking the law of Exod 23:2, which commands against following the multitude (i.e., his brothers) in an effort to pervert justice. Finally, Joseph's brothers' actions were the result of their covetousness towards their younger brother (37:4, 8, 18–20), a breach of the tenth commandment.

The events of the Joseph account show that the breaking of the commandments of God does not just affect the perpetrators; it brings with it a lifetime of heartache for everyone involved, especially the innocent. This was not only the case for Joseph, but Tamar, an innocent widow, who was pulled into the realm of deception because of Judah's failure to fulfill the laws of the levirate.

Levirate Laws

Next to the book of Ruth, which presents a levirate-like marriage, the story of Judah and his two sons' interactions with Tamar gives one of the clearest depictions of what levirate marriage was supposed to look like and what happens to those who reject this command found in Deut 25:5–10.[43] In other words, here is an actual example of case law showing the repercussions of breaking God's Law.[44] The instructional value of the Judah and Tamar account is bolstered by the fact that later rabbis actually made sure it was read in the synagogue (m. *Meg.* 4:10). This was just the opposite of the position which they took on the text that records the sin of Reuben with Bilhah.

---

41. Carmichael, *Origins of Biblical Law*, 112–13.
42. Ibid., 184–85.
43. Bruckner, *Implied Law*, 15; Carmichael, *Women, Law, and the Genesis Traditions*, 66–68; Allis, *God Spake*, 47; and Polin, "Jewish Law," 39.
44. Polin (ibid., 39) suggests that Levirate marriage also appears in 36:2: he argues that Esau's wife's name Oholibamah means "the tent of the levirate wife."

Genesis as Torah

According to Deut 25:9, the man who refused to perform the levirate requirements was to be disgraced by the spurned woman. She was to remove her brother-in-law's sandal from his *foot* and *spit* in his face. Some have seen sexual nuances/euphemisms in these actions, that is, in the "spitting" and the uncovering of the "foot."[45] In a tribal setting, the preservation of a deceased loved one's lineage was of vital importance (see Num 27:1–11; 36:1–13). So important was this act, that God took offence when someone refused to perform their duty. Onan died before the Lord because of his actions and Judah's refusal to honor his word by having his youngest son Shelah raise up a child for his deceased brother forced Tamar into a no-win situation.

In this vein, Judah's withholding of Shelah from Tamar led to further violation of key Mosaic laws. First, Judah in essence forced his "daughter" to play the role of a sacred prostitute (Deut 23:17). Second, Judah broke the command of not having sex with one's daughter-in-law (Lev 18:15), although some have posited that the law of the levirate may have in fact allowed for the overriding of this law.[46] While the latter act was done in ignorance—because Tamar was disguised—the former was not. Here the proverbial domino effect is put on display showing the importance of obedience to the Law. Of course this is abundantly clear when one considers the prohibitions of marrying Canaanites (see more below). The text begins by noting that Judah had married outside of his family. By noting this, the author makes a clear case that Judah's marital choice had started the downward spiral. Finally, procreation, which was established by God in Genesis 1, appears to be the driving force behind the levirate law.[47] The need for Judah's line to continue was of vital importance not only to Judah but to God himself. God had promised that Abraham would become a great nation. It is possible that this was one of the main reasons God killed Onan in the first place. God's creation laws were not to be abrogated, a similar picture discussed in relation to Genesis 19.

Teaching on Marriage

Chapter 38 also offers instruction on acceptable marriage practices for the Israelites. Early on, Jewish sages repudiated the actions of Judah in marrying

---

45. Carmichael, *Women, Law, and the Genesis Traditions*, 68–70.
46. See Niditch, "The Wronged Woman," 148.
47. Brett, *Genesis*, 113–14.

a Canaanite woman (see *Gen. Rab.* 85:1). One of the primary Torah laws for Israel was for them not to marry Canaanites (Exod 34:15–16; Deut 7:3). As I have noted in previous chapters, this is a recurring motif in Genesis. Here Judah's marriage to a Canaanite teaches the reader about what types of curses can come upon an immediate family when this marriage law is ignored.

Beyond this clearly stated law, Carmichael suggests that the Levitical and Deuteronomic laws of mixing seed and cross breeding (Lev 19:19; Deut 22:9) may lie, in a figurative sense, behind the mixing of Judah's sons with a Canaanite woman, Tamar.[48] While this is possible, there is nothing explicitly in the text telling the reader that Tamar was Canaanite. However, we do know that Judah's wife was Canaanite and it is possible that she may have influenced the wicked behavior of her two oldest sons, Er and Onan, whom the Lord killed (38:7, 10). Furthermore, Judah's blaming of Tamar (implicit) for the death of his two evil sons instructs Israel that they should not blame others for their own sin (cf. 3:12–13). Judah's circumstances were the result of his failure to obey the basic marriage law implicit throughout the book of Genesis and explicit in the Mosaic Law.[49] Again, according to the instruction in the Joseph narrative it was not Judah, but Joseph who was the best exemplar for Israel to emulate. It should therefore not be surprising that one can find numerous parallels between the life of Joseph and that of Israel.

Joseph as a Type of Israel

It goes without saying that Joseph's trek to Egypt, Potiphar's mistreatment of him, and Joseph's rise to prominence in the sight of pharaoh has distinct parallels with the experiences of Israel while they were in Egypt (and to a degree while they were in the Babylonian exile).[50] We also can see how the

---

48. Carmichael, *Law and Narrative*, 185–93; and Carmichael, *Law, Legend, and Incest*, 92–93. See also his connections between Judah and Tamar and Deut 22:11 (Carmichael, *Law and Narrative*, 197–205). Carmichael (*Law, Legend, and Incest*, 94–100) draws a similar parallel between the laws against mixing seed and Joseph's marriage to an Egyptian woman.

49. When speaking of the didactic features of the Joseph account, Humphreys (*Joseph and His Family*, 157) correctly notes that sometimes "the best instruction is the least obvious."

50. Briggs and Lohr, *Theological Introduction*, 20. See also comments by Coats, *From Canaan to Egypt*, 92.

sovereign plan of God to redeem Joseph parallels God's sovereign plan to redeem Israel in Egypt (Gen 50:20; Jer 29:11).[51] Moreover, Jacob's adoption of Joseph's two sons reflects the adoption of Israel by God (Exod 4:22; cf. Deut 32:10–20; Isa 1:2; 66:13; Jer 31:8; Ezek 16:6).[52] What is more, in the same way Joseph went into Egypt for the divine purpose of saving his family and the whole region, so, too, Israel went into Egypt and were meant to be, in a sense, "saviors" of the world as the people of God. They were supposed to be a light to the nations (12:3; Exod 19:4–6; Isa 49:6).

For an audience in the implied setting of the exodus period, the account of Joseph made sense; Joseph was in prison on no account of his own yet he remained faithful in a foreign land. Indeed, Joseph, a Hebrew (although "Egyptianized"; cf. Jeremiah 29), could flourish in Egypt without compromising his faith in his God.[53] Similarly, the enslavement of Israel at the hand of pharaoh was not of their own doing either; yet they could learn from Joseph's life that remaining faithful to God would bring blessings. And despite whatever Israel's current situation was, the life of Joseph proved that God is always faithful to his promises.[54]

Having noted these obvious parallels between Joseph and Israel, two further didactic points lay just below the surface of the narrative. First, the Joseph account teaches that God deals with pride in whomever it is found (cf. Saul—1 Sam 15:7, Uzziah—2 Chr 26:16–20, Nebuchadnezzar—Dan 4:29–37 etc.). Joseph, the favored child of Jacob and favored by God, still needed to go through a period of growth and spiritual maturity in order to overcome his apparent prideful attitude. As a youth he flaunted his position in the family and his God-given dreams (37:2, 5–11). It was not until he found himself humbled and in a pit/prison, twice (37:20–24; 39:20),[55] that he finally began to focus more on the role of God in his life as the one who gave him insight, elevated him, and protected him (40:8; 41:16).[56] Nevertheless, it is clear that while God protected Joseph God did not necessarily

---

51. Hamilton, *Pentateuch*, 126; and Klein et al., *Biblical Interpretation*, 431.

52. Hepner, *Legal Friction*, 638–40, 644–45.

53. Greifenhagen, *Egypt*, 35–36.

54. Sailhamer, *Pentateuch*, 211.

55. Rashi (commentary on 39:6), as did other Jewish commentators, suggests that Joseph curled his hair and reveled in his good looks. This is what attracted the attention of Potiphar's wife.

56. Kaminsky, "Election," 139–40.

Genesis 37–50

keep him from hardships that were intended for his spiritual growth.[57] Israel needed to learn the same lesson both early in their existence, and as time went on. The wilderness period helped shape them so that they would learn to trust in God for their future and their success in conquering the land. They could not take the land without God (Num 14:40–45), and they could not return to Egypt (Num 14:3–4; Deut 17:16).

Second, and closely related to the first didactic point, is the fact that even though Joseph was called for a special purpose he had to learn what that divine calling actually looked like. Joseph only attained this calling after a period of testing. For Israel, their calling would be no less marked by periods of testing and tribulations to make them into the nation God had intended them to be. For all intents and purposes, Israel, as they waited on the banks of the Jordan prior to entering Canaan, had reached at least a degree of readiness to embark on their calling to fulfill the plans of God, namely, the conquest of the Promised Land and the fulfillment of the land promise to Abraham (Gen 12:1; 15:16).

In light of these facts, it is clear that spiritually mature people of God was what YHWH expected from Israel. For those who refused to learn from the instructions of Moses, especially those of a later period, one of the curses of the law was exile (Lev 26:33; Deut 4:27; 28:63–67); however, one of the blessings of keeping the commands of God, no matter where Israel lived, was the fact that God would bless the work of Israel's hand (Deut 30:9). God's blessing upon Joseph is a clear reflection of this promise: God blessed everything that Joseph set his hand to do (Gen 39:3, 23; 41:38). Despite his circumstances he put God first and was blessed for it. Instructionally, Joseph's life presented a clear picture of how Israel should have lived in exile, or in Canaan even when their God appeared silent and oblivious to their cries for help.

The Proper Response to a "Silent" God

Another key factor, as many scholars have noted, is the absence of any direct interactions between God and Joseph as is common in the other patriarchal accounts.[58] Yet this should not be construed as though God's blessings were not upon Joseph in a similar fashion as his forefathers. There may be a very logical reason for the "silence" of God in the Joseph account. Joseph's life in

---

57. Jacobs, "Conceptual Dynamics," 328.
58. Von Rad, "The Story of Joseph," 28.

many ways becomes instructional for the nation on how to live when God does not speak directly to them. Joseph is a picture of trust knowing that God had called him for a purpose—through two separate dreams—to save his family from certain death (45:5; 50:20). In the midst of hardships and a silent God (Exod 32:1, 23; cf. 1 Sam 3:1),[59] Joseph's life became a picture of what true trust and reliance on God looked like. This is displayed in a number of ways. God provided for Joseph and God protected him from those who sought to do him harm. Even though he suffered unjustly, God vindicated him in the end. Similarly, Israel had suffered unjustly at the hands of the Egyptians, but in the end was elevated and released from their "prison."

This message would be particularly poignant for the wilderness generation. When faced with the need to trust in God, even when he was silent, Israel had failed miserably. Particularly relevant is the case of Moses' time on the mountain prior to the Golden Calf incident. After a period of only forty days Israel lost faith and hope in Moses and God. For Joseph it was a period of years, yet he remained faithful. Of course it is also true that this message would resonate with a number of periods within Israel's history. The diminished direct role played by God in the account of Joseph also would speak to the time immediately following the deaths of Moses and Joshua: until the time of Samuel, the word of the Lord was rare in Israel (1 Sam 3:1). Despite the silence, there can be no question that God was with Joseph as he was with Israel even though the direct revelation of God's will was only implicit. For Joseph this resulted in his complete trust in God, something Israel would have done well to abide by and learn from. Interestingly, whereas God was silent with Joseph, God revealed himself directly to Moses.

Joseph and Moses

Some scholars have also noted how the account of Joseph has parallels with the life of Moses.[60] For example, Moses was forced from his home due to a self-inflicted fault and had to live in Midian for an extended period of time. Similarly, Joseph was forced from his home by a somewhat self-inflicted fault (he was prideful of his dreams and flaunted them before his jealous

---

59. On the progression of God's interaction with humanity in Genesis and Exodus, see Schmid, *Moses Story*, 90–91.

60. Hepner, *Legal Friction*, 587–89. This list comes predominantly from Hepner. For just the opposite position, see Wildavsky, "Survival," 38, 48.

brothers) and was forced to live in Egypt. Both saved their people from certain death and hardships and both married the daughter of a priest (41:45; Exodus 2). As I have noted throughout the preceding chapters, whoever was writing these accounts intentionally related certain facts for the purpose of drawing these connections with Moses. Some may see in these connections further evidence of Mosaic material and/or authorship.

Theological Instruction on the Nature of God

While the overt workings of God are indeed subdued in the Joseph account,[61] it is clear that one of the most instructive facts learned about Israel's God in this block is that of God's providence. Joel Kaminsky highlights this point well.[62] For example, he notes that the mysterious man who met Joseph in the field while he was searching for his brothers certainly smacks of God's oversight (37:15–17). Furthermore, God's giving of dreams (in pairs) and Joseph's perfectly timed presence to interpret the dreams of the cupbearer, baker, and pharaoh shows God's design and timing. In this vein, the timing of many of the events in Joseph's life in Egypt leading up to the famine clearly reveals that God was providentially directing the paths of his people. He was to be trusted!

The account also teaches that God is sovereign and does not need the help of others to bring about his purposes. Walter Brueggemann notes this point well: "in the face of arrogant and strident ingenuity, the Eternal Spirit has his own purpose. And even if delayed, that purpose will not be defeated."[63] Israel may have had their plans about their future and what their role would be vis-à-vis their God but God would have the final say in the matter, be that through periods of wilderness wandering, exile, or prosperity, for as Ezekiel records, "As I live declares the Lord GOD, with a strong hand and an outstretched arm and with wrath poured out I will be king over you" (Ezek 20:33).

---

61. Brueggemann, *Genesis*, 289, 348; and Miscall, "Jacob and Joseph Story," 33.

62. Kaminsky, "Election," 145–47. My discussion on God's providence is a summary of Kaminsky's findings.

63. Brueggemann, *Genesis*, 347. See also Miscall, "Jacob and Joseph Story," 39.

Genesis as Torah
Some Final Thoughts

With a text as rich in intrigue and instruction as the Joseph narrative it is hard to draw to a close one's observations on the didactic aspects of the account. Nevertheless, before concluding this chapter it seems appropriate to examine two final instructive features of this narrative. The first deals with the need for unity within the family/tribal structure of Israel and the second focuses on the role of covenant.

A Call for Unity and Brotherly Love

A dominant theme of the Joseph account is the unfortunate fallout between Jacob's sons due to family dysfunction and disunity. From this vantage point, the Joseph account offers instruction on the need for brotherly love while warning of the dangers of inter-tribal/internecine strife, a reality that would later threaten the existence of not only the Transjordan tribes (Josh 22:9–34) but also the tribe of Benjamin (Judges 19–21), the very tribe that had issued from the son whom the rest of the brothers went to great lengths to protect in the Joseph account.

Next, as part of maintaining unity within the nation of Israel, the Joseph account serves to explain why Ephraim and Manasseh received an inheritance in the nation of Canaan/Israel.[64] Despite the laws governing the inheritance rights of the firstborn (Deut 21:15–17; cf. 1 Chr 5:1), Jacob's adoption of Joseph's two sons proves that Joseph had in fact received the double portion as the oldest son of his beloved Rachel. As such, the rest of Jacob's sons needed to accept the decision of their father to allow the two sons of Joseph to serve as Joseph's replacement in the inheritance rights in Canaan. Within the context of Joseph's life's story the reader is alerted to the fact that some of the reason for this double blessing upon Joseph stemmed from the fact that he had feared God and was in turn blessed by God, something lacking in the lives of Reuben, Simeon, Levi, and Judah.

Instruction on Covenant

It is also important to note that Joseph's brothers, the forefathers of the tribes of Israel, appear to have entered into a covenant together—although not with God—when they sold Joseph into slavery. The eating of a meal

---

64. See also comments by Syrén, *Forsaken First-Born*, 139; and Redford, *Story of Joseph*, 23.

Genesis 37–50

immediately after plotting to kill/sell Joseph was an ordinary way of sealing a covenant in the ancient world (37:25; cf. 31:54; Exod 24:11; Mark 14:22–25; Matt 26:26–28; Rev 19:9). As such, throughout the Joseph narrative the brothers often appear represented in collective terms as "Joseph's brothers" or "Jacob's sons" (e.g., 37:12, 17, 18, 31; 42:3, 6–17, 18, 21, 30–32; 43:18–22; 44:7–9; 50:15–18, 20, 24).[65] Moreover, in their guilt they are seen in a collective sense regardless of what role each played (44:16). Even Reuben, who had tried to help Joseph, was implicated (37:21–22, 29–30). The idea of collective guilt and/or blessing, a concept prevalent in the covenanted community of Israel, would have resonated with Israel in any period. This account would have aided in their understanding of why even the innocent sometimes suffered with the wicked (see Joshua 7). This is nowhere more applicable than in the wilderness period and in the time of the exile to Babylon.

Conclusion

The Joseph account certainly boasts some of the most important and memorable teaching on the dangers of family dysfunction in the entire book of Genesis. Furthermore, the instruction for the nation on how to behave and remain spiritually upright in the midst of exile finds no more fertile soil than in the life and example of Joseph. The instruction on sexual ethics and the importance of procreation (as seen in the instruction on levirate marriage) serve to highlight recurrent motifs within the book. Apart from these major motifs, I also noted a number of miscellaneous laws found within the account of Joseph that may not necessarily play a central role but are nonetheless very much representative of later Torah legislation. Indeed, a number of other miscellaneous laws could have been proposed.[66] What is clear within this final block of material is the importance of spiritual maturity evidenced in Joseph's unfaltering trust in God. For those of any generation facing unforeseen hardships, the Joseph narrative would have offered not only instruction, but a glimmer of hope that YHWH was still in control and would indeed have the final say as long as Israel remained faithful to the Sinai covenant.

---

65. On the collective language of the text, see Jacobs, "Conceptual Dynamics," 318.

66. For example, Carmichael (*Origins of Biblical Law*, 201–3) notes that chapters 42–44 have affinity with laws against oppressing the sojourner (Exod 23:9).

8

Conclusions

As I have worked through the book of Genesis my hope for the reader is that it has become clear that the stories preserved here served more than the simple function of giving a prehistory of the nation of Israel. Time and again I have shown that beyond the general instruction present in most chapters, a number of specific texts could easily reflect case law, which in turn helped explain later legislation. In other words, the Israelites could learn what a specific law looked like in practice as they learned the prehistory of the patriarchs along with the stories of the creation and flood. At other junctures I highlighted specific laws (e.g., food laws, tithing, sexual laws). These laws are easily discerned because they are plainly stated in the text. I also noted that a number of the accounts, especially those related to Genesis 1–11, served a polemical purpose against Mesopotamian, and more frequently, Egyptian mythological and religious thought processes (e.g., who was the creator, the origin of evil, the purpose of humanity vis-à-vis God, the reason for the flood etc.). No matter from what period these accounts are derived, instruction would have been gained on a variety of legal and theological levels.

In this regard, of central importance for the nation was the legal corpus known as the Decalogue. A number of the Genesis narratives reflect central teaching and truths directly related to the heart and soul of the Law as revealed in the Ten Commandments. Again, the narrative portions of Genesis served as an effective means of teaching Israel what the breaking of these ten vital laws actually looked like in practice. While those who

Conclusions

lived prior to the giving of the Ten Commandments may have not appreciated the full gravity of breaking these laws, a number of the Ten Commandments would have been understood based upon God's revelation in creation (e.g., monotheism, adultery, murder). What is more, according to Genesis, every nation could trace their roots back to Noah and his sons. As such, the Noahic covenant and the stipulations delivered by God once Noah departed from the ark would have been disseminated throughout the then-known world. It is for this reason that most ancient cultures had basic regulations and prohibitions very similar to those found within Jewish law (e.g., legislation against adultery, murder, stealing, etc.). Indeed, Fretheim has drawn a similar conclusion. He notes,

> The parallels to many Israelite laws in the cultures surrounding Israel must be placed within this [i.e., the context of Genesis] theological context. Few of the social laws are in fact uniquely Israelite, and there are many parallels to various ritual activities (e.g., sacrifices); what is unique is the particular configuration of material collected here and its being related in specific ways to Yahweh. But the existence of much of this legal material in the surrounding cultures is testimony to God's work as creator among these peoples. One result of this divine activity is the development of law for the ordering and preservation of human life, and this is prior to and independent of God's redemptive work. God uses such laws for the benefit of life, quite apart from both redemptive activity and the world's knowledge of the origins of the laws. This is further evidence for the fact that the law does not grow out of redemption but is brought into the light of day for Israel as the law of God for the sake of creation. It is now made clear to the redeemed people what their responsibilities are in God's reclaimed world. The law is given to be of service in the ongoing divine task of the reclamation of creation. In the obedience of the law, Israel in effect becomes a created co-reclaimer of God's intentions for the creation.[1]

Of course the natural conclusion is that if the nations understood the basic laws of creation through God's self-revelation within that creation, how much more was Israel responsible before their God seeing how they actually were given, in written and/or oral form, the very words and laws of God? Israel experienced the revelation of God's laws for the purpose of demonstrating to the nations what following the creator of the universe actually looked like. One can see this very reality in the words of pharaoh

---

1. Fretheim, "Reclamation," 365.

when speaking of Joseph: "Can we find a man like this, in whom is a divine spirit?" (41:38 NASB).

Yet, these laws were not only written in pedantic and laconic form with which Israel was unable to relate or recall. On the contrary, as we have already seen, many were related through narrative for the purpose of relatability and memorability. This conclusion is reinforced by God's declaration to Moses to tell the Israelites to speak of these laws regularly to their children (Deut 4:9–10; 6:7; 11:19). While some of the more pithy laws could have been written, literally, on one's doorposts (Deut 6:9; 11:20), the narratives of Genesis allowed fathers, mothers, and grandparents to teach their children as they communed together throughout the day, whether in the fields, in their homes, or walking along the road. Children and people of any age could relate to a good story told with the purpose of instructing them on the morals of the Mosaic Law.

The narratives of Genesis thus became more than a good story for entertaining people. As I noted in my introduction, these accounts are memorable even for a non-oral society like we live in today. One can easily ponder the stories of Genesis over and over again and draw more value from them each time they are told or mentally rehearsed. The average Israelite may not have drawn every piece of legal nuance and meaning from a narrative account the first time they read it, but after a dozen or more times of hearing or reading the narrative I am sure they would have begun to see the many layers of legal meaning within their texts. This conclusion is supported by the numerous rabbinic citations—a fraction of which I have given—that I noted throughout this work. The more familiar the Jewish people became with their Torah the more connections they made.

Now to be sure, the average person may not have drawn every connection that the rabbis did in their midrashic approach, but they certainly would have gained an appreciation for the heart of the Law, and more importantly, for the nature of their God. YHWH was not just another ANE deity to be feared when one chose to do so: YHWH was the God of all creation who was loving, just, kind, relational, longsuffering, and who enacted judgment when needed. From this vantage point, by learning the narratives of Genesis, Israel learned how to please their God for indeed, to love God is to keep his commandments! For as God himself declared through his servant Moses,

> "See, I have set before you today life and prosperity, and death and adversity; in that I command you today to love the LORD your

Conclusions

God, to walk in His ways and to keep His commandments and His statutes and His judgments, that you may live and multiply, and that the LORD your God may bless you in the land where you are entering to possess it." (Deut 30:15–16 NASB; cf. 1 John 5:2–3).

Bibliography

Albertz, Rainer. *A History of Israelite Religion in the Old Testament Period*. Vol. 1, *From the Beginnings to the End of the Monarchy*. Translated by John Bowden. OTL. Louisville: Westminster John Knox, 1994.
Alexander, T. Desmond. *From Paradise to the Promised Land: An Introduction to the Pentateuch*. Grand Rapids: Baker, 2012.
Allis, Oswald T. *God Spake by Moses: An Exposition of the Pentateuch*. Nutley, NJ: Presbyterian & Reformed Publishing, 1958.
Alt, Albrecht. *Der Gott der Väter*. Beiträge zur Wissenschaft vom Alten und Neuen Testament 48. Stuttgart: Kohlhammer, 1929.
———. *Essays on Old Testament History and Religion*. Translated by R. A. Wilson. Oxford: Blackwell, 1966.
Alter, Robert. *The Art of Biblical Narrative*. Rev. ed. New York: Basic Books, 2011.
Amit, Yairah. *Hidden Polemics in Biblical Narrative*. Translated by Jonathan Chipman. BibIntSer 25. Leiden: Brill, 2000.
Arnold, Bill T. *Genesis*. New York: Cambridge University Press, 2009.
Assmann, Jan. "State and Religion in the New Kingdom." In *Religion and Philosophy in Ancient Egypt*, edited by W. K. Simpson, 55–88. YES 3. New Haven: Yale Egyptological Seminar, 1989.
Balentine, Samuel E. *The Hidden God: The Hiding of the Face of God in the Old Testament*. Oxford: Oxford University Press, 1983.
Bartlett, John R. "The Brotherhood of Edom." *JSOT* 4 (1977) 2–27.
Beale, G. K. *The Temple and the Church's Mission: A Biblical Theology of the Dwelling Place of God*. Downers Grove, IL: InterVarsity, 2004.
Beyerlin, Walter. *Origins and History of the Oldest Sinaitic Traditions*. Translated by S. Rudman. Oxford: Blackwell, 1965.
Blenkinsopp, Joseph. *Abraham: The Story of Life*. Grand Rapids: Eerdmans, 2015.
———. *The Pentateuch: An Introduction to the First Five Books of the Bible*. New York: Doubleday, 1992.
Brett, Mark G. *Genesis: Procreation and the Politics of Identity*. Old Testament Readings. New York: Routledge, 2000.
Brichto, Herbert C. "Kin, Cult, Land, and Afterlife: A Biblical Complex." *HUCA* 44 (1973) 1–54.
Briggs, Richard S., and Joel N. Lohr. *A Theological Introduction to the Pentateuch: Interpreting the Torah as Christian Scripture*. Grand Rapids: Baker, 2012.

Bibliography

Brodie, Thomas L. *Genesis as Dialogue: A Literary, Historical, and Theological Commentary.* Oxford: Oxford University Press, 2001.

Brooks, Peter. "Literature as Law's Other." *YJLH* 22 (2010) 349–67.

———. "Narrative Transactions—Does the Law Need a Narratology?" *YJLH* 18 (2006) 1–28.

Bruckner, James K. *Implied Law in the Abraham Narrative: A Literary and Theological Analysis.* JSOTSup 335. Sheffield: Sheffield, 2001.

Brueggemann, Walter. "David and His Theologian." *CBQ* 30 (1968) 156–81. Reprinted in *David and His Theologian: Literary, Social, and Theological Investigations*, edited by K. C. Hanson, 1–28. Eugene, OR: Cascade Books, 2011.

———. *Genesis, Interpretation.* Atlanta: John Knox Press, 1982.

Budd, Philip J. *Numbers.* WBC 5. Waco, TX: Word, 1984.

Carmichael, Calum M. *Law and Narrative in the Bible: The Evidence of Deuteronomic Laws and the Decalogue.* 1985. Reprint, Eugene, OR: Wipf & Stock, 2008.

———. *Law, Legend, and Incest in the Bible: Leviticus 18–20.* Ithaca, NY: Cornell University Press, 1997.

———. *The Laws of Deuteronomy.* 1974. Reprint, Eugene, OR: Wipf & Stock, 2008.

———. *The Origins of Biblical Law: The Decalogue and the Book of the Covenant.* Ithaca, NY: Cornell University Press, 1992.

———. *Women, Law, and the Genesis Traditions.* Edinburgh: Edinburgh University Press, 1979.

Carr, David. "*Biblos geneseos* Revisited: A Synchronic Analysis of Patterns in Genesis as Part of the Torah: Part 1." *ZAW* 110 (1998) 159–72.

———. "*Biblos geneseos* Revisited: A Synchronic Analysis of Patterns in Genesis as Part of the Torah: Part 2." *ZAW* 110 (1998) 327–47.

Carson, D. A. *Matthew.* EBC 8. Grand Rapids: Zondervan, 1984.

Cassuto, Umberto. *A Commentary on the Book of Genesis: Part II.* Translated by Israel Abrahams. Jerusalem: Magnes, 1964.

Chesson, Meredith S. "Remembering and Forgetting in Early Bronze Age Mortuary Practices on the Southeastern Dead Sea Plain, Jordan." In *Performing Death: Social Analyses of Funerary Traditions in the Ancient Near East and Mediterranean*, edited by Nicola Laneri, 109–39. UCOIS 3. Chicago: OIUC, 2007.

Chilton, David. *Paradise Restored: A Biblical Theology of Dominion.* Tyler, TX: Dominion, 1987.

Clark, Robert T. Rundle. *Myth and Symbol in Ancient Egypt.* London: Thames & Hudson, 1959.

Clark, W. Malcolm. "A Legal Background to the Yahwist's Use of 'Good Evil' in Genesis 2–3." *JBL* 88 (1969) 266–78.

Clements, Ronald E. *Abraham and David: Genesis XV and its Meaning for Israelite Tradition.* Studies in Biblical Theology 2/5. London: SCM, 1967.

Clines, David J. A. *The Theme of the Pentateuch.* JSOTSup 10. Sheffield: JSOT Press, 1978.

Coats, George W. *From Canaan to Egypt: Structural and Theological Context for the Joseph Story.* CBQMS 4. Washington, DC: Catholic Biblical Association of America, 1976.

———. *Genesis, with an Introduction to Narrative Literature.* Forms of the Old Testament Literature 1. Grand Rapids: Eerdmans, 1983.

———. "The Joseph Story and Ancient Wisdom: A Reappraisal." *CBQ* 35 (1973) 285–97.

———, ed. *Saga, Legend, Tale, Novella, Fable: Narrative Forms in Old Testament Literature.* JSOTSup 35. Sheffield: JSOT Press, 1985.

Bibliography

Collins, C. John. *Did Adam and Eve Really Exist? Who They Were and Why You Should Care*. Wheaton, IL: Crossway, 2011.

———. "A Historical Adam: Old-Earth Creation View." In *Four Views on the Historical Adam*, edited by Matthew Barrett and Ardel B. Caneday, 143–75. Grand Rapids: Zondervan, 2013.

Cover, Robert M. "Nomos and Narrative." *HLR* 97.4 (1983) 4–68.

Crenshaw, James L. "Method in Determining Wisdom Influence upon 'Historical' Literature." *JBL* 88 (1969) 129–42.

Crüsemann, Frank. "Der Pentateuch als Tora: Prolegomena zur Interpretation seiner Endgestalt." *EvT* 49 (1989) 250–67.

———. *The Torah: Theology and Social History of the Old Testament*. Translated by Allan W. Mahnke. Minneapolis: Fortress, 1996.

Curley, Christine, and Brian Neil Peterson. "Eve's Curse Revisited: An Increase of 'Sorrowful Conceptions.'" *BBR* 26.2 (2016) 1–16.

Damrosch, David. *The Narrative Covenant: Transformations of Genre in the Growth of Biblical Literature*. 1987. Reprint, New York: Cornell University Press, 1991.

Daube, David. *The Exodus Pattern in the Bible*. Westport, CT: Greenwood, 1963.

———. *Studies in Biblical Law*. Reprint, Cambridge: Cambridge University Press, 1947. Reprint, 2008.

Davidson, R. *Genesis 1–11*. CBC. Cambridge: University Press, 1973.

Dietrich, Walter. "Joseph." In *RPP* 7:35–36.

Douglas, Mary. "The Forbidden Animals in Leviticus." *JSOT* 59 (1993) 3–23.

———. *Purity and Danger: An Analysis of Concept of Pollution and Taboo*. 1966. Reprint, with a new Preface. New York: Routledge, 2002.

Dozeman, Thomas B. *The Pentateuch: Introducing the Torah*. Minneapolis: Fortress, 2017.

———. "The Wilderness and Salvation History in the Hagar Story." *JBL* 117 (1998) 23–43.

Embry, Brad. "The 'Naked Narrative' from Noah to Leviticus: Reassessing Voyeurism in the Account of Noah's Nakedness in Genesis 9:22–24." *JSOT* 35 (2011) 417–33.

Emmerich, Martin. "The Temptation Narrative of Genesis 3:1–6: A Prelude to the Pentateuch and the History of Israel." *EvQ* 73 (2001) 3–20.

Erlich, Tvi. "The Story of the Garden of Eden in Comparison to the Position of Mount Sinai and the Tabernacle." *Alon Shvut for Graduates of the Har Eztion Yeshiva* 11 (1998) 20–34.

Fensham, F. Charles. "The Curse of the Dry Bones in Ezekiel 37:14 Changed to a Blessing of Resurrection." *JNSL* 13 (1987) 59–60.

Forrester-Brown, James S. *The Two Creation Stories in Genesis: A Study of Their Symbolism*. 1920. Reprint, Berkley: Shambhala, 1974.

Fox, Michael V. "Wisdom in the Joseph Story." *VT* 51 (2001) 26–41.

Fraade, Steven D. *Legal Fictions: Studies of Law and Narrative in the Discursive Worlds of Ancient Jewish Sectarians and Sages*. Journal for the Study of Judaism Supplements 147. Leiden: Brill, 2011.

Frankena, Rintje. *Kanttekeningen van een Assyrioloog bij Ezechiël*. Leiden: Brill, 1965.

Frankfort, Henri. *Kingship and the Gods*. Chicago: University of Chicago Press, 1978.

Fretheim, Terence E. "The Book of Genesis." In *NIB* 1:321–674.

———. *The Pentateuch*. IBT. Nashville, Abingdon, 1996.

———. "The Reclamation of Creation: Redemption and Law in Exodus." *Int* 45 (1991) 354–65.

Bibliography

Gaiser, Frederick J. "Homosexuality in the Old Testament." *Word & World* 10 (1990) 161–65.

Galling, Kurt. "Joseph." In *RGG* 3:859–60.

Garrett, Duane A. *Rethinking Genesis: The Sources and Authorship of the First Book of the Bible*. New ed. Fearn, UK: Mentor, 2000.

Gemser, Berend. "God in Genesis." In *Adhuc Loquitur: Collected Essays of Dr. B. Gemser*, edited by A. Van Selms and A. S. Van Der Woude, 12–29. Pretoria Oriental Series 7. Leiden: Brill, 1968.

———. "The Religion of the Patriarchs." In *Adhuc Loquitur: Collected Essays of Dr. B. Gemser*, edited by A. Van Selms and A. S. Van Der Woude, 30–61. Pretoria Oriental Series 7. Leiden: Brill, 1968.

Gevirtz, Stanley. "Curse Motifs in the Old Testament and in the Ancient Near East." PhD diss., University of Chicago, 1959.

Gnoli, Gherardo, and Jean-Pierre Vernant eds., *La mort, les morts dans les sociétés anciennes*. Paris: Éditions de la Maison des Sciences de l'Homme, 1982.

Golka, Friedemann W. "Genesis 37–50: Joseph Story or Israel-Joseph Story?" *CBR* 2.2 (2004) 153–77.

Gorman, Frank. *The Ideology of Ritual: Space, Time and Status in the Priestly Theology*. JSOTSup 91. Sheffield: JSOT Press, 1990.

———. "Priestly Rituals of Founding: Time, Space, and Status." In *Cult and Cosmos: Tilting Toward a Temple-Centered Theology*, edited by L. Michael Morales, 351–66. BTS 18. Leuven: Peeters, 2014.

Greenberg, Moshe. "More Reflections on Biblical Criminal Law." In *Studies in Bible* 31, edited by Sara Japhet, 1–17. Jerusalem: Magnes, 1986.

Greengus, Samuel. *Laws in the Bible and in Early Rabbinic Collections: The Legal Legacy of the Ancient Near East*. Eugene, OR: Cascade Books, 2011.

Greenspahn, Frederick E. *When Brothers Dwell Together: The Preeminence of Younger Siblings in the Hebrew Bible*. New York: Oxford University Press, 1994.

Greenstein, Edward L. "Biblical Law." In *Back to the Sources: Reading the Classic Jewish Texts*, edited by Barry W. Holtz, 83–103. New York: Summit Books, 1984.

Greifenhagen, F. V. *Egypt on the Pentateuch's Ideological Map: Constructing Biblical Israel's Identity*. JSOTSup 361. Sheffield: Sheffield, 2002.

Gunkel, Hermann. *Genesis*. Translated by Mark E. Biddle. Mercer Library of Biblical Studies. Macon, GA: Mercer University Press, 1997.

Hamilton, Victor P. *The Book of Genesis 1–17*. NICOT. Grand Rapids: Eerdmans, 1990.

Hartley, John. *Genesis*. NIBC. Peabody, MA: Hendrickson, 2000.

Hasel, Gerhard F. "Sabbath." In *ABD* 5:849–56.

Heard, R. Christopher. *Dynamics of Diselection: Ambiguity in Genesis 12–36 and Ethnic Boundaries in Post-exilic Judah*. SBLSS 39. Atlanta: SBL, 2001.

Henn, T. R. *The Bible as Literature*. London: Lutterworth, 1970.

Hepner, Gershon. *Legal Friction: Law, Narrative, and Identity Politics in Biblical Israel*. SBLit 78. New York: Lang, 2010.

Hillers, Delbert R. *Covenant: The History of a Biblical Idea*. Baltimore: Johns Hopkins University Press, 1969.

Hinckley, Robert. "Adam, Aaron, and the Garden Sanctuary." *Logia* 22.4 (2013) 5–12.

Ho, Craig Y.S. "The Stories of the Family Troubles of Judah and David: A Study of Their Literary Links." *VT* 49 (1999) 514–31.

Bibliography

Hoffmeier, James K. "Some Thoughts on Genesis 1 & 2 and Egyptian Cosmology." *JANESCU* 15 (1983) 39–49.

Holter, Knut. "The Serpent in Eden as a Symbol of Israel's Political Enemies: A Yahwistic Criticism of the Solomonic Foreign Policy?" *SJOT* 1 (1990) 106–12.

Humphreys, W. Lee. *Joseph and His Family: A Literary Study*. Columbia: University of South Carolina Press, 1988.

Jackson, Bernard S. "Ideas of Law and Legal Administration: A Semiotic Approach." In *The World of Ancient Israel*, edited by R. E. Clements, 185–202. Cambridge: Cambridge University Press, 1989.

———. *Wisdom Laws: A Study of the Mishpatim of Exodus 21:1—22:16*. Oxford: Oxford University Press, 2006.

Jacobs, Mignon R. "The Conceptual Dynamics of Good and Evil in the Joseph Story: An Exegetical and Hermeneutical Inquiry." *JSOT* 27 (2003) 309–38.

Joines, Karen R. "Serpent in Gen 3." *ZAW* 87 (1975) 1–11.

Josipovici, Gabriel. *The Book of God: A Response to the Bible*. New Haven: Yale University Press, 1988.

Kaiser, Walter C., Jr. *Toward Old Testament Ethics*. Grand Rapids: Zondervan, 1983.

Kamin, Sarah. "Rashbam's Conception of the Creation in Light of the Intellectual Currents of His Time." In *Studies in Bible* 31, edited by Sara Japhet, 91–132. Jerusalem: Magnes, 1986.

Kaminsky, Joel S. "Reclaiming a Theology of Election: Favoritism and the Joseph Story." *PRSt* 31.2 (2004) 135–52.

Kearney, Peter J. "Creation and Liturgy: The P Redaction of Ex 25–40." *ZAW* 89 (1977) 375–87.

Keiser, Thomas A. *Genesis 1–11: Its Literary Coherence and Theological Message*. Eugene, OR: Wipf & Stock, 2013.

Kikawada, Isaac M. "The Double Creation of Mankind in *Enki and Ninmah*, *Atrahasis* I 1–351, and Genesis 1–2." *Iraq* 45 (1983) 43–45.

———. and Arthur Quinn. *Before Abraham Was*. Nashville: Abingdon, 1985.

Kirsch, Jonathan. *Moses: A Life*. New York: Ballantine, 1998.

Klein, William W., Craig L. Blomberg, and Robert L. Hubbard Jr. *Introduction to Biblical Interpretation*. 3rd ed. Grand Rapids: Zondervan, 2017.

Knierim, Rolf P. "The Composition of the Pentateuch." In *SBLSP 1985*, edited by Kent H. Richards, 393–415. Atlanta: Scholars, 1985. Reprinted in *The Task of Old Testament Theology*, 351–79.

———. *The Task of Old Testament Theology: Substance, Method, and Cases*. Grand Rapids: Eerdmans, 1995.

Lambert, W. G. "Three Unpublished Fragments of the Tukulti-Ninurta Epic." *AfO* 18 (1957–58) 38–51.

Legrand, Lucien. *The Bible on Culture: Belonging or Dissenting*. Faith and Culture Series. Maryknoll, NY: Orbis, 2000.

Levenson, Jon D. *Creation and the Persistence of Evil: The Jewish Drama of Divine Omnipotence*. Princeton: Princeton University Press, 1988.

———. *The Death and Resurrection of the Beloved Son: The Transformation of Child Sacrifice in Judaism and Christianity*. New Haven: Yale University Press, 1993.

Lim, Johnson T. K. *Grace in the Midst of Judgment: Grappling with Genesis 1–11*. BZAW 314. Berlin: de Gruyter, 2002.

Bibliography

Lioy, Dan. *Axis of Glory: A Biblical and Theological Analysis of the Temple Motif in Scripture*. SBLit 138. New York: Lang, 2010.

Lohfink, Norbert. "Die Erzählung vom Sündenfall." In *Das Siegeslied am Schilfmeer*, 81–101. Frankfurt: Knecht, 1965.

———. *Theology of the Pentateuch: Themes of the Priestly Narrative and Deuteronomy*. Translated by Linda M. Maloney. Minneapolis: Fortress, 1994.

Long, Burke O. *The Problem of Etiological Narrative in the Old Testament*. BZAW 108. Berlin: Töpelmann, 1968.

Longacre, Robert E. *Joseph: A Story of Divine Providence: A Text Theoretical and Textlinguistic Analysis of Genesis 37 and 39–48*. Winona Lake, IN: Eisenbrauns, 1989.

Longman, Tremper III. *Genesis*. The Story of God Bible Commentary, Old Testament Series 1. Grand Rapids: Zondervan, 2016.

———. *How to Read Genesis*. Downers Grove, IL: InterVarsity, 2005.

Luther, Martin. *Commentary on Genesis I*. Translated by J. Theodore Mueller. Grand Rapids: Zondervan, 1958.

Machinist, Peter. "Literature as Politics: The Tukulti-Ninurta Epic and the Bible." *CBQ* 38 (1976) 455–82.

Mathews, Kenneth A. *Genesis 1—11:26*. NAC 1a. Nashville: Broadman & Holman, 2001.

———. *Genesis 11:27—50:26*. NAC 1b. Nashville: Broadman & Holman, 2005.

McKeown, James. *Genesis*. Grand Rapids: Eerdmans, 2008.

Mendenhall, George E. "Covenant Forms in Israelite Tradition." *BA* 17.3 (1954) 50–76.

———. "Puppy and Lettuce in Northwest-Semitic Covenant Making." *BASOR* 133 (1954) 26–30.

Merrill, Eugene. *Kingdom of Priests: A History of Old Testament Israel*. 2nd. ed. Grand Rapids: Baker, 2008.

Meyers, Carol L. *Discovering Eve: Ancient Israelite Women in Context*. New York: Oxford University Press, 1988.

———. "Gender Roles and Genesis 3:16 Revisited." In *The Word of the Lord Shall Go Forth: Essays in Honor of David Noel Freedman in Celebration of His Sixtieth Birthday*, edited by Carol L. Meyers and M. O'Connor, 337–54. Winona Lake, IN: Eisenbrauns, 1983.

———. *The Tabernacle Menorah: A Synthetic Symbol from the Biblical Cult*. ASOR Dissertation Series 2. Missoula, MT: Scholars, 1976.

Milgrom, Jacob. *Leviticus 17–22*. AB 3A. New York: Doubleday, 2000.

———. *Leviticus 23–27*. AB 3B. New York: Doubleday, 2001.

Miscall, Peter D. "The Jacob and Joseph Story as Analogies." *JSOT* 6 (1978) 28–40.

Moberly, R.W.L. *The Old Testament of the Old Testament: Patriarchal Narratives and Mosaic Yahwism*. OBT. Minneapolis: Fortress, 1992.

———. *The Theology of the Book of Genesis*. OTT. Cambridge: Cambridge University Press, 2009.

Moore, Rickie D., and Brian Neil Peterson. *Voice, Word, and Spirit: A Pentecostal Survey of the Old Testament*. Nashville: Abingdon, 2017.

Morales, L. Michael ed. *Cult and Cosmos: Tilting Toward a Temple-Centered Theology*. BTS 18. Leuven: Peeters, 2014.

Morris, Paul. "Exiled from Eden: Jewish Interpretations of Genesis." In *A Walk in the Garden: Biblical, Iconographical and Literary Images of Eden*, edited by Paul Morris and Deborah Sawyer, 117–66. JSOTSup 136. Sheffield: Sheffield, 1992.

Bibliography

Na'aman, Nadav. "The 'Conquest of Canaan' in Joshua and in History." In *From Nomadism to Monarchy: Archaeological and Historical Aspects of Early Israel*, edited by Israel Finkelstein and Nadav Na'aman, 218–81. Jerusalem: Israel Exploration Society, 1994.

Neusner, Jacob. *Genesis and Judaism: The Perspective of Genesis Rabbah: An Analytical Anthology*. BJS 108. Atlanta: Scholars, 1985.

Nicholson, E. W. "The Pentateuch in Recent Research A Time for Caution." In *Congress Volume Leuven 1989*, edited by J.A. Emerton, 10–21. VTSup 43. Leiden: Brill, 1991.

Niditch, Susan. "The Wronged Woman Righted: An Analysis of Genesis 38." *HTR* 72 (1979) 143–49.

Niehaus, Jeffrey. *God at Sinai: Covenant and Theophany in the Bible and Ancient Near East*. Grand Rapids: Zondervan, 1995.

———. "In the Wind of the Storm: Another Look at Genesis III 8." *VT* 44 (1994) 263–67.

Nigosian, S. A. "Moses as They Saw Him." *VT* 43 (1993) 339–50.

Noble, Paul R. "Esau, Tamar, and Joseph: Criteria for Identifying Inner-biblical Allusions." *VT* 52 (2002) 219–52.

Noth, Martin. *A History of Pentateuchal Traditions*. Translated by Bernhard W. Anderson. Englewood Cliffs, NJ: Prentice-Hall, 1972.

———. *Numbers: A Commentary*. Translated by James D. Martin. OTL. Philadelphia: Westminster, 1968.

Och, Bernard. "Creation and Redemption: Towards a Theology of Creation." In *Cult and Cosmos: Tilting Toward a Temple-Centered Theology*, edited by L. Michael Morales, 333–50. BTS 18. Leuven: Peeters, 2014.

Parry, Donald W. "Garden of Eden: Prototype Sanctuary." In *Temples of the Ancient World: Ritual and Symbolism*, edited by Donald W. Parry, 126–51. Salt Lake City: Deseret, 1994.

Patrick, Dale. "The First Commandment in the Structure of the Pentateuch." *VT* 45 (1995) 107–18.

Patrick, Dale, and Allen Scult. *Rhetoric and Biblical Interpretation*. JSOTSup 82. Sheffield: Almond, 1990.

Peterson, Brian Neil. "Does Genesis 2 Support Same-sex Marriage?: An Evangelical Response." *JETS* 60 (2017) 681–96.

———. "Egyptian Influence on the Creation Language of Genesis 2." *BSac* 174 (2017) 283–301.

———. *Ezekiel in Context: Ezekiel's Message Understood in Its Historical Setting of Covenant Curses and Ancient Near Eastern Mythological Motifs*. PTMS 182. Eugene, OR: Pickwick Publications, 2012.

———. "The Sin of Sodom Revisited: Reading Genesis 19 in Light of Torah." *JETS* 59 (2016) 17–31.

———. *What Was the Sin of Sodom and Gomorrah: Homosexuality, Inhospitality, or Something Else?* Eugene, OR: Wipf & Stock, 2016.

Polin, Milton H. "Genesis as a Source of Jewish Law." *Tradition* 4 (1961) 36–43.

Postell, Seth D. *Adam as Israel: Genesis 1–3 as the Introduction to the Torah and Tanakh*. Eugene, OR: Pickwick Publications, 2011.

Pritchard, James ed. *Ancient Near East in Pictures Relating to the Old Testament*. 2nd ed. Princeton: Princeton University Press, 1969.

———. *Ancient Near Eastern Texts Relating to the Old Testament*. 3rd ed. Princeton: Princeton University Press, 1969.

Bibliography

Rad, Gerhard von. *Genesis: A Commentary*. Translated by John Marks. OTL. Philadelphia: Westminster, 1961.

———. *God at Work in Israel*. Translated by John Marks. Nashville: Abingdon, 1980.

———. "The Joseph Narrative and Ancient Wisdom." In *From Genesis to Chronicles: Explorations in Old Testament Theology*, edited by K. C. Hanson, 75–81. Fortress Classics in Biblical Studies. Minneapolis: Fortress, 2005.

———. *Old Testament Theology*. Vol. 1. Translated by D. M. G. Stalker. New York: Harper & Row, 1962.

———. *The Problem of the Hexateuch and Other Essays*. Translated by E. W. Trueman Dicken. 1966. Reprinted, London: SCM, 1984.

Rashkow, Ilona N. *Taboo or not Taboo. Sexuality and Family in the Hebrew Bible*. Minneapolis: Fortress, 2000.

Redford, Donald B. *A Study of the Biblical Story of Joseph (Genesis 37–50)*. VTSup 20. Leiden: Brill, 1970.

Rendsburg, Gary A. "David and His Circle in Genesis xxxviii." *VT* 36 (1986) 438–46.

Richardson, Seth. "Death and Dismemberment in Mesopotamia: Discorporation between the Body and Body Politic." In *Performing Death: Social Analyses of Funerary Traditions in the Ancient Near East and Mediterranean*, edited by Nicola Laneri, 189–208. UCOIS 3. Chicago: OIUC, 2007.

Rofé, Alexander. "Defilement of Virgins in Biblical Law and the Case of Dinah (Genesis 34)." *Bib* 86 (2005) 369–75.

Rogerson, John W. *Myth in Old Testament Interpretation*. BZAW 134. Berlin: de Gruyter, 1974.

Rogerson, John W., R. W. L. Moberly, and William Johnstone. *Genesis and Exodus*. Sheffield: Sheffield Academic, 2001.

Rosenbaum, Stanley N. "Israelite Homicide Law and the Term 'Enmity' in Genesis 3:15." *JLR* 2.1 (1984) 145–51.

Rosenberg, Joel. "Bible: Biblical Narrative." In *Back to the Sources: Reading the Classic Jewish Texts*, edited by Barry W. Holtz, 31–81. New York: Summit, 1984.

Ross, Allen P. *Creation and Blessing: A Guide to the Study and Exposition of Genesis*. Grand Rapids: Baker, 2002.

Sailhamer, John H. *Genesis Unbound: A Provocative New Look at the Creation Account*. Sisters, OR: Multnomah, 1996.

———. *The Pentateuch as Narrative: A Biblical-Theological Commentary*. Grand Rapids: Zondervan, 1992.

Sanders, James A. *Torah and Canon*. Philadelphia: Fortress, 1972.

Sarna, Nahum. *Genesis*. JPSTC. New York: Jewish Publication Society, 1989.

Schmid, Konrad. *Genesis and the Moses Story: Israel's Dual Origins in the Hebrew Bible*. Translated by James D. Nogalski. Siphrut 3. Winona Lake, IN: Eisenbrauns, 2010.

Schmidt, Ludwig. *Literarische Studien zur Josephsgeschichte*. BZAW 167. Berlin: de Gruyter, 1986.

Schwartz, Regina M. *The Curse of Cain: The Violent Legacy of Monotheism*. Chicago: University of Chicago Press, 1997.

Shinan, A., and Y. Zakovitch. "Midrash on Scripture and Midrash within Scripture." In *Studies in Bible* 31, edited by Sara Japhet, 257–77. Jerusalem: Magnes, 1986.

Sigmon, Brian Osborne. "Between Eden and Egypt: Echoes of the Garden Narrative in the Story of Joseph and His Brothers." PhD diss., Marquette University, 2013. http://epublications.marquette.edu/dissertations_mu/263.

Bibliography

Soden, John M. "From the Dust: Creating Adam in Historical Context." *BSac* 172 (2015) 45–66.
Speiser, E. A. "The Biblical Idea of History in Its Common Near Eastern Setting." *IEJ* 7 (1957) 201–16.
———. *Genesis*. AB 1. New York: Doubleday, 1964.
Sperling, S. David. *The Original Torah: The Political Intent of the Bible's Writers*. New York: New York University Press, 1998.
Spinoza, Baruch. *Theologico-Political Treatise*. Translated by Martin D. Yaffe. Newburyport, MA: Focus, 2004.
Stager, Lawrence E. "Jerusalem and the Garden of Eden." In *Cult and Cosmos: Tilting Toward a Temple-Centered Theology*, edited by L. Michael Morales, 99–116. BTS 18. Leuven: Peeters, 2014.
Stahl, Nanette. *Law and Liminality in the Bible*. JSOTSup 202. Sheffield: Sheffield, 1995.
Stavrakopoulou, Francesca. "Ezekiel's Use and Abuse of Corpses." Paper presented at the annual meeting of the SBL, Boston, November 24, 2008.
Steck, Odil H. *Wahrnehmungen Gottes im Alten Testament: Gesammelte Studien*, 9–116. Theologische Bücherei 70. Munich: Kaiser, 1982.
Stratton, Beverly J. *Out of Eden: Reading, Rhetoric, and Ideology in Genesis 2–3*. JSOTSup 208. Sheffield: Sheffield, 1995.
Syrén, Roger. *The Forsaken First-Born: A Study of a Recurrent Motif in the Patriarchal Narratives*. JSOTSup 133. Sheffield: JSOT, 1993.
Trible, Phyllis. *Texts of Terror: Literary Feminine Readings of Biblical Narratives*. OBT. Philadelphia: Fortress, 1984.
Tsevat, Matitiahu. *The Meaning of the Book of Job and Other Biblical Studies: Essays on the Literature and Religion of the Hebrew Bible*. New York: Ktav, 1980.
Tucker, Gene M. "The Legal Background of Genesis 23." *JBL* 85 (1966) 77–84.
Van Seters, John. *Prologue to History: The Yahwist as Historian in Genesis*. Louisville: Westminster John Knox, 1992.
Vawter, Bruce. *On Genesis: A New Reading*. New York: Doubleday, 1977.
Visotzky, Burton. *The Genesis of Ethics: How the Tormented Family of Genesis Leads Us to Moral Development*. New York: Crown, 1996.
Vogels, Walter. "The Cultic and Civil Calendars of the Fourth Day of Creation (Gen. 1:14b)." In *Cult and Cosmos: Tilting Toward a Temple-Centered Theology*, edited by L. Michael Morales, 133–48. BTS 18. Leuven: Peeters, 2014.
Walton, John. *Genesis*. NIVAC. Grand Rapids: Zondervan, 2001.
———. *Genesis 1 as Ancient Cosmology*. Winona Lake, IN: Eisenbrauns, 2011.
———. *The Lost World of Genesis One*. Downers Grove, IL: InterVarsity, 2009.
Watts, James W. "The Legal Characterization of Moses in the Rhetoric of the Pentateuch." *JBL* 117 (1998) 415–26.
———. *Reading Law: The Rhetorical Shaping of the Pentateuch*. Sheffield: Sheffield, 1999.
Wenham, Gordon. *Exploring the Old Testament: Volume 1: A Guide to the Pentateuch*. Downers Grove, IL: InterVarsity, 2003.
———. *Genesis 1–15*. WBC. Nashville: Nelson, 1987.
———. "The Religion of the Patriarchs." In *Essays on the Patriarchal Narratives*, edited by A. R. Millard and D. J. Wiseman, 157–88. Leicester, UK: InterVarsity, 1980.
———. "Sanctuary Symbolism in the Garden of Eden Story." In *"I Studied Inscriptions before the Flood:" Ancient Near Eastern, Literary, and Linguistic Approaches to Genesis*

Bibliography

1-11, edited by Richard Hess and David Toshio Tsumura, 399-404. SBTS 4. Winona Lake, IN: Eisenbrauns, 1994.

———. *Story as Torah: Reading Old Testament Narrative Ethically*. Grand Rapids: Baker, 2004.

Westermann, Claus. *Genesis 1-11: A Commentary*. Translated by John J. Scullion. CC. Minneapolis: Augsburg, 1984.

———. *Genesis 12-36: A Commentary*. Translated by John J. Scullion. CC. Minneapolis: Augsburg, 1985.

———. *Genesis 37-50: A Commentary*. Translated by John J. Scullion. CC. Minneapolis: Augsburg, 1986.

Wevers, John W. *Notes on the Greek Text of Genesis*. SBLSCS 35. Atlanta: Scholars, 1993.

White, Leland J. "Does the Bible Speak about Gays or Same Sex Orientation? A Test Case in Biblical Ethics: Part 1." *BTB* 25 (1995) 14-23.

Whybray, R. N. *The Making of the Pentateuch: A Methodological Study*. JSOTSup 53. Sheffield: JSOT Press, 1987.

Wildavsky, Aaron. "Survival Must Not Be Gained through Sin: The Moral of the Joseph Stories Prefigured through Judah and Tamar." *JSOT* 62 (1994) 37-48.

Wolde, Ellen van. *Words Become Worlds: Semantic Studies of Genesis 1-11*. BibIntSer 6. Leiden: Brill, 1994.

Wright, G. R. H. "The Positioning of Genesis 38." *ZAW* 94 (1982) 523-29.

Subject Index

Aaron, 42, 64, 67
Aaronic Blessing, 102, 120
Abel, xiii, 41–42, 50, 53, 53n72, 54–57, 59–60
Abimelech, 8n39, 11, 24, 78, 83, 85, 93–95, 99, 102, 105, 129
Abraham, xiii, 8n40, 14–15, 35, 37, 48, 62–63, 74–86, 88–98 98n70, 98n73, 99–101, 103–5, 108, 111, 114, 121, 123–24, 132, 135
Adam, xiii, 14, 18, 20, 24, 29, 31–33, 33n60, 35–37, 39, 41–43, 43n11, 44–47, 47n42, 48–53, 55–60, 60n103, 62–63, 65, 65n10, 70, 77, 80, 115
Adapa Myth, 27, 53
Adoption, 112, 134, 138
Adultery, 24, 35, 59–60, 65, 68, 84, 86–87, 88n36, 94–95, 106, 117n66, 123, 127, 129, 141
Amarna Letters/Period, 27, 53–54
Ammonites, 87
Apodictic (law), xv
Ark of the Covenant, 32–33, 47, 67
Atrahasis Epic, 28, 50, 63
Attributes of God, 38–40, 56, 60, 71
Authorship (Mosaic), 10–13, 16, 137

Babel, xiii, 61, 64, 71–75
Babylon/ian, 21, 26n28, 27–28, 46, 46n35, 49, 55, 62, 65, 67, 72–73, 77, 86, 97, 109, 121, 130, 133, 139
Barren/ness, 37, 41, 49–51, 85
Benjamin, 107, 138
Bestiality, 35, 68, 87, 118n70

Bethel, 77, 83, 100, 104, 110–11, 120
Bilhah, 106, 112, 119, 131
Biography (of Moses), 13–14, 14n69, 15, 91
Blessing/s (of God), v, 14, 24, 35, 37, 43, 49–50, 62, 69, 71–72, 75, 79–80, 90, 93, 102, 111, 130, 134–35, 138–39

Cain, xiii, 15, 24, 41–42, 50, 53–57, 59, 63–65, 74
Canaan, 9, 19, 24–25, 27, 34, 36–37, 39, 41–47, 60–62, 65, 67, 69, 72–73, 77–83, 87–88, 93–94, 96, 98, 102, 105, 108–10, 114–16, 119–21, 123–24, 126, 130, 135, 138
Canaanite(s), 8, 26, 26n27, 45, 46n35, 47–49, 60–61, 64, 76, 80, 88, 90, 98, 98n73, 103, 103n16, 106–8, 116, 118–20, 124, 126, 130, 132–33
Canonical/Canon, 3, 8, 11, 117, 127
Capital Punishment, 5, 61, 68, 89, 127
Case law, xiv, xv, 3–4, 4n21, 60, 72, 75, 77, 83–86, 106, 113, 116, 120, 122, 127, 131, 140
Casuistic (law), xv, 4n21
Chaldean, 8, 79
Circumcision, xv, 5, 70, 92, 115–16
Covenant, xv, 11, 24, 26, 30, 34, 37, 44, 55, 64, 66, 69–70, 80, 92–93, 96, 99–100, 102, 104, 110–11, 119–20, 138–39

155

Subject Index

Covenant
  Abrahamic, 69–70, 92, 92n56, 93, 115
  Book of the, 2, 5n29, 39
  Davidic, 92, 92n56
  Edenic, 70
  Noahic, 68–70, 92, 141
  Sinai/Mosaic, xv, 22–23, 43, 49, 60, 64, 68–70, 92, 111, 115, 139
Covet/ing, 8, 8n39, 24, 59–60, 84, 94, 131
Creation, xiii, 5, 8, 16–19, 19n5, 20–32, 34–37, 39, 42–43, 46, 50–51, 53n72, 62–63, 68, 70, 75, 84–87, 132, 140–42
Curse, 37–38, 41–44, 48–51, 62, 62n3, 66n11, 69, 75, 81, 85, 90, 106–7, 127, 133, 135

Dan, 8
David, 9n43, 26, 80, 97, 114, 116
Decalogue, 2, 16, 19n5, 20n11, 79, 140
Deuteronomic, 2, 13n65, 47, 113n50, 133
Deuteronomist, 101
Dinah, 8n39, 69, 107, 116–17, 117n63, 117n66, 118, 118n70, 119, 124–25
Divorce, 36, 84
Dysfunction (family), 88, 112, 120, 126, 138–39

Eden, Garden of, 20, 24, 29, 32, 32n53, 32n55, 33–34, 42–47, 49, 55, 60, 70, 115, 123–24
Edom, 42, 99–100, 108, 114, 115n57, 120
Egypt, 16, 21, 23, 25, 27–29, 37, 39, 42, 51, 53–54, 62, 66, 73, 77, 79–83, 89–94, 101, 105, 107, 109, 118, 121, 123–25, 130, 133–35, 137
Egyptian, 21, 27–30, 34, 39, 46n35, 51, 55, 77, 82, 86, 91, 98, 124–25, 128, 133n48, 134, 136, 140
Election of Israel, 57, 57n87, 76, 125
Elohim, 10, 18, 22, 24–26, 29, 39, 104
Endogamous, 5, 89, 103n14
Enuma elish, 28, 31n48
Ephraim (Joseph's son), 15, 125, 138

Esau, 8n39, 15, 35, 42, 57, 99–109, 114–15, 120, 128n26, 131n44
Etiology, xiii, xiiin1, xiv, 11, 41, 98, 116
Eve, xiii, 18, 24, 29, 32–33, 35–39, 41–43, 43n11, 44–46, 46n36, 47–53, 55–60, 62–63, 65, 70, 77, 80, 115
Exile (Babylonian), 21, 27, 44, 46, 47n44, 48–49, 55, 62, 65–67, 73, 81, 88, 94, 96, 98, 102, 110, 121, 130, 133, 135, 137, 139
Exilic, 4, 5n27, 8–9, 12, 44, 77, 93, 103n14, 123
Ezra, 7, 65

Fall (the), 24, 27, 33, 41–42, 45–47, 50–51, 53, 57–60, 62–63, 77, 81
False Witness/Lying, 24, 59, 68, 95, 104, 107, 130–31
Famine, 42, 50–51, 66, 81–83, 101, 119, 124, 128, 137
Flood (the), xiii, 37, 55, 60–61, 63–67, 67n14, 68–72, 74–75, 78, 85, 140
Food laws, 11, 20, 48, 53, 61, 100, 140
Foreign/Foreigner, 14, 23, 25, 47, 64, 90, 104, 111, 123, 129–30, 134
Form-critical, 10–11

Genealogy, xiii, 7, 61–62, 62n3, 108, 120
Gibeonites, 25, 48, 80, 119
Gilgamesh Epic, 28, 51, 63
Golden Calf, 45, 56, 64, 66, 71, 136

Hagar, 8n39, 37, 81–82, 86, 90–92, 95
Ham, 62, 69, 72, 87
Haran, 79, 82, 94, 105, 107, 109, 112, 114, 121
Hatshepsut, 30, 54
Holiness Code, 2, 39

Idols/Idolatry, xv, 20, 56, 65, 94, 104, 111
Implied audience/reader, 1, 8–9, 9n47, 10, 12, 15, 17, 19, 21, 28, 40, 49, 78, 81, 101, 134
Implied author, 15
Implied setting, 28, 134

Subject Index

Incest, 35, 68, 87, 87n33, 88n36, 106
Infanticide, 124
Inheritance (rights), xv, 35, 100, 106–8, 112, 138
Intermarriage, 64–65, 102–3, 117–19,
Isaac, xiii, 15, 24, 37, 63, 80–81, 88–89, 93–103, 105, 108
Ishmael/ites, 15, 77, 86, 91–92, 95, 103, 127, 131

Jacob, xiii, xv, 8n39, 11, 14–15, 24, 35, 37, 42, 47n43, 62–63, 66, 78–80, 82, 93, 99–100, 100nn1–2, 101–5, 105n25, 106, 106n30, 107–9, 109n42, 110–13, 113n50, 114–21, 124, 126, 126n19, 127–28, 128nn25–26, 130–31, 134, 138–39, 139n65
Jerusalem, 26, 32, 32n53, 33n56, 36, 89, 96–98
Joseph, xiii, xiiin1, xv, xvin15, 8n39, 15, 24, 42, 66, 78–80, 85, 91, 100n1, 101–2, 105, 107, 112, 119–21, 121n1, 122, 122n5, 123–28, 128nn24–26, 129, 129n33, 130, 130n35, 131, 133, 133nn48–49, 134, 134n55, 135–39, 142
Joshua, 6, 48, 67, 111, 115, 118–19, 136
Judah, 25n26, 73, 103, 119, 121n1, 124, 126–30, 130n35, 131–33, 133n48, 138

Khnum, 29, 29n42, 30
Kidnapping, 68, 127

Laban, 88n38, 93, 104, 106, 109, 109n42, 110, 112–13, 113n50, 114, 119–20
Leah, 49, 112–13
Legend, xiii
Levi, xvi, 105, 105n28, 107, 116–17, 119, 138
Levirate Marriage, 128–29, 131, 131n44, 132, 139
Lot, 49, 76, 83, 86–87, 89–90, 94–95, 98, 102, 107–8
Lying (see False Witness)

Manasseh (Joseph's son), 15, 125, 138
Marduk, 28
Marriage, 11, 24, 34–37, 40, 61, 64–65, 70, 84–85, 89, 99, 102–3, 103n14, 112–13, 116–18, 118n68, 125–26, 129, 131, 131n44, 132–33, 133n48, 139
Melchizedek, 98, 98n73, 111
Mesopotamia/n, 16, 21, 21n15, 26–28, 50, 53, 63, 140
Midian/ite, 25, 27, 125, 131, 136
Miriam, 64, 67
Moab, Plains of, 9, 11, 17, 73
Moabites, 87
Monogamy/ous, 34–35, 35n70, 36–37, 84
Monotheism/Monotheistic, 9, 20, 25, 28, 34, 69, 94, 141
Moon (see also Yarikh), 18–21, 21n15, 22
Moses, xv, 1, 4, 8–14, 14n72, 15, 19, 23, 25, 27, 29, 30–31, 38–39, 42–43, 54, 56, 58, 66–68, 70–71, 78, 88, 91–93, 97, 110, 120, 125, 135–37, 142
Murder, 24, 52–53, 55, 60, 68, 74, 106–7, 117, 127, 141
Myth/Mythological, xiv, xvi, 4n18, 21, 26–28, 28n38, 29–30, 35, 40, 50–51, 53, 63, 128n26, 140

Naked/ness, 55–56, 72
Narrative, xiii, xiiin1, xivn5, xv–xvi, 2, 2n6, 3–5, 5n29, 6–10, 11n55, 12, 12n63, 13, 15–17, 20–21, 24–25, 27, 30, 37, 40–41, 45–47, 50, 53, 57–61, 63–64, 66, 69–72, 76–77, 79, 83–85, 87–89, 89n39, 93–98, 100, 108, 112, 114, 116, 120–23, 127, 128n26, 133–34, 138–40, 142
Nebo, Mt., 11
Noah, xiii, 14, 62–65, 65n10, 66–72, 75, 87, 141
Novella, xiii, xiiin1

Passover, 93, 115
Peniel, 106n30, 116, 120

Subject Index

Pentateuch (see also Torah), xv–xvi, 1–2, 2nn5–6, 3–14, 56, 59, 67
Plague/s (see also Curses), 82, 85, 89n40, 97, 111
Polemic (In Genesis), 27, 29–30, 50–51, 53, 60, 63, 69, 73–74, 83, 88, 104, 117, 118n68, 129, 140
Polygamy/ous, 35, 37, 60, 64, 85–86
Polytheism/Polytheistic, 21, 94
Postexilic, 5n27, 7, 9, 12, 19, 65, 77, 93, 103, 117, 118n71
Potiphar/Potiphar's wife, 78, 85, 123, 125, 129–30, 133, 134n55
Pre-exilic, 12, 19
Priestly source, 18, 19n3, 19n5, 22, 67
Primogeniture, 15, 15n79, 57
Procreation, 28, 50–51, 61–62, 70, 87, 132, 139
Ptah, 28–29

Rachel, 49, 104, 107, 112–13, 119, 138
Rahab, 25, 80, 95, 130
Rape, 68–69, 86, 107, 116–17, 117n66, 118
Rebekah, 49, 88n38, 89, 102, 120
Red Sea, 19, 34, 91
Reuben, 106, 112, 114, 119, 131, 138–39

Sabbath, 5, 5n23, 23, 23n18, 31, 43, 68, 70
Sacrifice (child), 77, 95–97
Sacrifice(s), xvi, 11, 55, 55n82, 56, 60–61, 63, 68, 77–78, 95–98, 141
Saga, xiii
Sarah, 8n39, 37, 49, 80, 82–86, 90–92, 94–95, 99
Seth, 15, 62, 64
Sexual ethics, 76, 85–89, 99, 128, 139
Shechem/ite, 8n39, 69, 100, 102, 105–7, 116–17, 117n63, 118–19, 119n72, 120, 125
Shem, 60, 62, 72
Shemesh/Shamash (see also sun), 21
Simeon, 105–7, 116–17, 119, 124, 138
Sinai (Mount), xv, 5, 5n27, 6, 8, 15–17, 26, 28, 30, 34–35, 41–44, 46, 50, 56–58, 67, 69, 74, 83, 85, 90, 93, 110–11
Slavery/slaves, 23, 25, 30, 73, 82, 90–91, 113, 123, 128–30, 134, 138
Snake/serpent, 41, 45–46, 46nn35–36, 47, 47n43, 48–49, 51–53, 55, 58, 60
Sodom, 11, 64, 69, 74, 78, 85–89, 89nn39–40, 90, 95, 98, 102, 107, 116
Solomon, 33, 65, 114, 122n4, 129
Source-critical, 10, 18
Steal/ing, 51, 59, 104, 107, 141
Sun (see also Shemesh), 18–22

Tabernacle, 31–32, 32n54, 33, 33n56, 34, 48, 67
Tamar, 11, 49, 103n16, 128–33, 133n48
Temple, 27, 30–32, 32n55, 33, 33n56, 34, 55, 58, 97, 98, 118n68
Ten Commandments (the), xiii, 20, 23–25, 58, 59n100, 60, 72, 94, 97, 103, 125, 140–41
Theological instruction on God, xiv, 2–3, 7, 20, 20n10, 38–39, 54, 56, 65, 71, 75, 78n8, 120, 129n33, 137, 140–41
Theophany, 57–58
Tiamat, 28
Tithe/Tithing, 11, 98, 100, 111, 128, 140
Toledoth (formula), 61–62
Torah (see also Pentateuch), xiv–xvi, 1–2, 2n6, 3–7, 11, 13, 16, 18–19, 21–23, 25–26, 33, 39–40, 43, 49, 58, 60–63, 68, 70–71, 75–80, 84, 96–97, 99–100, 109, 112, 122, 125, 133, 139, 142
Transjordan, 100, 114, 138
Tree of Life, 29, 33, 49, 52, 59
Tree of the Knowledge of Good and Evil, 43, 49

Ugarit, 21, 77

Wandering in the Wilderness, 28, 45, 56, 66–68, 74, 83, 96–97, 115, 120, 124, 137

Subject Index

Wisdom Instruction, 51–52, 115, 122–23
Yahwism/Yahwist/ic, 9, 12, 19, 19n3, 78
Yarikh (see also moon), 21

YHWH (Yahweh), xvi, 2, 9, 18, 20–22, 24, 26, 26n28, 29–32, 34, 36, 38–39, 49, 51, 57–59, 59n100, 66, 69, 71, 73, 77, 79–80, 94, 96–98, 104, 109–11, 124, 135, 139, 142

Scripture Index

Old Testament/Hebrew Bible

Genesis

Reference	Pages
1:1—Exodus 18	6, 20n12, 103
1–11	4n18, 25, 140
1–2	27, 34
1:1—2:4	5
1	18–19, 19n5, 20, 22, 24–26, 28, 31, 38–39, 70, 87, 132
1:1–10	34
1:4	18
1:10	18
1:11	20, 37
1:12	18, 20, 37
1:14–16	22
1:14	19
1:16	21
1:18	18
1:21	18, 20
1:22	39
1:24	20
1:25	18, 20
1:26–28	36
1:26–27	29, 32, 36, 62
1:28	36, 39, 45, 51, 76
1:29	30, 34, 37
1:30	37
1:31	18
2	18–20, 22, 24, 26, 29, 31–32, 34, 35–36, 38–39, 44, 65, 70, 76, 84, 87
2:2–3	23
2:2	5
2:3	31–32, 39
2:4	26, 61
2:5	26, 37
2:6	37
2:7–8	30
2:7	18, 21, 26, 29
2:8–25	30
2:8	26, 30, 34
2:9	26, 43
2:10–14	32–33
2:11–12	32
2:15	26, 45
2:16–17	39
2:16	26
2:17	29, 43, 47, 56
2:18–25	35
2:18	18, 26, 39
2:19	18, 26, 30
2:21–22	18
2:21	26
2:24	24, 36
3–6	50
3–4	59n100
3	29, 41, 44, 48–50, 56–57, 59–60, 81
3:1	26
3:5	52
3:6	24
3:8	26, 33
3:9	26
3:12–13	24, 133
3:13	26
3:14	26, 48
3:15	52, 75

Scripture Index

Genesis *(continued)*

Reference	Pages
3:16–19	81
3:16	49, 49n52
3:17–18	38
3:21	26, 55–56
3:22	26, 52–53
3:23	26
3:24	29, 34, 58
4	41, 53, 55–56, 59–60
4:1	49
4:7	56–57
4:8–9	24
4:9	54
4:11–15	56
4:11–12	50
4:14–16	55
4:14	120
4:15	56
4:17	74
4:23	24, 60
4:26	53
5–11	61–62
5	61–62
5:1	61–62
5:2	39
5:24	62
5:28–31	62
6–9	56
6	65
6:1–8	24
6:1–7	21, 87
6:1–4	61, 65, 85, 103
6:3	70
6:4	74
6:5	62, 66
6:6	71
6:9	61
6:12	67
6:17	67
6:18	66, 69
6:19–20	70
6:22	68
7:1	66
7:2	68
7:3	70
7:4	67
7:24	67
8	11
8:1	71
8:3	67
8:11	68
8:20	55, 68
8:21	62, 66, 66n11
9:1–17	69
9:1–6	61
9:1	39, 51, 72, 75
9:4	5, 68
9:5–6	5, 68
9:13–17	70
9:15	64
9:18–27	62, 69
9:20–27	24, 61, 85
9:22	72
9:23	72
10	62, 66
10:1	61–62
10:18–19	62
10:21–31	62
10:32	61–62
11	62
11:3	73
11:4	72, 74
11:8–9	72
11:10–26	62
11:10	61–62
11:27	61–62
11:28	8
11:31	8, 79
12–36	12n60
12–25	76–77, 85
12	8n39, 11, 79, 83–85, 94, 96
12:1–3	79
12:1	80, 82, 96, 135
12:3	39, 48, 80, 102, 117, 134
12:6–7	78
12:7	39, 55, 108
12:8	90, 110
12:10–20	24, 77, 82
12:10	50, 81, 101
12:11–20	81
12:13	101
12:15	82
12:16–20	82
12:16	82–83
12:17	56, 82

Scripture Index

12:19	82	17	xv, 92–93		
12:20	82	17:2–6	87		
13	11, 83, 93	17:8	80–81		
13:1	82	17:10–11	70		
13:2	83	17:11–27	5		
13:3–4	110	17:14	92		
13:3	83	17:15–21	87		
13:4	55	18–19	11		
13:6	108	18	86, 88		
13:7	8	18:9–14	87		
13:10	45	18:10	49, 93		
13:11	94	18:14	93		
13:12–13	74	18:19	88		
13:12	107	18:20–32	88		
13:13	69, 85–86	18:23–33	14		
13:14–17	80, 83	18:23–32	88		
13:15–17	81	18:24–32	56		
13:15	39	18:25	21, 87		
13:17	108	19	69, 74, 76, 86–87, 89, 132		
13:18	55, 78, 90	19:1–29	56		
14	74, 98	19:13	21		
14:14	8	19:24	21		
14:18	97, 98n73	19:26	107		
14:20	11, 98, 111	19:29	71		
14:24	98n70	19:31–38	49, 87		
15	11, 92–93, 98	19:30–38	87, 87n33, 107		
15:1	81	20	8n39, 11, 83–84, 94		
15:4	93	20:1–18	24		
15:5	62	20:2	101		
15:7	8, 79–80, 108	20:3	56, 94n61		
15:9	98	20:6	85		
15:13–16	42, 81, 90, 123	20:7–8	99		
15:14	21, 93, 98	20:7	14, 85, 93		
15:16–18	39	20:16	99		
15:16	78, 80, 118, 125, 135	20:17–18	85, 87		
15:18	69, 81, 108	21	11, 95		
16–21	87	21:1–8	87		
16	8n39, 86, 90	21:1–6	99		
16:1–16	81, 87	21:1–2	49		
16:1–4	112	21:1	93		
16:5–6	95	21:6	v		
16:5	91	21:8–21	90		
16:6	90, 120	21:9–14	86		
16:7–14	91	21:10	91		
16:7	91	21:15–16	92		
16:8	120	21:16–21	95		
16:11	91	21:22	93		
16:13	91	21:32	102		

Genesis *(continued)*

Reference	Pages
21:33	78
22	77, 96–97
22:2	96
22:5	97
22:7	105
22:9	55, 94
22:11	105
22:17	62
23	11
23:3–20	80
24	11, 89
24:1–4	88
24:1	39, 93
24:3	126
24:5–8	81
24:7	108
24:12–14	89
24:37	88, 126
24:50	89
24:55	88n38
25	99, 109
25:8	105, 126
25:9–10	80
25:12	61, 77
25:19	61, 77, 100n2
25:21	49
25:22–23	108
25:23	15, 108, 120
25:29–34	107
25:30	108
26–36	100
26	11, 83, 100n2
26:1–5	81
26:1–2	101
26:1	50, 81
26:2–5	120
26:3–4	101
26:3	108
26:4	62
26:4b–5	101
26:5	1, 100
26:6–11	101
26:7–10	24
26:10	105
26:12–14	93, 101
26:15–22	101
26:24	101
26:25	55
26:28	102
26:30–31	93
26:34–35	24, 102
27	8n39, 104, 107
27:1–4	105
27:1	105
27:6–13	105
27:7–46	24
27:9–25	24
27:19–29	105
27:35	24
27:36	107
27:40	108
27:41—31:55	113
27:41–45	106, 110
27:41	105
27:46—28:9	5
27:46	102
28	100
28:1–8	126
28:1–5	103
28:1–4	24
28:4	108
28:6–9	103
28:11–22	111
28:12–17	120
28:13–14	83
28:13	108, 111
28:15	101
28:18	78
28:19	8
28:22	11, 78, 100, 111
29–30	100
29	14, 112
29:15	110
29:17	113n52
29:18–30	113
29:26	16
29:30	112
29:31—30:24	112
29:31	49, 112, 120
29:32	112
30:3–4	112
30:9	112
30:14–16	49
30:15–16	112

Scripture Index

30:17	120	32:24–31	115
30:20	112	32:24–29	120
30:22	49, 71, 112, 120	32:28	116
30:27–30	93	32:30	120
30:27	114	32:32	11, 100, 114, 116
30:37–42	120	33	11
30:43	93	33:1–3	115
31	11, 107	33:8	115
31:1–2	109	33:10	120
31:3	14, 79, 82, 110, 120	33:14	107–8
31:5	109	33:18–19	107
31:9	109	33:20	55
31:11–13	110, 120	33:25–33	105
31:11	105	34–35	104
31:12	109	34	8n39, 69, 74, 100, 107, 116–17
31:13	79	34:1–5	105
31:16	109	34:1–2	107
31:19	104, 107	34:2	119
31:23	110	34:9	118
31:24	120	34:15	92
31:25–55	105	34:23	102, 118
31:28–31	109	34:25–26	106
31:29	56, 106	34:26	117
31:32	107	34:27	111
31:35	104, 107	34:29	107, 118–19
31:38	51, 105	34:30	105, 117, 119
31:39	113	35	11
31:41	105	35:1–15	108, 111
31:42	109	35:1–7	55
31:43	113	35:1–4	104
31:44–55	110	35:1	120
31:45	78	35:2–4	21n12, 103
31:47–55	93	35:2–3	104, 119
31:50	112	35:2	111
31:53	104, 119	35:5	119
31:54	139	35:6	8
32	100	35:7	120
32:1—33:16	106	35:10	116
32:1–20	110	35:11–12	111
32:1–2	115, 120	35:11	51
32:3	108	35:14	78
32:3–7	120	35:16–20	105
32:4—33:16	105	35:16–19	119
32:7–8	115	35:22	106
32:9–12	115	35:29	105
32:12	62	36	120
32:13–21	115	36:1	61, 108
32:24–32	106n30	36:2	131n44

Scripture Index

Genesis *(continued)*

36:6–8	83
36:6	120
36:7–8	108
36:8–9	108
36:8	108
36:9	61
36:19	108
36:31	8
36:43	108
37	8n39, 127
37:2	61, 134
37:3–4	126
37:4	131
37:5–11	134
37:7	118
37:8	131
37:12	139
37:13	105
37:15–17	137
37:17	139
37:18–20	131
37:18	139
37:20–24	134
37:21–22	139
37:25–36	86
37:25	139
37:26–33	105
37:28–36	27
37:29–30	139
37:31–35	119, 131
37:31–32	24, 131
37:31	139
37:34–35	126
38	11, 126–27, 128nn24–25, 129–30, 132
38:1–10	119
38:1–2	126
38:1	130n35
38:7–10	126
38:7	133
38:10	133
38:12	129
38:14–30	49
39	127, 129–30
39:3	135
39:6	134n55
39:9	85–86, 129
39:17	130
39:20	134
39:21–23	129
39:23	135
40:8	134
41:14	122
41:16	134
41:34	128
41:38	130, 135, 142
41:40–44	122
41:45	125, 137
41:54–57	119
41:54	50, 81
42–47	121
42–44	139n66
42	128n25
42:3	139
42:5	81
42:6–17	139
42:9–16	130
42:18	122, 139
42:21–22	127
42:21	139
42:30–32	139
43	128n25
43:3	120
43:5	120
43:18–22	139
44:7–9	139
44:9	107
44:14–34	130
44:16	127, 131, 139
44:23	120
44:26	120
45:5–8	122, 124, 129
45:5	136
45:17–20	82
46:2–4	82, 118, 124
46:2–3	107
46:2	105
46:4	101
46:27	62
46:32–34	124
47:9	105
47:13	81
47:14–26	129
47:28	105

Scripture Index

47:29–31	79–80	3:10	14, 91
48:14–20	15	3:13–15	10
48:22	112	3:22	109
49	14, 47n43, 124, 128n24	4:14	72
49:3–4	106	4:22–23	65
49:4	106	4:22	134
49:5–7	105	4:24–26	92
49:5–6	107	4:31	109
49:6	118	5:6–19	109
49:7	107	5:7	73
49:8–10	130	5:21	21
49:29–33	123, 126	6:3	10
49:29–32	79–80	6:4–5	92
49:29	126	6:5	39, 71
50:3	126	6:8	92
50:5	79	9:14	82
50:10	126	9:16	34
50:12–13	126	9:30	26
50:15–18	139	10:11	91
50:15	124	12:16	20
50:19–20	123	12:25	92
50:20	124, 134, 136, 139	12:30–33	82
50:21	122	12:35–36	82
50:24–25	79, 123	12:36	109
50:24	139	12:38	25, 80, 82
50:25	80	12:39	91
		12:40–41	27
		12:43–50	93
		12:48	92
Exodus		12:49	1
1	77	13:5	92
1:7	37	13:9	1
1:8–22	124	13:11	92
1:8–16	109	13:13	97
1:9–22	82	13:15	97
1:9	62, 66	13:17	73
1:11	74, 109	14:8–10	110
2	14, 137	14:17–28	21
2:15	110	15:22	91
2:16	125	15:22–27	95
2:22	110	15:23–25	81
2:23–25	30	15:24	92
2:24	39, 71, 92	16:3–29	81
3:1	110, 125	16:4	2
3:2	91	16:11–19	34
3:6–22	110	16:15	30
3:7–8a	39	16:29	23
3:7	91, 109	16:33–34	32n54

Exodus (continued)

Reference	Pages
16:35	30
17:1–6	95
17:5–7	34
17:8–13	116
18:1	125
18:3–4	110
18:16	1
19	3
19:1–2	34
19:3–5	16
19:4–6	34, 134
19:5	39, 92, 110
19:10	111
19:16	57
19:22–24	75
20	2
20:2	79
20:5	50, 69, 91
20:6	69
20:7	22
20:8–10	23
20:9–11	5
20:11	5n23, 23
20:12	59, 105
20:13	60, 129
20:14	84, 106, 123
20:15	59, 107
20:16	39
20:17	59, 84
20:18–19	58
20:18	57
20:19—23:33	39
20:20	97
20:22—23:33	2
21:4–6	113
21:4	113
21:7–11	113n50
21:10	112
21:12–14	106
21:12	127
21:14	127
21:15	68
21:16	68, 127
21:17	131
22	117
22:8	104
22:10–11	113
22:16–17	117
22:18	68
22:19	68, 118n70
22:20–22	90
22:20	104
22:21–24	118
22:21	86
22:28	77
23:1	131
23:2	131
23:9	139n66
23:12	23
23:21	53
23:24	78
23:25	62
23:26	49, 51
23:32–33	102
24:11	139
24:12	2
25–31	31
25:1	31
25:7	32
25:9	34
25:18–22	34
25:31–35	33
26:31	34
28:4	56
28:9–14	32
28:20	32
28:40	56
30:11	31
30:17	31
30:18	33
30:19–21	111
30:22	31
31:1	31
31:12–17	23
31:12	31
31:13	23
31:14	43, 68
31:15–17	70
31:17	23, 31
32–34	xv, 56, 64, 66
32:1	136
32:10	14, 66
32:13	92
32:14	56

Scripture Index

32:23	136	17–26	2, 39
32:26–35	53	17:10–15	68
33:1–3	66	18	69, 76, 86–87, 87n33
33:1	92	18:8	106
33:3	75	18:9	84
33:12–17	66	18:11	15, 84
33:12–16	14	18:15	132
33:18–20	38	18:18	15, 100, 112
33:21–23	38	18:22	68
34:5	57	18:25–30	80
34:6–7	38	18:27–30	88
34:7	50, 69, 91	19:12	119
34:10	34	19:18	127
34:11–16	102	19:19	133
34:12–16	65	19:26	53n68, 68
34:12	102	19:29	129
34:13	78	19:33–34	118
34:15–16	133	19:33	86
34:16	61, 103, 118	20	69, 76, 86–87, 87n33
34:20	77, 97	20:10–11	106
34:21	23	20:10	68, 84
35:1–3	23	20:12	68
35:2	23	20:13	68
35:9	32	20:15–16	68
35:27	32	20:17	15, 84
39:6	32	20:27	68
39:13	32	22:29	73
39:42	68	23:1–3	23
40:34–38	34	23:2–37	19
		24:16	68
		26	43, 69
## Leviticus		26:1	78
		26:4	50
1–7	68	26:12	33, 58
1	98	26:18–19	89
1:10	98	26:19–20	50
1:14	98	26:30	75, 127
7:12–15	73	26:33	135
7:26	68	27:30–32	111
8:35	33		
10:1–5	56		
10:2	21	## Numbers	
10:8–11	xv		
10:11	6	1	68
11	20, 48, 68, 114	3:7–8	33
13:34	111	3:7	33
14:8–9	111	3:8	33
15:20	104	3:10	33

Scripture Index

Numbers *(continued)*

3:28	33
3:32	33
3:38	33
4:20	47
4:23	33
4:24	33
4:26	33
6:24–26	102, 120
8:26	33
10:9	71
10:29	25
11–14	56
11	21, 64, 81
11:1	72
11:7	32n54
11:9	30
11:10	72
11:31–32	34
11:32–34	53
12	21, 64
12:1–9	42
12:3	71
12:9	72
13–14	64, 74
13	96
13:2	82
13:23–25	68
13:28	74
14	21, 55, 66
14:3	96
14:3–4	73, 135
14:9	116
14:11–12	66
14:13–19	14
14:18	50, 69
14:34	67
14:40–45	81, 135
15:30–36	23
15:32–36	68
16	21
18:5–6	33
18:15	97
18:24–28	111
20	42, 114, 120
20:2–11	95
20:5–11	34
20:14–21	99
21:8–9	56
21:23–35	110
21:34	116
22:22	72
24:5–7	45
24:9	80
25	21, 64
25:3–4	72
25:11	72
26	68
26:31	119
27	xv
27:1–11	132
30:1–16	60n103
31:1–5	116
31:19–20	111
31:24	111
32:10	72
32:13–14	72
32:22	45
32:29	45
33:52	75
33:52–55	73
36:1–13	132

Deuteronomy

1:1	8
1:5	8
1:21	116
1:26–30	73
1:29	116
1:30	116
2	120
2:1–23	108
2:4–5	108
2:10–12	8
3:2	116
3:9	8
3:20	45
3:22	116
4:2	47
4:5–6	43
4:6	92
4:9–10	142
4:9	43

Scripture Index

4:11	57	8:16	30, 43, 97
4:19	22	9:3–5	73
4:23–24	75	9:7	53
4:23	43	9:18–19	72
4:25	72	9:24	53
4:26	43	10:19	86
4:27	135	10:20	119
4:37	63	11:9–15	37
4:40	43	11:9–12	30
4:41	8	11:9	43
4:46–49	8	11:14	50
5	2, 20n11	11:15	37
5:9	50, 69, 91	11:17	50
5:10	69	11:18–20	6
5:12–15	23	11:19	142
5:14	23	11:20	142
5:16	43, 59	11:23–25	73
5:17	60	12–26	2
5:18	84, 106	12:2	75
5:19	59, 107	12:5	98
5:20	59	12:5–6	75
5:21	59, 84	12:6	111
5:22	57	12:10	45
5:25	58	12:11	98, 111
5:29	43	12:16	68
5:33	43	12:21	98
6–26	20n11	12:25	43
6:2–3	43	12:28	43
6:4–6	22	13:1–10	68
6:5	22	13:1–3	46
6:6–9	6	13:5	53
6:7	142	13:17	72
6:9	142	14	20, 48, 68
6:10–11	74	14:1	65
6:13	119	14:2	57
6:15	72	14:3–21	114
6:18	43, 73	14:22–29	111, 128
7:2–5	102	14:23	98
7:2–3	102	14:24	98
7:3–4	88	15:9–12	113
7:3	61, 65, 118, 133	15:18	113
7:7	16, 62	15:23	68
7:12–13	62	16:2	98
7:14	49, 51, 72	16:6	98
8	96	16:11	98
8:1	73	16:21–22	78
8:2	96	17:3	22
8:3	30	17:14–20	47

171

Deuteronomy (continued)

17:16	73, 135
17:19	6
17:20	43
18:10	53
18:16	58
19:15–21	68, 95
19:15	89
20:4	116
21	84
21:10–14	84, 113
21:11	113n52
21:14	90
21:15–17	15, 35, 100, 106, 112, 138
21:18–21	68, 102
22	100, 117
22:7	43
22:9	133
22:10	118
22:11	133n48
22:22	84, 94, 94n61
22:23–27	117n66
22:23–24	87, 90
22:25–27	68
22:28–29	117
22:30	106
23:2–3	50, 87
23:3	87
23:7	108–9
23:8	50
23:14	33
23:17	132
24:1–4	36, 84
24:5	99
24:7	68, 127
24:16	88, 117
24:17	86
25:5–10	131
25:9	132
25:15	43
25:19	45
26:2	98
26:12	111
27:22	84
28	43, 69
28:1–14	93
28:4	52
28:12	50
28:13	114
28:18	50
28:23–24	50, 89
28:26	127
28:63–67	135
28:63	43
29:20	72
29:22	37
29:23–24	72
29:27–28	72
30:5	43
30:6–10	130
30:9	135
30:15–20	43
30:15–16	143
30:15	43
30:18–19	43
30:20	43
31:8	116
31:9–13	38
31:10–13	6
31:17	72
31:27	53, 66
31:29	72
32:8–9	16
32:10–20	134
32:16	72
32:21–22	72
32:21	72
32:24	50
32:35	127
32:47	43
33	14
33:10	6
34:6 7	56
34:7	71

Joshua

1:8	6
1:13	45
1:15	45
2	95
2:12	119
3:10	73
5:3–7	92

Scripture Index

5:3–8	115	3	87
5:11	115	3:2	81
5:13–15	115	3:6–7	61
6	95	3:6	65, 103, 118
6:2–5	116	8	86
6:17–25	26	8:24	86
6:23–25	130	10–12	87
7	139	11:26	27
7:1–26	56	11:31	107
7:1	130	13	49
7:16–26	130	19–21	138
8	100		
8:1–4	116		
8:1	116	### Ruth	
8:30–33	119		
9–10	26	1:1	50
9	119		
9:7	119		
9:23–27	48	### 1 Samuel	
10:8	116		
10:11–14	116	1	49
10:25	116	1:5	112
11:19	119	1:19	112
13:1	73	3:1	136
13:6	73	7:16	100, 110
15:63	73	8	83
17:14–18	73	8:1–22	46
18:1	45	10:3	100, 110
21:38	114	14:24	107
21:44	45	15:7	134
22:4	45	15:12	74
22:9–34	138	15:23	52n67
23:1	45	16:12–13	15
23:12–13	61	17:44	127
23:12	65	21:10–15	116
23:13	73	28	52n67
24	100		
24:1–27	111		
24:1–25	119	### 2 Samuel	
24:14	111		
24:23	111	2:8–9	114
		5:5–9	26
		6:7	47
		7	92
### Judges		7:6–7	33
		7:25	26n31
1:19–33	73	13:11–16	117
2:3	73	17:24	114
2:10	126	18:18	74

Scripture Index

2 Samuel *(continued)*

19:32	114
21:1–14	119
21:1	50
21:10	127
24:16–25	97
24:18–24	26

1 Kings

3:3	75
4:14	114
6:1	27
6:23–29	34
6:23–28	34
7	33
11:1–13	65
11:1–10	103
11:1–8	65
12:4	129
12:29–32	110
12:32	75
13:2	75
17:1	89
19:11–12	57

2 Kings

18–20	116
19:19	26n31
21:3	22
22:20	126
23:2–3	7
23:4	110
23:5	22
23:11	22
23:15	110
25:27–30	122

1 Chronicles

5:1	138
17:16	26n31
17:17	26n31
18:8	33
21:21–25	26
22:9	15
28:20	26n31

2 Chronicles

1:9	26n31
4:2–15	33
6:41	26n31
6:42	26n31
17:7–9	6
26:16–20	134
34:28	126
34:30–31	7

Ezra

9–10	65, 102–3
9:11–12	117
9:12	118

Nehemiah

8:1–5	7
8:13	7
8:18	7
9	13
9:3	7
13	93, 102
13:23–28	65

Job

26:12	34

Psalms

34	116
46:4	33
59:6	26n31
72:18	26n31
77:16–20	57
80:4	26n31
80:20	26n31

Scripture Index

82:6–7	65
84:9	26n31
84:12	26n31
94:1	127
119	52

Proverbs

1:7	52, 122
5–6	123
17:14	115
22:17—23:14	27

Isaiah

1:2	134
1:9	67n13
1:10–17	57
2:2–4	80
10:20–22	67n13
11:11	67n13
11:16	67n13
13:19–22	89
14:12–16	52
14:28–32	47n23
34:13–15	89
37:31–32	67n13
42:6	80
49:6	80, 134
51:3	45
51:9	34
60:3	80
66:13	134

Jeremiah

3	34, 36
5:8	88n36
8:1–3	127
8:2	22
8:17	47n43
9:11	89
10:22	89
13:27	88n36
14:1–6	89
15:3	127
15:11	67n13
16:18	88
17:19–27	23
23:3	67n13
27:5–6	80
29	134
29:11	134
31:7	67n13
31:8	134
34:20	127
46:22	47n43
48:13	110
49:33	89
51:37	89

Ezekiel

1:4–28	57
6:5–7	127
6:8	67n13
6:9	88n36
8:16	22
11:13	67n13
14:22	67n13
16	34, 36
16:6	134
16:22	88n36
16:43	88n36
16:47	88n36
16:49	86
16:58	88n36
17	119
18:6	88n36
18:11	88n36
18:12–13	88n36
18:15	88n36
20:12	23
20:20	23
20:32	46
20:33	137
22:11	88n36
23:36	88n36
29:5	127
32:4	127
33:24–29	130
33:26	88n36
33:27	127

Scripture Index

Ezekiel (continued)

36:35	45
38–39	93
39:4	127
39:17–20	127
40–48	121n1
47	33
47:12	33

Daniel

1–3	130
2	122n5
4	122n5
4:29–37	134
5	122n5

Hosea

1–3	34, 36
4:1–6	47
4:6	47
4:13–14	88n36
9:14	51
12:4	115

Joel

2:3	45
2:32	67n13
3:2	93

Amos

1–2	93
3:14	110
4:4	110
5:5–6	110
5:15	67n13
7:10–13	110

Obadiah

	42

Micah

1:3	89
2:12	67n13
5:3	67n13
5:7–8	67n13
6:1–12	57

Habakkuk

2	93

Zephaniah

2:2b	57
2:7–9	67n13

Haggai

1:12	67n13
1:14	67n13

Zechariah

8:6	67n13
8:12	67n13

Malachi

1:6–14	57

New Testament

Matthew

1:2	130
1:5	130
5:28	94
19:4–6	36
19:8	36
24:37	64
24:38–39	75
26:26–28	139

Scripture Index

Mark
14:22–25	139

Luke
17:26	64
24:27	13
24:44	13

John
1:17	13
1:45	13
5:46	13
7:19	13
7:22	13
8:44	46n35

Acts
3:25	80
10	48, 49n50
28:23	13

Romans
1	59
4:13	80
5:14	3
12:19	127
14	48

1 Corinthians
15:22	3
15:45	3

2 Corinthians
11:3	46n35
11:14	46n35

Galatians
1	49n50
2	48
3:8	80
3:16	80

Ephesians
5	34

1 Timothy
2:13–14	3

Hebrews
10:30	127
11:7–22	3
11:9	81
11:31	130

James
2:25	130

2 Peter
2:5	66, 71, 75

1 John
3:15	106
5:2–3	143

Revelation
12:9	46n35
19:9	139
20:2	46n35, 52
20:10	52
22	33
22:2	33

Scripture Index

Apocrypha

Wisdom
2:24	46n35

Ben Sira
50:25–26	118n68

Pseudepigrapha

Jubilees
3:10–12	32
33:10–20	106

Testament of Abraham
12:4–9	53n72
12:15	54n72
13:1–3	54n72

Testament of Levi
5:1—7:3	118n68
5:3	117
6:7	105

Qumran Literature

Genesis Apocryphon (1QGen Apoc)
20	82
31–32	82

Jewish Writings

Mishnah

Megillah
4:10	131

Pirqe Aboth
5:1	19n5

Qiddushim
4:14	101

Babylonian Talmud

Ketubot
57b	88n38

Sanhedrin
57a	65
58a	36
59a	68
108a	65
109a	86

Yoma
28b	101

Midrash

Genesis Rabbah
3:9	44
19:9	43, 44
20:5	48
21:1	44
21:9	44
41:7	89

Scripture Index

45:1	82
45:6	90
80:6	117
84:11–12	128
85:1	133
85:9	128
85:11	128
87:6	128
89:2	125

Pirqe de Rabbi Eliezer

26.190	82
36.272	125
38.287–88	125

Targums

Neofiti

Gen 41:45	125

Onqelos

Gen 41:45	125

Pseudo-Jonathan

Gen 16:1	82
Gen 34:27	111
Gen 41:45	125

Maimonides

Mishneh Torah

Hilchot Melakhim

9.3	3n12

www.ingramcontent.com/pod-product-compliance
Lightning Source LLC
Chambersburg PA
CBHW031433150426
43191CB00006B/490